In the Dark and Still Moving

Anne Geraghty works as a psycho-spiritual counselor with individuals, relationships and groups. She has explored many different cultures and religions on her search for freedom, meaning, truth, love, God, herself … and although the name of what she was seeking changed many times, the search continued.

She now lives in the wilds of Cumbria with Martin, her husband, Harry, the dog, and what she found – and keeps on finding.

Also by Anne Geraghty
HOW LOVING RELATIONSHIPS WORK
UNDERSTANDING LOVE'S LIVING FORCE
LEARNING TO LOVE AND BE LOVED

In the Dark and Still Moving

A DIFFERENT VERSION OF WHAT IS GAINED WHEN
A PARADISE IS FOUND AND THEN LOST

Anne Geraghty

The Tenth Bull

First published in the UK 2007 by
The Tenth Bull
31 James Street
Whitehaven
Cumbria
CA28 7HZ
www.thetenthbull.co.uk

ISBN 978-0-9554954-0-3
Copyright © 2007 Anne Geraghty

Cataloguing-in-Publication CIP Data is available for this book from the British Library

Edited by Stuart Booth
Designed and typeset by cbdesign
Printed in the UK by Biddles Printing

Contents

Preface

This is the story of a great coming together. It is one, when, for the first time in history as many women as men travelled all over the world in search of new freedoms, love and the latest dance moves. It tells of what can happen when you see visions, dream dreams and then try to live them. Yet, though it offers a different version of what is gained when a paradise is found and then lost, some things, never change. Every Eden has its snake, and in this story too, the serpent plays a starring role.

We did our best to make love and not war, but all love leads to some kind of war, if only because it takes a lot of fights these days before we realise what we love will insist on being itself and not what we wish it to be. That includes ourselves too – should we become an object of our own desire, the apple of our own eye. And too there was a fall. Though our fall, when it came, was not only with gravity, it was in all directions; just as was the coming together.

Though this fall was neither from grace nor into grace, the dancing, however, was often very graceful indeed, because a generation which does not have to march to the drums of war is free to dance to its own music. Yet, despite our new dance moves, we found what every generation before us has found, the lessons of love and war are the same – love needs us as much as we need love. And though at first we fall in love, and that can happen in an instant, later the love must fall into us, which is a far longer story.

ANNE GERAGHTY
Cumbria UK
Spring 2007

There's a thousand ways to be lost and only one to be found.
But I am drunk and you're insane, so who will lead us home?
Let's sing another love song while we stumble in the dark.

With respects to Jalal Al-Din Rumi (1207–1273)

We all have a light inside; but trying to look at it turns it black.

Ummon, a Chinese Zen Master of the
T'ang Dynasty (AD 864–949)

PART ONE

Born a Long Way From Home

*In which my first eye opens
and I see The World*

Chapter 1

The Refuge of Lies

On hearing me say 'I hate you!' to one of my sisters, my mother grabbed my arm and yanked me into the kitchen.

'You must never say that! You must never hate anyone!'

'But shouldn't we hate the devil?', I asked – my four-year-old eyes wide with innocence.

My grin gave the game away and I was sent to my bedroom to draw pictures of hell to teach me the error of my ways. But I liked drawing graphic horror scenes, people burning in agony in the eternal fires of damnation, devils laughing and poking at them with pitchforks. Perhaps because there was a little devil lived in me.

'She's got a little devil in her!', my mum explained when I asked Father Neary whether baby Jesus ever did a wee-wee on Mary.

That devil taught me different lessons, because the next time my sister pulled my hair, I thought to seek peace at any price might end up costing you more than a war, and kicked her back. But then my parents knew the wounds of more enduring wars than sibling rivalry. When they fell in love during WW II, their families fell out and into their own war.

My mother, an Irish catholic, would not marry my father, an English protestant, unless he took 'instruction' and was thereby baptised into the 'One True Faith'.

When he converted, his family were outraged. They saw my mother's family, where out of seven children only three survived the diseases of poverty, as vastly inferior to their more ordered life, where cleanliness was next to godliness and every piece of furniture was moved daily to sweep under it. In my mother's house there was just the godliness and the furniture moved only when sold or chopped for firewood. But the fault lines that cracked through this family went even deeper.

My father's father had fought in the notorious 'Black and Tans', the ostensibly unofficial military regiment that, nevertheless, had terrorised and killed so many in Ireland. My mother's family had left their home in Ireland in order to escape the brutality and poverty there.

When my parents married, the Irish family went to the Catholic Nuptial Mass, but not one of them to the wedding reception. The English family went to the reception, but not one of them to the Mass. Only my parents were at both.

When I was born a year later, both families came to claim me, though not, of course, at the same time. Apparently I smiled indiscriminately at them all and whether with the healing of time or my smiles with a bit of each family in the dimples, an uneasy truce arrived.

I graduated from drawing devils to writing letters. I copied them off the Weetabix packet, the tomato sauce bottle, the Catholic Herald, anywhere I could find them. I hoped tracing the shapes of the letters would persuade them to reveal their secrets. I liked the curly letters 'e', 'g' and 'c', but 'w', 'y' and 'v' seemed to have a bit of the devil about them. And the Devil could be anywhere, even in the Weetabix. Though not, of course, in the Catholic Herald. My favourite words were on the Golden Syrup tin above a picture of bees flying out of a dead lion. 'Out of the strong came forth sweetness'. Though Father Neary had already told me the after-life was sweeter than this one.

With all my copying, before I went to school I could read. I didn't go to the local school, but to the Catholic Infant School run by the nuns from the Notre Dame convent, and to reach it, I had to travel across Northampton on two buses. My mother arranged for an older girl to take me. On the first day she picked me up, we made our way across town together and she brought me home. The next day she called for me, smiled and held my hand as we walked down the road. We turned the corner.

'Gi' us yer money!' she ordered. I handed it over and she ran off. Each morning we went through the same routine. She'd smile at my mother, hold my hand, until round the corner, when she ran off with my bus fare and dinner money.

For several weeks I was late until I had sorted the numbers of the buses and their stops in my mind. The conductors were friendly. They let me travel without paying the fare. People were kind to this five-year-old girl travelling alone. They showed me my stop, smiled and gave me sweets. I would thank them politely, though put the sweets in my pocket to be thrown away later. One day I forgot they were poisoned and popped one in my mouth. My tongue curled round the chewy sweetness so recently off rationing. I remembered the danger, but too late. I was never going to spit this deliciousness out. Was I going to die on the bus or later? Would it be like going to sleep or would it hurt like when you fell over? I chewed on. Anyway even heaven could not be sweeter than this.

At school I forgot I was about to die and remembered only on the bus home. Maybe there were other things not as I had been told. A crack appeared in the cosmic egg.

My mother had enough on with four younger children, so I didn't bother her with stories of my adventures. The school must have eventually asked why I never had any dinner money, as one day the girl stopped taking it. But by then I had found travelling alone, reliant only on the kindness of strangers, rather suited me. Once you've tasted the freedom of the road, even if only down town on the Number 32 bus, you don't relinquish it easily. Not if you have a devil in you, anyway.

We kids learned about the world through street gossip as there was no TV, except at Mrs Green's who had a 9-inch screen with a giant magnifying glass in front of it. She'd let you watch it for five minutes if you cleaned her windows. Before I went to school I had heard you stood in lines, got told off if you didn't finish your food and were not allowed home if you cried. On my first day I dreaded a future where I queued all day, possibly all night too if I cried and didn't eat my cabbage. When I saw the class-rooms with chairs and desks I cried anyway, but with relief.

Six of us were new that Spring term and the teacher lined us up to see if we could read any of the letters on her sheet. No one could. I was the last.

'I can read.'

'Don't be silly. Do you know any of these letters?'

'Yes, I know them all and I can read.'

'No you can't. You haven't been taught yet.'

'But I can, I really can!'

'Stop being naughty and sit over there.'

She pointed to the table for the new children who couldn't yet read anything.

It was wrong not to do as I was told, but it was not true that I could not read. For once that devil was on the side of the truth and stubbornly refused to let my little legs move. I stood there defiant, though shaking with fear. The teacher became impatient and pulled out a book, opening it at random.

'OK, then read this!' She ordered abruptly. Clearly she did not expect me to do anything other than stare at the pages.

I read it.

'Well, well, you can read, after all!' She smiled at me.

Even then I knew better than to say 'I told you so!' and, eyes wide with innocence, simply smiled back.

When I was seven, we moved to Nottingham, into a house with our own toilet – inside! No more making a hole in the ice with your pee in winter. No more tin bath on the kitchen tiles every Friday either, we now had a proper bathroom, with hot and cold running water. And a garden big enough for war games in which all five of us could fall about in elaborate, twitching, drawn out deaths. Though Paul's were usually the best. He didn't have to worry about his knickers showing like us four girls.

Despite the plumbing and the garden, my mother was depressed. She said the ceilings were too low and pressed down on her, but I thought she was probably lonely. In our other house, people had popped in and she'd read their fortunes in the tea leaves. The terraced houses had had thin walls, we all knew each other's business; and with shared toilets and no gardens, our lives had mixed on the streets. When the twins were born it had been a complete surprise. The street had clubbed together and bought her a double-ended pram. It wasn't like that in this street of detached houses, each with their own toilet and garden. Some even had a car.

I tried to make her happy by peeling potatoes, making cups of tea and doing the ironing, but got in her way. I was better at helping her with my three sisters and brother. I taught them to tie shoelaces, cuddled them when they fell over, told them stories and explained when mum said 'we all have our cross to bear', there was not an angry beast out to eat them. But despite my efforts, that devil kept peering up out of where he lived in my soul and made me bad. It might have been something to do with my unruly red hair. I was supposed to brush it one hundred times before I went to bed, but it was impossible to get a brush through it.

'Your hair has a mind of its own', my mother told me, wrestling with it as I squirmed. 'You look like you've been dragged through a hedge back-wards!'

I knew it was wrong to have wicked red hair like mine, yet neither the devil nor my hair would change. And though I tried to be good, they kept making me naughty.

Each Thursday our class went swimming. If you had a cold or a verucca, you stayed behind to work on your own. A group of us forged notes from our parents and stayed behind to play Postman's Knock and I kissed Adam Kusak and Michael O'Leary in the stationary stock room. The devil made us like it so much, we forged more notes for the next week.

Our childish writing gave us away. Either that or the leprosy Michael claimed meant he could not learn backstroke that week. The sin was so wicked, the normal punishment of the strap, a leather belt with three strips of leather on the end, was switched for the cane. No one had ever had the cane in our school before and Sister Agnes had to order it especially from school supplies. The whole school waited with glee during the four days it took to arrive. They could have flogged tickets for up front seats as well, and made money for the African missions.

The cane arrived. Sister Agnes called us to the front in assembly.

'You have committed a wicked sin and this is to teach you the error of your ways. Afterwards we will kneel and pray to St Teresa to save you from eternal damnation.'

'Yes, sister.'

'Why am I going to cane you?'

'To teach us the error of our ways sister.'

'And what will we pray for?'

'That we'll be saved from eternal damnation, sister.'

But we weren't saved, not yet anyway. Adam, Michael and I met after school behind the bike sheds for more Postman's Knock. Then I read a Catholic Truth Society pamphlet about Our Lady of Fatima and all that passion promptly transferred into my new project, to become a saint. Adam and Michael tried to persuade me back behind the bike shed with sweets, ginger beer and their best collection of cigarette cards, but I had turned away from the devil and all his works, and scorned them. I was soon to be delivered from such temptations anyway as the next year I was due to go to the Loreto Convent Grammar School for Girls.

During the school holidays that summer a letter arrived for my parents. My mother walked into my bedroom early that morning and thrust a letter at me as she told me abruptly,

'Read this, but don't let it go to your head, and don't tell anyone!'

My mother was very keen on everyone being equal. She once sent shock waves through the Parish when she told a meeting of the Parent-Teachers Association that coloured people should not only have equal rights in law, coloured men should be allowed to marry our daughters if they wanted to; provided, of course, the daughters wanted to as well.

I read the letter. I had come in the top three of the Midlands in the 11 plus, and had won a scholarship to a special school for gifted children. I had also won a bursary that would be paid to my parents each term.

I knew we should never shine and put others in the shade but must hide our lights under a bushel, which I think was a cross between a bush and a shovel. To be better than others at anything was almost a sin, as was going to a non-Catholic school; yet the devil made me feel a flash of delight I was 'gifted'. I immediately hid my pleasure under the nearest bushel, of course, and felt guilty for feeling 'special'. In my next confession I would have to confess.

'Bless me father for I have sinned. It is two weeks since my last confession and since then I have answered back my parents, argued with my sisters and was tempted with ideas above my station.'

Neither the scholarship nor the money was mentioned again, and the following September I went to the Catholic Convent Grammar School up the road. But when I was eighteen, my parents gave me a cheque for all the money that had been paid to them. They had kept it safe for me and despite being poor, had not spent a penny of it.

I was taught first by the nuns of Notre Dame, then by The Sisters of Mercy, and then by nuns of the Loreto Order, a matriarchal Trinity that made sure we grew up good Catholic girls, who would marry good Catholic husbands, and have lots of good Catholic children. Even better was to become a nun, a bride of Christ.

After reading about Our Lady of Fatima who was like the Queen, only more so because she was the Queen of Heaven, the Star of the Ocean, Our Lady of Sorrows, the Immaculate Conception, and a host of other titles, I was keen on becoming holy. Even now I can recite chunks of the Catholic Catechism, a little blue book, about the same size as Mao's little red one. We chanted the questions and answers about dogma and doctrine in religious instruction classes until we had learned them by heart. Now I planned to be a saint when I grew up, I threw myself into all this with gusto.

Q: 'Who made you?'
A: 'God made me.'
Q: 'Why did God make you?'
A: 'To know him, love him and serve him in this world, and to be happy with him forever in the next.'

There's no doubt who is the star of this show.

I joined the church choir and sang soprano in the Gregorian chants of the Latin Mass. I swooned at the smell of frankincense during

Benediction, this must be how it smelled in heaven. I offered up regular novenas and nine first Fridays, murmured decades of the rosary, chanted litanies and prayed to the nine choirs of angels and the community of saints.

To speed up the transformation from sinner to saint, I 'mortified the flesh'. I got ideas from reading the lives of saints and stopped leaning on the backs of chairs, tied scratchy string round my waist and slept on toy building bricks. One Sunday, in a fit of intense piety, I threw a small teddy bear I loved onto the fire. I cried while he burned but took consolation in how holy I must be by now. I regularly slipped into church after school and stared for ages at the statue of Our Lady, which I hoped would smile at me, or maybe a tear would fall gracefully down her cheek. I prayed regularly for the conversion of Russia, worried about all those communists who didn't know their souls were in mortal danger and would get a dreadful shock when they died.

One of the heaviest responsibilities came on All Souls Day. On this day you could gain a plenary indulgence for a soul in purgatory if on each visit to church you said an Our Father, a Hail Mary and a Glory Be. This meant a soul was released straight to heaven from the fires of purgatory, which were said to be as agonising as those in hell, except you didn't get the devil poking you with pitchforks, and when your soul was burned clean of all trace of sin, you made it to heaven. I thought it better to be burned in purgatory, however, than to lie in a bed for eternity, among millions of other beds in neat rows full of un-baptised babies in Limbo, where everything was white and the only thing that happened was an occasional visit from an angel. At least you got out of purgatory eventually. Though when I mentioned this to Sister Veronica, she told me I was wrong. It was better to die with only original sin on your soul than to live and do even venial sins.

On All Souls Day I would kneel in church, say the three prayers, save a soul, and leave. Outside I'd think, why not save one more soul from such terrible torment? And I'd go back in. A short while later, I'd come out again. But just another five minutes on my knees and another soul would be freed, so I'd slip back in for more prayers. Each time I emerged blinking into daylight, pictures of poor souls in torment, screaming in agony as the flames burned them, would force me back in – though I made sure each time I stood with both feet on the ground outside the church, else the prayers didn't count.

Many hours of this and I am hungry, thirsty and feeling faint. Perhaps next year I should bring sandwiches and some lemonade. Why is no one else running in and out saving as many people as they can, it'll be another year before we have this chance again? To speed things up, I hit the prayers running, muttering them before I even genuflect. Our Fathers run into Hail Mary's run into garbled Glory Bes. It's getting dark. My sister arrives panting on her bike.

'Mum says you've got to come home for dinner!'

I prayed to God to give me a vocation to be a nun. I wanted to be a Carmelite, one of the contemplative orders where you retire completely from the world, take a vow of silence and are never seen again except from behind a screen and an iron grill with spikes. But it's not what you want that matters, it's what God wants, so I asked God to give me a sign. A holy picture fell out of my prayer book during Mass that Sunday and on it, a prayer from St Therese of Lisieux, a Carmelite saint. 'I desire to reserve nothing for myself but freely and most willingly to sacrifice myself and all that is mine to Thee.' The sign!

Each morning while the rest of the family were asleep, I dressed and tiptoed downstairs, onto my bike and rode to early morning Mass at the Loreto Convent. One morning, full of holiness with not a devil in sight, I pedalled home down Aspley Park Drive, past trees, gardens, houses and driveways, all completely familiar to me from thousands of similar journeys to church, school and the convent and back, and suddenly my life stretched out before me in utter clarity. I knew, without a shadow of a doubt, that I had simply to follow the teachings of the Catholic Church, die, and then live forever in heaven. I wondered why so few others seem to have worked out what a good deal this was, to sacrifice one insignificant life for an eternity of bliss.

I rode home, swinging my legs, in my last moments ever of absolute existential security. Though perhaps not the last, death must be equally absolute. Yet that is how far back I began my journey into life, from where death has more meaning than life. The same place, when I think about it, as a suicide bomber.

The international terrorism we were dealing with then however was nuclear war, or rather the threat of it, between Russia and the West. Praying for the conversion of Khrushchev was just one part of it. This was the time of MAD – Mutually Assured Destruction – being apparently the safest option. Though it escapes me how the same people who thought it a good idea to stockpile enough nuclear missiles to kill every single person on Earth many times over, could also have a sense of humour.

I knew about the 'Monster Bomb', the thirty-eight nuclear blasts of Operation Hardtrack, the three-hundred-and-thirty-one high altitude tests and the nuclear explosions detonated under the sea. I saw films of Little Boy dropped on Hiroshima and Fat Boy dropped on Nagasaki; black and white footage of people naked, skin burned off, melted eyeballs, rocking in shock, writhing in agony, proving beyond all doubt that hell really does exist, but not under the Earth, on it.

I watched films of Americans in rows of deck chairs and sunglasses, drinking cocktails and enjoying the spectacular jellyfish, mushrooming over the dessert with the 'light of a thousand suns'. I heard about the school children bussed to the area to witness the power of their glorious America.

What I did not hear about was the marines ordered into trenches just three miles from the explosions, told to cover their faces with their hands and wait, the light was so bright they could see the bones in their hands through closed eyes. Some died in the blast, others later of radiation sickness. Or the pigs and rabbits dressed in military uniforms squealing in a panic before being blasted to smithereens as their world turned inside out. Or the eye witness accounts from service men who survived, of groups of ten to twelve people, even closer to the blast, caged behind chain linked fences and barbed wire, with deformed hands and faces, hair falling out, blackened skin hanging off, more dead than alive. With wires attached to their heads.

Though I did know the heat from a 'nominal bomb' could burn you twenty five miles away, that radiation was lethal within a four mile radius, that radioactive particles from fall out could travel down wind hundreds of miles, to contaminate everything, that measures of the blast over twenty miles were measured along a scale of 'severe damage', 'irreparable damage', and 'total destruction'. I knew because my father was a member of the Royal Observer Corps that scanned the skies looking for early warnings of nuclear bombs headed our way.

Their motto was 'Forewarned is Forearmed'. Though when I suggested if we were not so dangerously armed we would not need the warning, he told me 'The price of freedom is eternal vigilance'. So I asked him if he thought it was worth being so vigilant to preserve a freedom that made such bombs. But he told me to shut up and stop being so clever. I can't say I blame him.

I sensed there must be a different kind of freedom, but couldn't see it anywhere. I asked Mother Pauline whether true freedom was the freedom to follow your desires, or freedom from your desires. And how could there be proofs of the existence of God if He wanted us to have free will to believe in Him or not? But she just cried 'Jesus, Mary and Joseph, have mercy on us! If you're asking questions like that, girl, you'd better offer up a Novena to the Sacred Heart!'

I now had two projects on the go, rather hard to reconcile – the on-going sainthood one and a search for freedom.

While I fought for a freedom I could not name, underground, in secret, not really knowing what I was seeking, my father and his friends in the ROC fought for another freedom, on underground exercises in secret nuclear bunkers. These were practice runs for when the bombs dropped and the government and military had to be protected in order they survive to continue to fight the war. The war must go on.

I asked why they didn't save some ordinary people, as maybe they would fight for peace rather than plot more war, but Dad told me to do something useful for a change and learn more aircraft recognition.

We kids learned aircraft recognition from cards of the silhouettes of planes. We tested each other for hours until we could tell a P1 Lightening fighter and a Vulcan Bomber from various enemy planes from just a quick flash of the wing. Though we never got to be as good as Dad. He could recognise a plane from just its lingering vapour trail.

We practised what we must do in the four-minute warning before the bomb dropped in order to Protect and Survive. There was a lot had to done very quickly. Though hopefully, with our aircraft recognition skills, we might gain a few extra minutes if we were peering up at the sky around the time the bomb was dropped. We were to whitewash windows, build an inner refuge of mattresses piled around a table in the hall for our 'fall out room', and gather what we would need for two weeks under the table. Three and a half gallons of water per person, a clock and calendar, a radio, tins of food, tin opener of course, and a sand tray for the toilet. You could also take a couple of books. Obviously one would be the Bible, but we argued so much over which comics to take, *Girl* or *Eagle*, *Bunty* or *Dandy*, Mum threatened us with the lives of saints instead. Dad would give the signal and we'd rush and squeeze against table legs and mattresses, squabbling over who had the best space in the middle while Dad read out what we would be hearing over the radio when the real thing happened – 'Though you cannot see it, smell it or sense it, fall out can kill you. There is danger outside.'

Yes, there was madness and danger out there. If you discover, while young, the world is both mad and dangerous, you begin a quest to understand what the hell is going on. When you've no power, that's your only hope, that there is some meaning in the madness. Though you may have to journey a lifetime to find it.

During the Cuban Missile crisis our practice runs became more frequent. Dad told us they reckoned only half of the personnel in these underground bunkers would show up if there really was a nuclear war, the rest would chance it with their families under the table. Mum wanted Dad to want to stay with us, but we all knew he would do his duty to Queen and country first. He rose to be a Wing Commander and one day met her, the Queen. They were possibly soul mates as I expect she also would have gone to the bunker rather than under the dining table in Buckingham Palace.

Mum's soul mate was the parish priest who came to bless our house so often there were holy water marks on the walls. After we had trailed through each room sprinkling holy water, and telling the devil and all his works to leave, we kids were banished too. Mum and the priest sat in the front room, sipping sherry as they discussed finer points of doctrinal liturgy. Once we used very holy water from the miraculous spring at Lourdes. I watched to see if it made any difference but I still answered back my parents, argued with my sisters and harboured rebellious thoughts.

To balance things, I offered up more mortification of the flesh. We were supposed to offer up everything, grazed knees, no seconds of pudding, and your hamster dying. Whatever happened we 'offered it up.' Even if you got polio and had to live in an iron lung for the rest of your life, you would know to 'offer it up.' Offering up was what you did with what happened to you, giving up was what you did yourself. Like giving up sugar and not reading comics for Lent. Though you got more grace if you gave things up outside Lent, for no reason other than just to give them up.

Despite the dangers of nuclear war, the holy water flying around, and all the offering up and giving up going down, there was always life on the street. Greendale Gardens was a cul-de-sac, and for a whole gang of us, this was our playground. We played pirates, Mr Wolf, hide and seek, colours, football, rounders, tag, marbles and conkers; we skipped, hop-scotched, juggled and span tops and hula hoops; we biked, made go-karts out of old prams and learned to roller skate. We fell out, fell in and fell over, marking the cul-de-sac with a secret history – that's where Ruth fell over and her chin needed stitches, that lamp-post is where Paul fell off his bike and bent his finger nearly completely backwards, that bush is where

Bridget and Clare got stuck trying to hide and Liam saw their knickers. In echoes of an ancient human connection with the land, our street became a living landscape and as much our home as the house.

When Dad bought us bikes, our playground extended out into Strelley, real countryside. There were trees to climb, streams where we splashed and built dams, hills to roll down, meadows with the long grass where you could read all day and not be seen by anyone.

After the duties of being holy were finished for the day, I would ride off to find a lonely field where I could lie undisturbed and read about ballerinas and horse riding, dreaming I was really a princess who had been adopted. On the days I read the lives of saints with their various flesh mortifying tips, fantasies of riding through palace gardens in a tutu were replaced with those of walking bare-foot over stones in sackcloth and ashes.

Growing up in a family with a crack right through its heart, you become divided against yourself. But then perhaps we all are.

In 1956, the year I made my first Holy Communion dressed, to my delight, in a virginal white bridal dress with a veil, Elvis could be seen on TV only from the waist up. His hip gyrations and leg movements were banned after they had been too 'suggestive' on the Ed Sullivan Show. That same year, the electron microscope was invented, dividing even matter against itself. What we saw was now no longer what it was before we saw it. Uncertainty had entered everything.

It was about to enter me.

Not long after my whole life had stretched before me in such chilling clarity on my ride home from early morning mass, I rode into a bluebell wood. It was May, and the evening air was warm and sweet with the scent of bluebells. The wood was fresh and bright with new growth, not yet faded into the heavier maturity of full summer. I ducked under the branches that stroked my face with their first leaves, skipped over mossy branches that had fallen across the path, delighting in my new red sandals, my bright pink socks and the goose pimples on my bare legs in the evening breeze. I loved the bright colours of my dress. I loved the mouldy smell of damp leaves, the dappled sunlight, the little creatures rustling, the bright green of the new leaves. I loved everything at that moment, even my wild and wicked unruly hair.

I arrived in a clearing and lay looking up through the fringed circle of trees at the deepening blue above me. A blackbird sang. Her song of sun and rain, of love and worms, rang out through the soft dusk and found its way into all things – including me. I flew through the wood on the black-bird's song to where a strange wind blew through my heart and, under that secret sky, I heard a different hymn from those sung in churches. One that made me want to fling my arms wide and sing. Dance with a new happiness, jump and laugh with the sheer delight of being alive. I rolled over and pressed my face into the bluebells- into this delicious earth.

I rode home but despite another level of passion in my fantasy ballet and tablecloth piano playing, no one noticed the new light shining in my eyes.

What had awoken in me in the bluebell wood penetrated my prayers. I began to sigh in a similar ecstasy looking at pictures of the Sacred Heart smiling down at me. I had pleasurable fantasies of being tied to an altar by devils and Jesus galloping in to save me on a white horse. Such feelings must be proof my saint-hood project was going well. So well in fact, I was becoming holier by the day. Then our parish priest, offered to give me private Bible readings.

He was a good priest. He gave interesting sermons, he joked with the parishioners, he wasn't a fanatic, he was thoughtful and said the Mass with feeling when most just gabbled the prayers as fast as they could. When he came to bless our house, he was friendly, and we kids saw he didn't grab the biggest bit of cake though it was his by right.

I went to the presbytery where he lived with his housekeeper. He ushered me into a small room, smiled and pulled down from the bookshelf a large Bible with red embossed leather binding and gold leaf along the pages. He placed it on the table. He pulled two straight backed chairs closer, patted one and said 'Come here my child', gesturing me to sit on one while he took the other. He opened the Bible reverently and asked me to read the Passion according to St Matthew. He leaned close. He reached over to turn the page brushing his hand against my budding breasts. I faltered but carried on reading in my best voice. He stopped me, and put his hand on my shoulder saying how he found reading about the sufferings and crucifixion of Jesus sexually excited him. He told me how he had to pray hard in order not to become sexually aroused. He began to breath heavily and the air was filled with a dense electrical charge, like before a storm. He began to massage my shoulder, breathing in my ear. The room became stifling and his pulse beat in my throat. My mouth went dry. I froze.

'I'm sorry, I have to go!' I squeaked, even in my terror apologising. I ran out the room, out of the presbytery, down the drive, not knowing where to run to as suddenly nowhere was safe. I said nothing to anyone. It must have been my fault. No one would believe me anyway. I could not believe it myself. This priest was such a holy man, Everyone knew that. I would have been told I was a liar, hysterical and crazy. I probably was. In the *Malleus Malificorum*, the handbook of the Spanish Inquisition, it tells you how to recognise a witch – she has red hair and can make a man's member move at a distance. I was not just crazy; I must be evil as well. I never even told my sisters.

Much later, in our forties, I learned one of my sisters had been invited to special confessions with this same priest. He had sat her on his knee and stroked her while she confessed. She had never told anyone either.

I was initiated, before I was ready, into the lonely understanding that the same man who preached to us every Sunday about how we should live, who heard our confessions, forgave us our sins, the man we called Father and treated with more respect that anyone else, this man had his own dark secrets which he kept hidden and did not confess to us. Perhaps we would have forgiven him, after all real forgiveness lies with our fellow creatures, the ones we have hurt, and not an invulnerable God that lives far away from us.

Looking back I can understand this priest, too, was a victim of the split between the spirit and the body, yet at the time, this premature meeting with adult sexuality shocked me. My landmarks were suddenly gone. A guilty knowledge sliced through my life. When the nuns asked with a smile how my vocation was getting along, I blushed with a secret shame. I had not only brought sin to a holy man of God, I knew my devotional ecstasies had had their source in that same polluted river. Every two weeks I confessed my sins to this priest, but the worst sin of all, that my holiness was really a corruption, I kept locked away in my heart.

This crack in my innocence, that was to widen into a chasm, between me and my family, me and the Catholic Church, proved to be a blessing in disguise. It set me off on a journey to heal the shock that had sent a petrified piece of my soul spinning off into outer space. Like a young mole emerging for the first time from its underground home, I began to sniff the air and blindly feel my way into the world outside the Mother Church.

I came across books by Marx, Freud and Sartre in our local library. I was curious. Many of these books were listed on the Catholic Church's Index, a list of books too dangerously evil to be read by any Catholic. What on earth could be in them? We had been told by the nuns that if a girl or a woman touched any of the sacred objects on the altar in church, our hands would erupt in boils; and as I gingerly opened these books, I was afraid they might burn my hands. Nothing happened to my hands, but a lot happened to my mind. I found myself looking into worlds beyond anything I had been told about at home, school, or by the Church. And these worlds invited me in.

My parents had left school when young, to earn money for their families. Working class people in the 30's and 40's kept to their station in life, and anyway it was the war. They had never thought to read such books, and never imagined I would either. The nuns and priests too would never have discussed with me such forbidden ideas, even if they had read them. So I struggled alone with what I was reading, and did not confess I was wandering off the straight and narrow. At this point it was more an intellectual slide into darkness anyway. Though another fall from grace was not far away.

The brother school to our Loreto Convent School was run by Jesuits, and each year was held a Christmas dance where we could meet and mix with the boys. The dances were supposed to be the waltzes and fox trots we had learned in deportment classes, and in these, hands could lightly rest on shoulders, but no other part of our bodies were allowed closer than 18 inches to any part of theirs. From 7.30pm when the boys arrived, the nuns had their rulers ready.

But nuns with rulers, cannot hope to control girls who have just heard a new kind of music, a music with a rhythmic beat that made you want to twist and shout well outside the routine of strictly ballroom.

In the crush in the middle of the dance floor, unseen by the jealous eyed nuns, new dances were being created. We moved closer. We touched each other. We twisted in moves not seen in a Loreto Convent before. A boy held me in his arms, bent down and kissed me. He put his tongue in my mouth. I nearly fainted. I would have fallen had he not been holding me tight in the crush. But I fell all the same.

The list of sins in my prayer book, to help jog your memory before confession, stated that to kiss with an open mouth for longer than five seconds was a mortal sin, so if I died before confessing this, I would be burned in the flames of hell forever. I was burning anyway. The flames of hell, the heat of desire, the melting of my petrified life, all ran into each other. And I came in from the cold.

After that first prince's kiss, I began to have boyfriends. We touched. We lay on beds and played as young people do everywhere when given the chance. Flirting, dancing, giggling, cuddling. There was always a point beyond which I would not go, but where I drew that line kept changing as my resistance wore away and the glacier melted. There was, however, a darker river running through me, its undertow continually threatening to pull me under and into the Hell that still lay menacingly beneath me.

Despite not being able to voice my worst sin, being so evil I had corrupted a priest, my many other sins needed regular forgiveness. After confession you performed an act of penance, usually a few Hail Mary's, maybe a decade of the rosary, but people with serious sins had to walk around the church doing the Stations of the Cross. And everyone stared. With my sins I would be stared at too as I genuflected at the fourteen stations placed around the church. Everyone would know what I had been up to, as apart from sex, the only other serious sins were becoming a lapsed Catholic and murder. I saved up my pocket money and bought a long blonde wig, which I wore whenever I went to confession, now in the more anonymous Cathedral in town.

One Saturday I walked up the aisle of the cathedral in my wig. I passed a nun from the convent. She looked straight at me as if recognising me. I stared unblinking, back. Under my blonde wig, not a flicker betrayed my sudden fear. She stared at me first accusingly, then bewildered, and then away.

A profound relief flooded me. For the first time in my life I felt I was safe and could breathe. Under God's patriarchal, omnipotent, omniscient, omnipresent eye and the strict, devout, matriarchal eyes of my mother and the nuns, it had been impossible to find any private space, have secrets or be myself. I had grown up in occupied territory, my inner world constantly penetrated and revealed to one or the other. Nowhere had been safe. My only escape had been to bury myself in a book and not to hear when spoken to, to go for long bike rides alone, to lie hidden in fields of bluebells. Even then I would have to return and explain where I had been, confess my thoughts, especially the most secret – the rebellious and the impure.

With the blank stare I gave that puzzled nun, I began to re-claim the territory of my own being, the sacred inner temple where I could become myself. I had at last found a sanctuary other than the one in church. Though I paid a terrible price in even more guilt. One of Satan's names is Beelzebub, 'the Lord of Lies'. Perhaps I was indeed on the side of the Devil.

I now know it is essential to be able to lie. Without the capacity to lie we can have no inner life and are transparently available to whoever cares to look. Living in such utter vulnerability, with no privacy or inner safety, destroys any personal self, as it nearly destroyed me. If we cannot be dishonest, tell lies, keep secrets, manipulate the truth or deceive, we are too exposed to the gaze of both friends and strangers. We would never leave our parents, enjoy dinner parties or relax in the company of others. Utterly incapable of gestating anything in the solitude of our own inner space, our privacy repeatedly violated by anyone's enquiry, we would have no creativity, no freedom, and no self. It is not only Satan who must be practiced at the art of deception.

We each need a forked tongue that can tell both truth and lies, even to God if needs be. An omnipotent, omnipresent, omniscient being, leaves us with nothing, unless we steal ourselves back. Surely the real subversion of God's authority and the beginning of true knowledge was not eating an apple, it was when Adam and Eve hid from Him.

The art of lying, however, lies in knowing which truth and which lie to tell to whom and when.

I never read that in the Catechism. Neither did I read what really made me had been the love my parents made. Or that life was for the living, not the dying. There were many things I had not read in the Catechism or the Catholic Truth Society Pamphlets on sale in the Church porch. I soon made up for it.

My subversive reading from the library took off in all directions: Nietzsche, Simone de Beauvoir, Camus, Jung, and beat poetry with its songs of freedom. All were books I could scarcely understand, but sensed in them whole worlds lay waiting to be explored. I hid my new knowledge under my long bond wig and went forth into a world full of unfamiliar colours, clothes, sounds, and tastes. My first taste of pure orange juice hit my taste buds like an electric shock. My first smell of real coffee hit me so hard it not only woke me up, it knocked me out. And there was the music.

The first generation that did not have to march to the drums of war, we were free to create our own sound track, dance to our own music and sing new songs of love and freedom. We took this opportunity and ran with it. Ran into the future, as completely and blindly as creatures run from a burning building.

Except that it was we who burned. We burned flags, bras, weed, law books and history. And we burned with a fervour to change everything. The old world was so rapidly changing, if we had looked back, we would have been petrified, turned to stone. So we didn't. We danced in the streets, fixed our sights on the far horizon, and ran as completely into the music as the music ran into us.

Chapter 2
Dancing to the Best Tunes

In the sixth form we were allowed to stay in during lunch break which saved us from hanging around in dismal huddles in corners of the playground, looking anything but the with-it dolly birds, French intellectuals or hardened sex-goddesses, we so much wanted to be. Kathryn, Sandy, Eileen, Patsy and I met every break in Room 6, and considered ourselves the most seriously cool in the school. For a start we were known to occasionally smoke and wear sling backs with heels at weekends. We lounged on desks, flicked our hair, waved around imaginary cigarettes, and discussed profound existential issues such as was it more cool to be a mod or a rocker, to scream for John or Paul. We rated boys on scales of 1 to 10 on various attributes and talents – and I don't mean their O-level grades. We dissolved into uncontrollable giggles about absolutely nothing, though that nothing was the funniest thing we had ever come across. Teenage girls all over the world know this.

After school 'The Room 6 Gang', would catch the 16A bus and go down town. On the top deck we would re-arrange our school uniforms, hitch up our skirts, stuff our white gloves into our satchels and try to hide our ridiculous panama hats. The Loreto Convent School uniform was known all over Nottingham, but not how we wore it.

We stuffed tissue paper down our bras, rolled up our skirts revealing our knees and backcombed our hair, though with my hair, I chewed gum instead. We may have been hanging out in Nottingham's High St but we were really cool, Californian cool. Or at least some of us were – it was a question of style. There were those who listened to Cliff Richards, Country and Western, Petula Clarke, those who listened to Dusty Springfield, Herman's Hermits and Cilla Black, and then there were those who listened to the Rolling Stones, the Animals, the Kinks, the Beachboys – and anything on the Tamla Motown and London American (Atlantic) labels. But we all listened to the Beatles, in our pale lipstick and as much mascara as you can load onto your eyelashes without poking your eye out bouncing around on the top deck of a 16A bus.

In a dark corner of the Co-op down town were four record booths where you could listen to the latest single before you bought it. We never had money or the hi-fi to play it on, but we'd pretend to contemplate a purchase, and then request all our favourites one after the other. After a day spent with nuns trying to teach us how young Catholic ladies should behave, to look at the bottom of our glass when drinking, wear demure clothes, never to slam doors, answer back our elders or have hair that touched our shoulders, we squashed together in the Co-op booths, giggling and picking up such good vibrations they were giving us excitations not forbidden by the nuns because they didn't know about them. And that was just the vinyl.

According to our school rules, we were not permitted to speak to any male while in school uniform, though we were allowed to nod should we meet our fathers or brothers, and, of course, any priest could have his way with us conversationally whatever we were wearing, but with the rest of the male population we were to caste our eyes down and walk demurely on. But who would see and report us if we whispered and jiggled with boys in this dark corner of the Co-op?

But God and the nuns do not look at the bottom of the glass when drinking; they look around and see everything. I was seen laughing with a boy, 'flirtatiously' and worse, 'without a hat.' I was sent to the Headmistress, Mother Frances Xavier, who towered above me in her black flapping habit, showering phrases on my unruly red hair, which I knew she disapproved of anyway: 'dreadfully disappointing...' 'terrible waste....' 'should know better...' and that kind of thing. But the effect was ruined as going through my head the whole time was a line I had just heard in The Animal's version of 'House of the Rising Sun' with its lyric of 'and it's been the ruin of many a poor girl, and God, I know I'm one.' Those sinful chords took me somewhere else.

'What are you smiling at girl, this is no laughing matter!'

'No, Mother Frances. You're right Mother Frances. Those sounds are to die for not just to smile for.' But, no; I didn't. I caste my eyes down demurely.

I knew someone who knew someone who's cousin was the producer of the new 'Top of the Pops', which was much more trendy than 'Ready, Steady,

Go' or 'Six-Five Special'. I kept trying to persuade my friend to persuade their friend to persuade their cousin to get us tickets for the show, but until they materialised the Co-op booths would have to do. Those, and the pirate radio stations that had begun broadcasting off the coast somewhere in the Channel. Dad found me an old reel-to-reel tape recorder and I spent hours bent over the radio twiddling with the dial tuning into Radio Caroline and Radio London trying to record my favourite songs onto long reels of tape with the minimum of hiss. I don't know how my friends, and I could sing new songs after hearing them only once or twice through crackly badly tuned tinny mono radios, but we did. 'I was a lonely soul, I had nobody...' until I found a generation out there, like me, who sang these same songs.

The music alone could make you stagger off the straight and narrow, but there was more turbulence on its way. I read Jack Kerouac's *On the Road*.

I was ill with a cold and off school. I lay in bed and began to read. I have no idea how many opened that book and got a blast of energy way beyond anything they might have expected. I imagine it was thousands. I was one. Lying in my bedroom in a house full of crucifixes, holy water stoops, pictures of the Sacred Heart and statues of Our Lady, I was blasted into another world. That book spoke to my generational soul like nothing I had encountered before. I suddenly understood that 'throwing caution to the winds' was not 'making a big mistake', but a vital spontaneity that made the fearful insurances, careful planning and deals with the real Devil, to swap this glorious life of the body for a disembodied one in heaven, look like the empty death it really is. My boyfriend could not believe his luck when I told him I would 'do it' next weekend if the weather was fine. The weather only figured as we had neither car nor bedroom where we would be undisturbed, so it had to be the fields.

The sun shone as we lay on the banks of the river Trent.

Within six months I was sleeping with my boyfriends and enjoying all night parties when my parents thought I was staying over with friends. It was wonderful. I loved it. We all loved it. The laughter; the sex; and the dancing. Every Saturday night we would meet in one of the new coffee bars that had sprung up all over the place to decide where to go.

There was the Palais de Dance with its massive mirrored ball twinkling over a different scene on Saturday night than during the week when it was strictly ballroom. There were the Boat Clubs, converted old boats on the River Trent, as well as other large dark rooms up rickety stairs, where you put your handbags on the floor and danced around them hoping a boy would ask you to dance. Maybe this boy was a good dancer. Maybe later he would be a good kisser. Maybe later still he could be a boyfriend. As apart from the sheer fun of dancing, the point of the exercise was to get a boyfriend.

A boy we all fancied, a real heartthrob, asked me to come to a party with him. He was a cool dancer, tall, good-looking and could borrow his father's car sometimes. What more could you want? I was stunned. Perhaps he had not seen my wiry red hair in daylight and had got the mistaken idea I was beautiful. He obviously hadn't seen the bump in my nose. Or worse ... my freckles. The night of the party arrived. I wished I could wear my long blonde wig, but being *seen* in the wig was not the point.

We began 'courting'. We went for walks. We went to the movies. We went to parties. But wherever or whatever we did, this was really the prelude to what would happen in the car later. His arm around me pulling me to him on the back seat. Touching. Close smells. Breathing slowly. A throbbing deep inside me with an insistent beat that grew into a heavy rhythm pulling us into its embrace. Down and down we fell.

In panic and guilt, I would pull out the wig and rush to confession. For a brief period I was free to be run over by a bus and not damned for eternity. Unfortunately confessions were always on a Saturday, and on Saturday night I would fall from grace all over again, until the anxiety and guilt became more than I could stand and I'd rush back to confession for my next hit of forgiveness.

An institution that has survived so many wars, regime changes, political upheavals, that has accumulated more wealth than can be calculated, is obviously going to be adept in the arts of dealing out that opium to the masses. Though I soon learned another way to dream from a different part of the poppy.

One night, after dancing at a club, I went back with a bunch of musicians to their flat. They rolled a joint and I smelled my first marijuana. These were not school kids living with parents and this was not your usual weed. It was intense straight from the American sinsemilla grass that released pure Californian sun into down town Nottingham. They passed it round and when it came to me I took it and stared.

'I've never had this stuff' I said, looking up at them helplessly.

'Hey, that's OK. We'll show you.' They showed me how to inhale it, keep it in my lungs, slowly breathe it out and let the high gently take me. They showed me how to roll pure grass. How to smoke it. How to use a roach clip. When and how to pass on different kinds of blow. How to hold it. How to suck it when it's hot and near the end. How to roll with tobacco. How to hang the Rizla cigarette papers together. How to balance an LP cover on your knees as a surface for this whole operation, though of course, John Mayall's Bluesbreakers, not Gerry and the Pacemakers. How to heat up the resin and crumble it into the joint. How to get high. In one evening I was taught the whole etiquette of dope.

That grass was strong. Every detail of this operation took on the significance of a sacrament. We were totally focused and each one of us completely understood this was a sacred substance to be treated with great respect through a series of holy and time-honoured rituals. At least that's what I thought, and what I thought they thought, and what I thought they thought, I thought. Totally focused on the ritualistic drama of rolling a joint, we could see all the great stories of the world came down to these same details– this, here, us. And then suddenly the world cracked open and I leaped up as the forces of the Earth came up from the ground and an earthquake rocked through me.

There was only one way to be with this massive power and that was to dance with it, surrender to it, let it move me wherever it would. I have no idea what music those musicians were hearing but they were making the most incredible sounds on their guitars. We had no choice but to let those great subterranean forces do their thing with us. One guy beat out a rhythm so compelling we all fell into it and travelled back through time to before all sound. In the silence someone made tea, the most amazing tea, a tea full of such exquisite tea-fulness it was the most tea-ful tea imaginable. I went to the loo saw myself in the mirror. My God! The pupils of my eyes were so wide open I could see a whole world in them. I leaned over the sink and travelled into and through my own eyes, and in that bathroom mirror, was stunned to discover that within me, lay a whole universe.

I had only recently discovered there existed an inner world; here I was falling right into it. And it was boundless. I fell through an endless darkness and suddenly panicked. I was about to disappear into a bottomless void. This inner universe was so vast, I was on the brink of annihilation. I leaned over the sink, but this sickness can't be relieved by being sick.

'Help I need somebody. Help, not just anybody...' I knew that when I raised my head, when I looked up into that mirror, I would see the awful truth – that I was nothing, worthless, an empty space not a person. I lifted my head and looked at this sad eyed lady of the Midlands. The whole of existence looked implacably back at me. I found myself gazing into the eyes of the first person I had met who I sensed might be able to help me. I made a promise. One day, I would become that person, the one I had glimpsed in the mirror – the one who maybe, just maybe, was going to be the one to save me.

As you know, with this kind of deep cosmic stuff there's no time, and after an eternity, the music being played next door called out to me and brought me back. I came out of that sacred toilet with new songs of myself, singing the body electric, celebrating the music of the spheres that, I now knew, was what these guys had been playing all along. I told them I hadn't realised I was hanging out with gods on Mount Olympus. That Walt Whitman must have read the Upanishads while stoned. That rock music plugged right into the soul of the universe. That I was picking up such good vibrations, and...

Maybe that was when I gently fell sideways and asleep.

After realizing musicians were naturally in touch with the 'forces', I began to hang out with them more. One of my boyfriends edited a magazine, and though it only ran for a couple of issues, I would interview the bands that came to Nottingham for a gig. This was great. I not only met these rock gods, I got into their performances free. I could not have afforded it otherwise.

My total income for the week was 17/6 (about 85p) from a Saturday job on the handbag sales counter at British Home Stores. Next to the handbag counter was the record counter and while unzipping purses and pointing out the inside pockets of handbags, to women who liked Perry Como and Russ Conway and had permed their hair into orderly curls, I jiggled my unruly mop to the sweet sounds coming from the next counter. The Four Tops, The Supremes, The Kinks, the Animals, the Beatles, the Rolling Stones, Dylan – and I sang all day long.

Everything I earned went on clothes and shoes. You had to have the gear to look like the cool dolly bird you knew you really were if you could only get your act together. I knew that with my inside info on the dope scene my cool credentials were, well, cool, but that was no good without the white boots and Empire line paisley dress to prove it. I thought the accounts department might give me my wages before lunch rather than at the end of the day, so I could go shopping in the lunch hour.

I went upstairs during the morning tea break and asked to see the accounts manager. He arrived with what I thought only ever appeared in books, strands of long hair drawn across a bald head and plastered down with Vaseline. He must have grown these few hairs specially, as they were so long I think he had them looped over his ear to anchor the arrangement. I did not want to hurt his feelings by staring so I rushed into my request instead.

'Can I have my wages at lunchtime rather than just before we go? You see…' I paused. I realised I was speaking to a guy would not understand that I just had to have that dress for tonight's dance. 'You see…' I was thinking fast now. 'You see … erm … I need it.' I finished lamely.

'Sorry. Can't. Not procedure.'

'OK. Fair enough. Worth a try though eh?' I smiled.

I had yet to understand the power of a young girl's genuine smile on a middle aged man with hair wrapped over his head, and as I turned away he sighed.

'Well, if you really need it, I suppose…'

'Oh I do, I do! You see there's this dress in C&A…'

'Never mind that. Come back before lunch and I'll have it here for you.'

And he did. Every Saturday. I would pop up during morning tea break and he would pass over the envelope with its ten-shilling note and the cash that slid around so promisingly inside it.

'Thanks Mr. Edwards. I really appreciate this.'

'That's fine, just don't spend it all at once.'

But of course I did. I popped over to C&A opposite to get my outfit for that night. I always knew exactly what I wanted to buy.

My family was not wealthy. We either wore clothes we made ourselves or those we had got from a jumble sale. When the school Christmas parties came, I had only my clumpy lace-up school shoes to wear, while the other girls had sparkly sandals. One year, for a change, I went in my slippers. The other girls laughed at me. My only defence was to pretend I didn't care. I pretended so well I nearly convinced myself – but not totally as after that, I spent hours pouring over the Littlewoods catalogue trying to work out how much I could afford each week for a pair of shoes and a jacket other than my school blazer.

All my money went on clothes, shoes, and dancing. Books I got from the library. Cigarettes and drinks from hopeful boys. Though to do this I had to pretend I only had two O-levels, as it didn't do to be too brainy at the bar in the Palais.

Interviewing musicians was simple in those more innocent days. There were no minders, no ultra violet stamps or wristbands, no back stage passes. I just made up a press identity card, stuck my photo on it and was always told 'Fine. In you go!' And although media images of that time were that we were all stoned and wearing beads, patchouli oil and hanging out with Rock stars, actually there weren't that many of us really, not in Nottingham anyway. Certainly none of my friends from school came with me to these more funky scenes. And none of them smoked dope. I once took a copy of the new International Times to school with its articles on expanded consciousness, the links between Zen and getting stoned, and interviews with Allen Ginsberg and Timothy Leary on the intelligence of dolphins. My friends looked blank and didn't get it. I wasn't sure what I was getting either, but all this held a promise of a land of milk and honey somewhere out there, and was manna from heaven to someone more familiar with scrabbling in dried grass in a desert. Though I could not explain exactly what drew me so strongly.

Mother Pauline found my copy. Horrified she took it to Mother Francis Xavier. I was called into see three of them this time. That was bad, but what was worse was they were truly distressed that my immortal soul was in danger. I tried to put their minds at rest.

'You see it's about new ways to find out what we don't know. And there's more that we don't know we don't know than even what we know we don't know. If you know what I mean.' Not surprisingly, they didn't. Neither did I really.

We stared at each other across an abyss. My punishment was to write out Thomas Aquinas's proofs of the existence of God. I was sad as I left that room, not about having to write about Prime Movers and First Causes, but because they were genuinely worried and upset about me and there was nothing I could do. Mother Francis, Mother Pauline and Mother Bernard, had each loved me as a daughter of the Church. They had smiled at me when I used to go to those early morning convent masses. They had nurtured my vocation and had high hopes of my future as a nun. They knew I had been playing around with boys a bit, but this was different. I knew it was and so did they.

I wanted to tell them that maybe they hadn't failed. Maybe their teaching had helped me develop a sense of real enquiry and my adventures were a sign they hadn't totally frozen me into blind obedience. Maybe they had done a better job than they ever imagined. But there was nothing that could be said to bridge a misunderstanding so deep it broke a piece of all our hearts.

At least with musicians you didn't have to explain yourself. Guitar riffs speak louder than words and are plenty proof enough of the existence of gods.

The musicians I interviewed would naturally try to get me into their beds. What else could they do when it became clear I hadn't a clue about music really, other than they were great, and their music fab, and wasn't it cool, man? But my primary mission was a meeting of minds, not the kinds of meetings they had in mind.

I told them – making love not war was about really listening to each other. They nodded – 'yeah babe, that's so where it's at, man.' It was about putting yourself into another's shoes, seeing through their eyes, and understanding each other. They nodded 'Yeah that is so real, really real.' I can see I am beginning to get through. I press on. 'It's about getting high and gazing deep into each other's eyes so that you can see the universe in each other. 'Yeah that is so right-on babe. Let's gaze into each other's universes back at to the hotel.' There were enough beautiful groupies around to help these musicians relax after their intense performances, well able to raise parts of their anatomy, but I was the only psycho-spiritual groupie trying to raise their consciousness.

Naturally there were times when my consciousness fell, along with my latest C&A dress. Then I too, along with the other groupies, smiled a knowing Mona Lisa smile when the same Rock gods who had sighed in my arms, strutted their stuff to thousands.

It was strange, the more seriously cool the bands, and the less I seemed to worry about my wiry red hair. Something else was going on that I had yet to fathom. Whatever the reason it was a relief to be less concerned about my wild rebellious hair, which resolutely continued in its own fashion, irrespective of what I wanted. I longed for the silky, long-swinging hair of Kathy McGowan or Sandie Shaw, and tried to iron my hair straight and slept with sticky tape holding it down over my cheeks. All I managed was a zigzag effect and rectangular red marks on my face. So when I came across the energy phenomena that was Jimi Hendrix, with his stratospheric level of cool, my wild unruly 'looking like I'd been dragged through a hedge backwards' hair did not come into it. Anyway, no one gave a damn about his hair and it was far worse than mine.

Several hundred of us were gathered in Nottingham's Rainbow Rooms waiting for the man we already knew was a rock genius. Most people had not yet heard of him, but through the instinctual grape vine and the jungle drums of cool, we, the hip most with-it guys in the Midlands, we knew.

I was six feet from the stage when Jimi leaped out and began to pour his music into us. We'd heard rumours from London, that his live performances were like nothing else on Earth, but we were not prepared for this.

We listened to sounds never heard before, to songs not yet sung in any time or space ever – certainly not in Nottingham. Waves of pure energy washed over us. This was not just music. It was an Earth shattering mind blowing raw primal winds of the universe sound tsunami. We none of us had any choice in the matter, the music ordered us and, submerged in the throbbing, pulsing, moving, living music, we danced. Jimi Hendrix, musician, poet, tantric shaman, energy phenomenon, made love with his guitar and released orgasmic sounds with feedback howls that went on and on and on...

His recorded albums do not have the electric spontaneity of his live performances; no record company would have released such sounds on any label in those days. It was pure energy. A hard, cruel father, a failure at school, hours alone in a garage with just his guitar as a friend, Jimi fell so deep into the music, he broke through, and gave it to us, heart, body and soul. And he took us with him. To a dark wilderness so raw, it bit into you and savaged your soul. Life would never be the same again.

We staggered out into down town Nottingham, several hundred of us disoriented, wild eyed, shocked, and strangely silent. What had gone on in there? We did not want to leave each other and hung out in bars, stunned victims of the same catastrophic event. We knew the world had changed. People think I am exaggerating; but this was before the Who smashed guitars on stage, before music videos, before dance routines, before any electronic wall of sound produced in studios. The Moog synthesiser had not even been invented. P .J. Proby had recently been banned just for splitting his trousers during a performance. Bob Dylan had not yet horrified fans at Newport or at the Royal Albert Hall when he used an electric back-up band – though I for one didn't feel betrayed, on the contrary. But that's how far back this was.

To my eternal regret I was so blasted, it never occurred to me to pull out my press card and actually meet Jimi. But then, as I was to learn much later, it rarely works out when a mortal meets their god.

I had been taught the fires of hell lie in wait to receive those who fall too far; but as I could not stop my freefall into sexuality, dancing, the life of the body, I split into two. Part of me flew as high as I could to reach the light, to re-negotiate my old deal with those who rule in heaven; and part of me fell and kept on falling deeper into darkness, into the interior of that dark continent – the body. So although England was swinging and having fun, I was swinging but confused, divided between songs of innocence at Mass and Benediction (*Introibo ad altare Dei. Ad Deum Qui laetificat juventutem meum*) and songs of experience ('But first are you experienced. Have you ever been experienced, well I have…')

Which was me? The bright light one, on the side of the angels, striving for love and peace everywhere? Or that dark hidden one, who had had secret meetings with a Devil who told me our hearts are of darkness, our liver and kidneys too. If they come to light, we die.

I began to hear the shadow side of the beat poetry, the hip culture, the darkness in those drug highs, that their howls were not only freedom songs, but also ominous warnings of sinister truths. The violence and horror of hell was also in there, maybe telling us the forces of darkness are as great as the forces of light. Or was this just my fear? I read that Freud had concluded in the dark years of WW II that Thanatos, the death instinct is more powerful, in the end, than Eros, the instinct for life. But he was old and had never smoked powerful weed or danced all night. In the mistake all generations must make if they are to give new forms to ancient wisdom, we thought we were different. Maybe we were.

The Apollo 8 spacecraft had recently sent back pictures of Earth from space and we saw our lovely blue and green planet for the first time, the only colour in a black and white universe, the home to so many living, breathing creatures as it floated through space. So beautiful. So alone. Even the astronauts had wept. Though all before us had failed, we were determined to bring peace and love to our precious planet Earth. That we had seen for the first time was one world – and so heartbreakingly vulnerable.

Yet while striving for the light, the forces of darkness found me anyway. They came up through the earth and made me dance. They beat their rhythm in music that demanded my surrender. They called to me in seductive songs and pulled me into a darker, more insistent freedom than any blackbird knows.

After the Jimi Hendrix experience, I found I had moved so far from the world of my childhood it was as if I was looking back on a village from half way up a mountain. The houses were tiny, the people specks moving in the distance and unrecognisable. I couldn't be seen by them either. I wanted to call out 'it's lovely up here! The air is sweet and fresh. Come and look at the view! I wanted to tell them about the wild flowers, the butterflies, the larks singing. I wanted to tell them how good it felt to walk on a path through unknown territory where round every corner was something new. I wanted to tell them about the music, about the dancing, how wonderful it was to be coming alive. But my words couldn't reach that far and were carried away in the wind.

I became a child of those times – less and less a child of my parents.

And all the while a great surge of collective energy was forming itself into a massive wave that would carry me, and so many, to shores beyond our wildest dreams. I heard it coming, singing its irresistible siren promise of liberation, love and dancing in the streets. I let go – fell into it – and was gone.

Chapter 3

A Friend of the Devil is a Friend of Mine

I had been gradually leaving my family for years, then, one October morning, I packed a suitcase and left. It was a bright crisp autumn with a bite in the wind that brought tears to your eyes; but not to mine. Nothing was going to dampen my spirits, not even those autumn mists that frizzed my hair. With my C&A dresses, my long boots, now dyed purple, and the most wicked of my books, I got ready to travel fifty miles up the brand new motorway to Sheffield University.

Eager to go, I bounced through my good-byes smiling. My parents would have preferred a more sombre affair, tinged with sadness, but I was too excited. I had anyway said so many secret good-byes to their world; this was just another step on a long march that had begun years before. My sisters and brother were very sad, two of them cried. I tried to tease them out of it.

'Did you know a leech has 32 brains. Maybe there'll just be a load of leeches there, it'll be so disgusting I come straight back!'

They looked at me unsmilingly.

'That's not funny.'

No. And neither was I coming back.

I went to Sheffield to study maths simply because at the interview we were given a set of strange problems to solve and I had several flashes of inspiration and solved them. They told me all I had to get was two E grades and I was in. Being so engrossed in my extra curricular activities, I went for this easy option as I could easily get two E-grades. I ended up getting all A grades anyway as I had a gift for abstract thinking, if not for some of the more important aspects of life.

At the registration desk for 'Pure Mathematics', my major subject, I was asked what subsidiary I wanted to study. I hadn't thought about it. I noticed the next desk was for 'Psychology'. No one from my family, or anyone we knew had ever gone to university before, I could hardly break through more cultural frontiers and study a weird subject like psychology.

'Psychology!' I told the lecturer at the desk.

'I don't think so', he told me. 'It should be physics, statistics or computing. Besides the timetables are not synchronised.'

With no status or wealth behind me, a person of no significance or worth on any social scale I knew about, I nearly gave way in front of the august power and might of this university system.

'But I'd really like to study psychology', I said despairingly as I stared at a future of numbers and graphs with little relevance to the real mysteries of life, such why we are as we are.

He sighed. But he wrote down 'Psychology'.

'Thank you, thank you!' I told him. Though I managed to rein in my excited explanations of why it was important to me to unravel at last, the crazy contradictory tangles in my own soul. If there were clashes between maths and psychology, there was no doubt which lectures I would be missing.

I did not yet know, academic psychology was more about rats in mazes than the human craziness that studies rats in mazes more than itself. Neither did I know the intellectual mind, far from trying to understand the less articulate heart, bullied it.

Several hundred female students lived in Halifax Hall where each Tuesday and Thursday we gathered for formal dinner and a lecture from the Head of Hall on how young women should comport themselves. 'If you could see what you looked like from behind wearing trousers, you would not wear them!' I thought only vicar's wives in Agatha Christie's books said that kind of thing. Has she never been to C&A where its changing rooms had mirrors at angles for exactly that purpose? In my psychedelic T-shirt and Levis, I gazed at her in her gown and pearls, across a socio-economic-class-generational divide, so vast I could see no possibility of it ever being bridged.

I looked around for comrades in the cultural revolution, happening right under their noses whether the straights knew about it or not, and found Denise. Denise and I smoked dope and said 'yeah man' a lot. We raved about the new mind blowing Doors album. We were outraged by Enoch Powell's Rivers of Blood speech. We knew the difference between

Afghani Red and Thai Black. As this was the mid-sixties in Sheffield, there were not many of us cool chicks around yet, so obviously we had to check out who were the hip guys to hang out with. There's no point rolling superb joints, on exactly the right LPs if your mates are not going to appreciate how dead trendy you are. Though there was a lot more to being with-it than just listening to the Doors, Hendrix and the Velvet Underground.

You had to wear Levis in the bath to shrink them to your legs, then scrub them with a pumice stone to fade them as if they'd been worn in a Californian sun all summer – preferably somewhere around Big Sur or hanging out with Janis Joplin and The Grateful Dead in San Francisco. You couldn't just sing the blues, sway to un-electrified folk music, jiggle your head in complex rhythms in jazz dives, you had to jump around and wave your arms in free flowing spontaneous movements to rock music. And there was the hair. To my delight, your hair could go its own way. In all directions: 'fab', or rather, 'far-out'.

As seriously heavy counter cultural revolutionaries, it was a political act in itself to be trendy, tie-dye your clothes in psychedelic colours, wear patchouli oil and second hand fur coats inside out. Being seen on the scene with with-it clothes and hip talk was helping turn on and expand the consciousness of the world, and such expanding consciousnesses, being raised to new heights daily, needed new language. As Wittgenstein pointed out, the way you say it is what you say. Or would that be Marshal McLuhan – the medium is the message? Both were pretty hip guys to be reading anyway. Out was 'fab', in was 'funky'. You could say 'Wow, man' as much as you liked, but not 'Groovy', and never 'Groovy, baby'. Yet, the coolest words came only hot from the lips of the beautiful people themselves; and they all hung out in London, which put us provincials at a disadvantage. We were always a few weeks behind. Before long, however, we discovered we now all lived in a global village, even those of us in Yorkshire. It was happening simultaneously everywhere – Big Sur, Greenwich Village, Chelsea, Tangiers, Afghanistan and yes, Sheffield – according to *Oz* magazine anyway.

Parties, lovers, friends to hang out with day and night, great music, walks on the moors, discussions into the night about the existence of God, the true nature of the class struggle and the best lay out for Rizla cigarette papers when rolling a joint … the first generation that had not had to go to war or join the army for National Service made good use of that freedom. Not forgetting what may have been the most important liberation of them all, at least for us women – birth control.

When still at school, I had gone through paroxysms of anxiety each month waiting for my period. I was very strict about birth control and made all my boyfriends wear condoms or only did it in 'the safe period'. But accidents could happen and for years I had carefully kept as a talisman a worn piece of paper with a phone number should I ever need an abortion. But now the pill was freely available on prescription. For the first time in history a whole generation of women could have both sexuality *and* freedom. The relief of that alone could account for the explosion of sexual activity that went on. Making love and not war was not only fun but also an imperative revolutionary act. So no guilt! (Well, not much anyway.)

I moved into a flat and even more freedom to mellow out and explore new ways of being. I soon stopped going to most lectures, there were far more important things to attend to – especially as the revolution could arrive on the streets of Sheffield at any moment. We had to be prepared.

My good works for the souls in purgatory and the 'poor of the parish' had faded long before, but all that caring had to go somewhere. I went on a few 'Ban the Bomb' marches; but the sandals with socks and earnest folk music (where you sat down and gently swayed), meant I couldn't give myself heart and soul. Plus there were a fair few vicars around and I was allergic to men of the cloth. I had then thought I would save what in those days we called 'The Third World', but during Freshers Week, when all the societies lay out their wares, the stand for this had been staffed by Christians. Wearing tweed skirts. One had coughed when I came near with my cigarette and said 'Do you mind?' with a phoney smile, when she was the one who minded and we all smoked then. There were so many cool postures that could only be adopted with a cigarette in your hand – especially of the 'fuck you' variety. A cigarette was in fact an essential fashion accessory unless you looked like Twiggy or Marianne Faithful who were so beautiful they could wear tweed skirts and still seem cool.

The stands further along, for the International Socialists, the Worker's Revolutionary Party, the Socialist Labour League and the International Marxist Group, were however packed with intense smokers who looked you in the eye with serious frowns rather than phoney smiles. I preferred this bunch. I already thought 'property was theft' – or at least I liked saying it, and 'when you ain't got nothing, you've got nothing to lose'.

The first priority according to the radical left – as opposed to the straight left, the Stalinist left, the bourgeois left, the democratic left and even the fascist left, though who they were was not quite clear, any group you disagreed with I think – was to confront our bourgeois individualistic conditioning so our commitment was at one with the dialectics of history and, when the time came, we could shoot to kill. I knew I could not shoot anyone. For me the socialist vision was 'to each according to their needs, from each according to their abilities' so everyone would be free to have as much fun as I was having. It was not about killing. What was the point in a Revolutionary Worker's Party if there was never any actual partying?

I was criticised a lot for this frivolous reactionary position by my comrades who interpreted Trotsky's speech at the Fourth International rather differently. Whether in the IMG, the WRP, the SLL or IS, we fought each other with far more vehemence that we did the true enemy, which I think was 'the Capitalist State', though it may have been Royalty and Religion as well. We hadn't yet decided that it was actually 'patriarchy'; that came a few years later. I think some of us, later still, decided the true enemy was in fact within, in the internalised oppression of individualistic conditioning and the fascist body armouring of fear. At least that was my view.

I remember walking back to the Psychology Department with my friend Steve, and in a brilliantly lucid explanation as to why my analysis of society was correct, I told him 'But I am right and they are wrong!'

He couldn't stop laughing. Since being laughed at was not the point of any of this, I learned to hide how often I was right about almost everything.

Every day reading the newspapers in the student's union, looking for signs of the coming revolution, endless analyses of the state of the class struggle, regular re-interpretations of interpretations of Trotsky, and I began to long for a deeper freedom than that from capitalism. I became restless sitting on those grey stackable plastic chairs on lino marked with burns made by the roll-ups we claimed to smoke as an expression of solidarity with the alienation and poverty of the working class, though the Rizla papers had other uses.

A comrade stood up to address one Tuesday evening meeting. He looked at me pointedly and then declaimed around the room.

'I would like to bring this meeting's attention to the behaviour of a particular comrade, who was selling the *Socialist Worker* outside the steel works in Attercliffe last Friday, wearing completely inappropriate bourgeois decadent clothing that marked her out as a potential class enemy and a recidivist revisionist individualist!'

Though this was not a rap duel. I knew this guy. He had hit on me in the bar when we were drinking after a meeting a few weeks earlier. I had not been exactly rude but, he was more Trotskyite than Trotsky, almost a Stalinist Maoist and everyone knows they never get down and funky; they're not into *any* music, except revolutionary chants at the barricades. I had sweetly declined the favour. Though perhaps he had noticed I had not declined the favours of some of his sexier comrades.

My turn.

'The sexual frustration in this comrade's revelation is really an expression of his emotional repression. He's got less instinctual anarchy, than an androgynous sick monarchy. There's no vibration, no flirtation' just an anal fixation. He's so beyond salvation, there's no point in arbitration, what he really needs is a total renovation!'

I spin in cool moves inviting the Sheffield Massive to applaud my killer rap attack.

No I didn't. It was nearly 40 years ago. Heavy rap sessions were what you got up to when getting into where it was at and what it was all down to, man – not hip-hop.

The comrades all turned and looked at me. I don't know which was redder, my hair, my face or my new oh so cool to die for Biba jacket that I had bought on my last decadent trip to London and where on Kensington High Street this new temple to style had recently opened its doors and half my term's grant went in one afternoon. Oh, but now when I walked into lectures and the students' union bar, heads turned. Even the coolest of the cool guys who organised the rock concerts wanted to know me. But this stalwart of the inexorable historical dialectic was not to be distracted even by wild red hair, long slim legs and a sexy Biba outfit.

I stood up.

'Well obviously I am totally dedicated to the class struggle and all that, but I have trouble combining the needs of the party with my needs to party. And though Marx is a far-out, cool guy and I'm totally with you on Trotsky's call for international communism, there's too much of a fascist bureaucratic state happening here, so I'm off to liberate the workers in a different kind of class action.' Or something like that anyway. And I quit.

At least I hadn't been accused of being petty bourgeois. That was worse than being called a fascist. Though I wasn't quite sure what was the difference between plain bourgeois and petty bourgeois. Maybe if you were petty it was because you were preoccupied with which fork to use for desert, how to address royalty, ironing handkerchiefs, petty things like that, rather than the grand sweep of the revolution. Though I did know that to be one was so far beneath contempt, even being a fascist was not as bad.

Obviously I still despised capitalism, and hoped workers would soon cease to be alienated from the means of production, giving them more time to smoke dope, listen to Velvet Underground and make love, just as I also demonstrated against the US in Vietnam and for freedom fighters in Africa, but I began to long for a world freed from inner anguish and torment too. Because of course, my old demons lived in me still.

Even though I was gradually swimming further from that Rock of St Peter, the Catholic Church continued to exert its deadly undertow. But when you have been brought up in intimacy with a rock, you have no bearings in an ocean. Especially when the Rock has terrified you with its tales of hell, petrified you, turned you to stone so that you not only belong to the Rock, you become the Rock. What had once been righteously solid had become fluid, and though I was learning to go with the flow, so many new uncertainties disoriented me as well as liberating me. I was adrift with no one to teach me how to swim. Around me were other young people in the same situation. It was inevitable that we turned to each other.

On a rock, your fixed reference point is where you stand; in the sea, the distant horizon. Perhaps that's why we set our sights on a horizon so far away, we had no other bearings. So when I heard R. D. Laing speak at the Dialectics of Liberation conference in the Round House in the summer of 1968, I was ripe for a new direction and a new teacher – and Ronnie Laing made more sense to me than any person I had ever heard speak before in my life.

It was the summer of 1968 and revolution, love and great music were in the air. My boyfriend was studying architecture at Nottingham University. We had met when I was still at school. He was cool. Very cool. He was the first person at Nottingham University to have long hair and we were stared at everywhere we went. Once, in Hyde Park, in the heart of swinging London itself, a group of Japanese tourists crowded around us. They excitedly called out 'Hiipppieees!' and took photos to show their friends back home the swinging sixties of London. I posed and played the part, not mentioning I was actually a convent school girl from the provinces, who was so out on the edge of the swinging sixties at that point, I could hardly roll a joint that didn't fall apart.

Pete wore a black leather jacket and, in real style, *black* Levis. I didn't even know black Levis existed. He read Nietzsche as well as Marcuse, painted his walls bright colours and rolled a mean joint on the back of LPs from the greatest collection I had ever seen. How could I have failed to fall in love with him? But even more of a wonder was he fell in love with me. He was my first deep love.

I had two lives. In Sheffield I had fun, played around, coolly played the scene. With Pete, in Nottingham, I was more vulnerable. Even thinking about some of the things I was up to was probably a mortal sin. And it was to Pete I whispered the secrets that I dared not tell elsewhere.

No one else seemed to suffer from the terrors I knew. One time in fun, some stoned friends wanted to say a Black Mass by turning a crucifix upside down and saying the Latin prayers backwards. I froze in complete and abject terror.

'No, no, no!' I screamed incoherently, seeing visions of demons laughing, getting ready to devour me, burn me, and take me to evil regions more dreadful than anything even my terror could imagine.

My friends assumed I was having a bad trip on a cocktail of speed, mandrax and the Afghani Black. I didn't tell them that these demons lived in me all the time, hiding in the hell of my own cracked up soul. What had fragmented my being in the first place and allowed such creatures to slide into me through the cracks, was still a mystery to me and I felt deeply ashamed of my terror. I saw it as a dreadful flaw, a debilitating crack in my sanity that ran through me like the San Andreas Fault, threatening destruction and complete mental breakdown at any moment. Perhaps I needed to tell someone about it. All the talking cures, from confession to psychoanalysis, recommended this.

One night after weeks of struggle, terrified that he would turn in shock and reject me in horror, I whispered to Pete,

'I have to let you know, I am actually basically mad.'

There was a pause.

'I'm so sorry,' I added in a small voice, apologising, as much to life as to Pete – I was clearly an existential failure as well as a personal one. To be mad was shameful, disgusting, cracked up and so pathetic, that no one could ever love me. In fact I was so insane I was beyond insane, I did not even have the courage to actually go mad. I admired crazy people. At least they were honest and dared to be themselves far more than I did. I faked it so real I was beyond fake, but the truth was, I was completely fucked up.

Pete turned to me.

'Doesn't everyone feel like that sometimes?'

I felt a relief that nearly broke my heart in its intensity. I had thought the world would end but instead, here I was, still lying in Pete's arms, crazy maybe, but still alive, still here. Though it was clear Pete had not really understood that he had a genuinely crazy person in his arms. A person who was only just managing to hold off complete schizophrenic break-down by sheer effort of will; helped, it has to be said, by a lot of distractions, such as my new long purple suede boots which, with my psychedelic slinky dress, would make me look sexy and cool at the party on Saturday.

How crazy is it after all to be pretending to be exactly who you are?

I heard about the Dialectics of Liberation Conference and was immediately interested in a meeting between all shades of the radical left from Black Power to Maoism, the politicised counter culture and anti-psychiatry with its explorations of the politics of experience. Surely such a great coming together of so many divided camps would not only raise our consciousness to stratospheric levels, it might also heal my own confused, fragmented, divided self. The atmosphere was electric when R. D. Laing took the stage. An existentialist, phenomenologist, anti-psychiatrist, with flashing dark Scottish eyes, a devil in each of them – and both of them spoke.

He explained how all of us are a little mad. Perhaps not so little. And however afraid we are of the chaos of madness, madness has a meaning and chaos can be creative. What is mad within one context may anyway be completely sane within another. A person walks along a road talking to someone who is not there. Maybe they are rehearsing lines for a play. Maybe they are praying. Maybe they are speaking to themselves because no one else understands or cares. To understand what we think is madness we need to find the context that gave rise to it.

His soft Scottish voice with its ever so slightly rolling rrr's caressed me as you would a terrified animal. A horse whisperer of broken hearts. A shamanic healer of despair. A priest of a greater spirit than can be found in churches.

Ronnie Laing kept on talking and I kept on listening, each phrase a Zen stick knocking on my door, seeking to be heard through the layers of my fear in my cracked up fragile psyche. His words were not just music to my ears, they fed my soul. He told me the fundamentalist religions of the world, with their righteous absolute division of life into right and wrong, had made schizophrenics of us all. So it was not only me that was cracked up. I wept. I was no longer so completely alone.

Even when the Maoists at the same conference, told us we were all Running Dogs and Paper Tigers and that it would be better that everyone in the world was killed rather than the Chinese Revolution fail, this could not distract me from Laing's existential antidote to all that sick religion.

Mao himself has always struck me as more of an existentialist than his followers seemed to be, in the west anyway. It was Mao who said to know a pear you had to eat it. And that a frog in a well who says the sky is no bigger than the mouth of the well is confusing his position with reality. Perhaps Mao and R. D. Laing would have understood each other. But then this was not the first time a guru has been profoundly misunderstood by his followers. And, as I was to discover later, neither was it the last.

Ronnie continued.

'Madness and insanity are not the same' his words rolling around the Round House in Chalk Farm, where just around the corner, many years later, I would be meditating furiously in the Kalptaru Rajneesh Meditation Centre to cathartically release my insanity in the Dynamic meditations. 'The worrrd madness is derrrived from a word meaning 'change', while insanity comes from a worrrd meaning 'unhealthy'; there's a worrrld of differrrence. What we call madness is simply the raw chaos of constantly changing life beyond the ordered constructions of the mind. It is the denial of these realities that is the real insanity. To lose touch with the life of the body is to go insane while thinking that what is alive is mad.'

That is my memory of what he said anyway, I was so transfixed I would never be able to remember it exactly. Though I got the message. The first steps had been taken on my own long march to freedom, whatever the Maoists thought. I now knew that to become sane would involve a journey back through what can look like madness. That it was OK to be mad. That there was a meaning in the madness and the true insanity was in the fear of madness, not the madness itself. And anyway it was perhaps society that was mad, not me. Great stuff!

The word 'schizophrenia' is derived from words meaning 'split knowledge' or 'split love', and Laing spoke to the fragmentation and broken hearts of all our schizophrenias. He certainly spoke to mine. Ronnie Laing was the first person to tell me that even someone as ontologically insecure and split off from the reality of their own being as I was, had a place in the universe where they could belong, where they could be loved, where they could be. Though he did tell me once, in one of the long meandering evenings with a group of us lounging around him, drinking and sharing psycho-political therapeutic gossip, he had never seen anyone with such a shattered self who was not diagnosed schizophrenic or out of it on heroin.

Many years later, R. D. Laing died of a heart attack. But only love can break your heart. Perhaps so much lonely visionary greatness and meeting so many broken hearts had broken his own.

The day after he had died, I went round to a friend's who had visited him in Switzerland not long before. People gathered in her large house in Kentish Town from all over London. We sat around and told our favourite stories of him to each other, some of us drinking whiskey, some tea, some rolling joints, things we had done with Ronnie many times. Probably in houses all over the world people gathered to tell similar stories. It usually happens this way when a person of wisdom and love dies, there's celebration of their life rather than a mourning of their death.

His partner showed me his personal notebook. The last thing he had written about was love. 'Love is the greatest untapped natural energy resource on this planet, in short supply simply because we have developed neither our capacity to love nor to be loved.' That's how I remember it anyway.

But he loved me, and I loved him. I know he had devils in him, I had seen them, one in each eye. But they had smiled at me. They had taught me forgiveness and redemption does not lie in the hands of priests but in our own understanding. They told me we are the ones who will heal and redeem us; we are the ones we are waiting for. They told me that even someone as fractured and with as many devils as me, could exist with meaning. They also told me that the quickest way to heaven is straight through hell.

And that's how I learned that a friend of the devil could be a friend of mine.

Chapter 4
The Smiles in the Eyes of the Wise

To be a university student in 1968 was definitely a lucky break in the karmic lottery. We really never had it so good.

Abortion was now legal. Birth control was free on prescription. With no anxieties about getting pregnant we could make love with even more abandon. The law had yet to catch up with us on other fronts. LSD was not yet illegal, neither were home grown grass and mushrooms. That's a lot of legal highs. The anti-Vietnam demonstrations were more than protest marches; they were parties. Grosvenor Square was a meeting of the clans, a gathering of the tribe. Random seminal conversations and wonderful plans for collaborative action sprang up all over the place. When they found they had a common enemy, the yippies, hippies who had been hit on the head by police and therefore politicised, linked up with the Black Power guys. The black guys brought black consciousness as well as cool dance moves to the party. The yippies brought the hallucinogens.

Then of course, there was Paris in spring. May 1968, when the dream of the radical student left, that we would one day unite with the workers and bring revolution to the streets, actually materialised. For one month we were euphoric, believing we were witnessing the downfall of western capitalism and the creation of a society based on freedom and love rather than power and wealth. Whatever darkness we had to encounter later, and there were already storm clouds gathering on the horizon, we would always have Paris.

In the north of England too we played our part. Several hundred of us hard-core counter-culturalists in Sheffield organised sit-ins, read-ins, swim-ins, party-ins, smoke-ins, lie-ins, etc. The difference between hanging out, having a good time with friends, and serious underground political action was a fluid one you understand – especially with so many mind altering substances going round. Many an elaborate critique of the cultural dialectics of society flowed into an equally elaborate rambling tale of our last acid trip. In the afternoon we chanted 'Victory to the NLF' in Ché Guevara T-shirts and struggled with the existential challenge of being an authentic individual in an inauthentic class-ridden capitalist society. In the evening we'd turn off our minds, relax and float downstream, to where all thought is an illusion, and we let it all be.

I wished I could have had the same philosophical acceptance of the contradictions within myself. I was full of the tensions of opposites with not a dialectical synthesis in sight. I flew upwards and hung out in heaven on the natural highs of dancing and all that loving, as well as of course the grass and LSD, then would crash to Earth, falling into my old despair and nameless dread. In another contradiction I wanted to change the world, turn it on, raise its collective consciousness, on the other hand, I wanted desperately to change myself, turn myself around, and change my own consciousness. That familiar sign of the cross was dividing me still.

For most of 1968, I was sufficiently distracted – there was so much to do. Write articles, hand out leaflets, organise the sit-in so that it didn't clash with the Grateful Dead concert, spray paint slogans – 'Paris Today, Sheffield Tomorrow.' So much to learn – the latest hip talk, where to get the best weed, the latest semiotic deconstruction of culture, how to operate the Gestetner Roneo machine… So much to read every month: *Rolling Stone*, *Oz*, *New Musical Express*, all those hand-duplicated articles. As well as keeping in touch with the music scene, the fashion scene, the intellectual scene, the cosmic consciousness scene. And then of course, all those people to love. How did we do it all?

Well, on a full grant, with no exams on the horizon, no student loans, cheap housing, and no worries other than which kind of high to go for that day, we had all the time in the world.

In November that year the USA halted its bombing of North Vietnam. We thought we had won. I am sure the body bags of dead young Americans being flown back daily, the determination of the Vietcong and many other factors played their part, but we felt flushed with victory. Thousands of young people with no military power and negligible economic power had managed to influence the most powerful nation this Earth has ever known. Another excuse for a party.

I was keen on everyone having the chance to make as much love and freedom as we privileged students and tried to take the partying to the factories. That summer I took a job to earn money for a holiday, plus that

Biba outfit I had to have, and worked for six weeks in Boots' factory in Beeston. D10 was a large hanger with a glass roof, in which forty belts ran continuously day and night. Seven hundred 'girls' stood in lines along these belts and repeated a single movement for eight hours – or more with overtime. We bio-machines were allowed two ten-minute tea breaks, an hour lunch break and two five minute pee breaks per day. The breaks were staggered and a roving set of relief girls stood next to you to first pick up the rhythm, then take over your action, like a baton change. The belt must go on. When the machine at the top ran out of labels, there was relief all round. We breathed deeply, flexed our muscles, cracked our stiff fingers and a few minutes later got into position for another interminable run of sorting pills, packing lozenges, sticking cotton wool into bottles, testing vacuum seals on tins, sticking on labels, or packing – whatever was our action for the day.

The sun shone that summer. With the glass roof the temperature rose. Women began to faint. The relief girls were on extra alert not just for breaks but also to take over from anyone who passed out. The belt must not stop; the belt was King. The temperature continued to rise. I knew from my Marxist studies of the class struggle that a copy of the Factory Act had to be displayed somewhere. I could not find it but demanded to see it and told the floor manager that it was illegal not to have it displayed. He frowned. One of those student trouble makers obviously. I brought a thermometer in. Underneath the glass it was over 110F. Everyone was complaining bitterly but did nothing about it. I called a meeting attended by the other students and a few of the more bolshie workers, where we had a wonderful time denouncing the capitalist system and oppressive industrialists and agreed to call a strike that afternoon.

'I know what you're up to' hissed the floor manager to me during my break, 'and if you persist in your Marxist ways I'll send you up to Boiling Sweets!'

I knew this was an empty threat however. Only men could work in Boiling Sweets. The temperature there was astronomical even in winter. You worked for only twenty minutes and then had a twenty-minute break to recover.

Our gang of fervent revolutionaries, with plans to integrate the workers and the students in Beeston's version of Paris, having synchronised watches, were just about to blow whistles and shout: 'Everybody out!', when there was a fire drill.

We spent the afternoon on benches and the lawn in front of D10 while the maintenance crew whitewashed the roof. This was not the breakdown of western capitalism with its alienating oppressive economy and class-ridden hierarchies that we had hoped for, but it was a lovely afternoon off and we claimed a victory of sorts. And I learned a good lesson in how adept big business is at protecting its own interests, as well as how ruthless is its revenge.

I was put to work packing Mepacrine, a drug for malaria. On my application form for the job you were required to list any allergies to pharmaceutical products. I had put down quinine, the primary ingredient in Mepacrine. I had to wear rubber gloves, a mask over my mouth and nose, glasses over my eyes and special protective clothing. In that heat. I quit.

But I also got *my* revenge. On my last day I visited various friends to say goodbye, especially those working on the amphetamine and mandrax belts. I stuffed my pockets with handfuls of speed and mandies and left to enjoy myself far more than any manager of D10 was likely to do that night. They may have won the day battle, but not the fight of the night.

I have often found that the best revenge is a kind of psychic Aikido, to be seen laughing, loving and having such a good time your enemies' envy turns back on themselves and fills them with jealous rage. (Only much later did I realise that such jealous rage would, of course, then spin back onto me.) The fun I was having in the nights was excellent revenge on the Catholic Church, on the priests and nuns of my childhood, on an economic and class system that had crushed my parents into defeat before they had a chance. Every time I held up a joint and inhaled, it went beyond the pleasure of the moment into a 'fuck you' to someone or something. Each time I turned to my lovers and made love, I was turning my back on what I hated and into an even more delicious 'fuck you' to the whole show.

But underneath all this bravado, a depression lay in wait for me. I could turn away all I liked, but this dark cloud lay on me and in me, and whenever the music stopped, threatened to overwhelm me.

In the darkness of the night I could fly, like a bat using instinctive radar to seek out the places I felt safe. I found friends with some of the same insecurities and nameless dreads that plagued me. Were we products of society or was it our own fault we were so fucked up? Was it the fault of the systems of society or were we to blame? It seemed clear to me every night that the fault lay elsewhere – why on earth would such lovely people as these friends of mine ever be ashamed of themselves? But all that goodness slipped away and evil was with me in the morning.

I lay in bed unable to face what was waiting for me when the harsher light of day showed up the cracks, revealed the flaws, laid bare the truths that could not be argued with – that really there was something dreadfully, shamefully wrong with me, though I hadn't yet worked out what it was.

I would lie in bed for hours staring at the ceiling, before turning sideways to stare at the wall. That I could not get up was further proof of the terrible wrongness in me. Around the middle of the afternoon, hunger and thirst would drive me into the kitchen to make some tea and toast. Once up, I shrugged off the torments, pulled on my Biba jacket and Levi's, and went down to the Union, where there would always be someone to gossip with about the doors of perception, the class struggle or the amazing Pink Floyd's 'Dark Side of the Moon'. And I could forget my own dark side of the moon lying in wait for me tomorrow.

Today I would probably have gone to student counselling and got some help for depression, but there wasn't so much awareness of these things then. Most of us had always been told 'never mind', 'pull your socks up', 'don't be silly', and so that's what we told ourselves. At least I did. Despite writing psychology essays on the nature of learned helplessness as the cause of depression. But that was about rats in cages given random electric shocks and not fed however many levers they pressed, and, surprise, surprise, they felt helpless and depressed.

I also learned, if children must always do as they are told and are punished when they do not, if they are given no power or self determination during their childhood, then they too, like those poor starving rats, learn helplessness and become depressed. But such a pathetic figure was so not my image, no way was I going there. Needy, depressed, helpless, pathetic! No fucking way! Don't 'Bogart' that joint my friend – pass it round!

We filled out a questionnaire in the Clinical Psychology course that was supposed to measure you on a scale of neurosis. I came out completely normal and non-neurotic. But then when asked the question – 'Are you depressed?', I had ticked the 'no' box – because I never even thought that I might be depressed. That was an illness and not really your fault, whereas what was going on for me was my own shameful fault – mea culpa, mea culpa, mea maxima culpa. Perhaps I was so neurotic I could not answer such questions. That made me psychotic didn't it? I must be so out of touch with my own reality I even invented myself. Laing was right I was divided against myself. On the one hand I was super normal, I think my score was minus two, less than zero neurosis, while on the other hand I was so fucked up I was off their scale completely.

It didn't help that my favourite revenge tactic was to say 'fuck you!' by having such a wild time. All that making love, getting high and dancing required those demons of mine to be well and truly locked away, behind triple deadlocks, chain locks and combination locks where I never wrote down the numbers and so forgot them. Forgot I'd ever done any locking up at all. Sex, drugs and rock and roll released energies imprisoned by rigid bourgeois culture. We all knew that – Article 1 of our new faith. It seemed in my case to also involve, locking away other energies – my fears, despair, insecurities and need. For a time anyway. Somewhere I knew that if I had allowed those genies out the bottle, I would have gone the way of my ancestors and been so completely ruled by my fears and insecurities, I would never have ever done anything at all. Desperate situations require desperate measures.

Writing essays about the nature of the unconscious while my own unconscious was so firmly packed away, meant that I at least had an illusion that my mind and its intellectual understanding was greater than the forces of chaos and darkness. And when, as did happen occasionally, those demons escaped during an acid trip, or in some wild unforeseen energetic let-go with a lover, or dancing, or suddenly out the blue, I had no tools to deal with them other than say 'Hello again!' and go to bed until they went back to sleep. I had learned so much helplessness that I thought not only could I do nothing with my demons, but that no one else could either. Then another great man arrived in my life to teach me differently and bring me in from this frozen cold.

D. W. Winnicott was a famous Child Psychiatrist whose wisdom and genuine caring for parents and the children he treated, led many to love as well as respect him. I met him when he came to give a seminar at the Psychology Department. He asked to meet some of the radical students to find out for himself what we were about. Three of us were invited to have tea with the great man. We sat around in the common room, drinking cups of coffee in hot plastic cups from the machine. Steve was wearing a home made badge stating 'You can play with my reality any day!', and a batik kaftan with ZAPU and ZANU slogans, cause of the week – African freedom fighters. Neal was wearing a maroon and orange striped jacket, which unfortunately clashed horribly with my Biba green silk dress and the purple boots.

'Are you going to Bickershaw for the Festival?' I asked, balanced awkwardly on the edge of the chair. Sitting down in a mini dress is an art I should have practiced more. 'Grateful Dead and Hawkwind are playing.'

'Yeah. Sure man' said Neal. 'I might write it up for Oz, from like a psychic politics of experience perspective, the music being a collective manifestation of the etheric vibrations of a whole generation. Woodstock meets R. D. Laing meets Ginsberg, know what I mean?'

'Yeah.' We all nodded meaningfully.

'But don't forget to take wellies and toilet paper' added Steve, 'remember the toilets at the Isle of Weight – Aaargh!' We remembered.

Steve had perfected the art of seminar guerrilla warfare. He would sit in the front row in strange attire and interrupt with surreal questions the lecturers were never sure meant they were dealing with a nutter or a brilliant student it was wise to respect.

'Turn to page 24 and you'll see a diagram of the relationship between cognitive maps and information retrieval.' Dr Warr stood in front of the blackboard in his smart suit, his pipe in his hand, and looked at us across a greater divide than the lectern. We reach into bags and back packs, leaning to release straps caught on desk legs, scraping chairs as we shift around.

'Come, come, don't let the grass grow under your feet. We haven't got all day.'

Steve, on this day, was wearing a 'Ban Agent Orange' headband and a Ché Guevara T-shirt over a greasy mechanics overall – to express solidarity with the victims of imperialist aggression in Vietnam, the third world peasant army of South America and the alienated factory workers of western capitalism, obviously. He leans forward, one eyebrow raised.

'Surely grass cannot grow under anything, so perhaps you are using grass as a metaphor for consciousness, like in Zen, sitting silently doing nothing the grass grows by itself.' We all snigger waiting for the punch line we know is coming, even if we haven't worked out what it is yet.

'Or are you referring to the grass that stands under us in the sense that smoking it leads to new under-standings – and you don't want it under us, you want to put it in your pipe and smoke it? Right on man! Expand the cognitive maps of your mind! See me later.' We erupt.

Poor guy! The lecturer, not Steve.

Neal is a musician who played guitar and sang dark side of the moon kind of stuff. 'The bird of paradise is dying in the wasteland of your mind. The system has seduced you and now you're tone deaf and blind.' That kind of thing. Some of what he wrote was so impenetrable it had to be brilliant.

He had been anointed into his position as a high priest of cool, when he became the first person at Sheffield University to plug headphones into his sound system. And let me tell you, the first time you hear the music directly INSIDE your own head is incredible. So many years of listening to sounds with the volume turned up as far as it could go, so you could get lost in the music without the noise from next door pulling you back into a more mundane reality, then one night you put on these big black headphones, and those sweet sounds are vibrating intimately, immediately and directly through your frontal lobes, your corpus collusum, in your obdulla oblata and your striate cortex, your whole brain vibrating as one. (We'd studied the physiology of the human brain that week obviously.) You are no longer hearing the music, you have *become* the music. Those guitar riffs, those complex back beat rhythms, those base chords, those multi-tracked feedback wall of acid rock sound are no longer out there, 'way out', 'far out', they are in here, in this, in the most intimate here and now of all – me. This very body the amplifier, this very Earth the music. The 'I' that had vibrated like those guitar strings would never be so rigid again.

Even now when I hear The Beatles' 'Abbey Road', I go back to that terraced house in Netheredge where Neal put headphones over my wiry red hair and said 'Listen to this. You're going to love it!' And I did. I love that album, like you love the first lover who makes you *feel* the love.

You have to remember, you modern i-Pod wearers, you MP3 downloaders, you E-generation ravers, that in the fifties when I grew up, the only music you were likely to hear, unless you were posh and your parents listened to classical music, were hymns in church and the Archers' theme tune. Rock music fed vibrational levels in us that had been frozen in permafrost, an ice age that had continued for generations. And when the ice of a polar winter first melts, what has been petrified in the freeze starts to breathe, move and dance with an ecstasy those who take such movements for granted, cannot know.

Perhaps having been born on the first day of Spring, I am particularly attuned to the time when winter fades into a fresh warmth. 'It's been a long cold lonely winter but here comes the sun...' Although here, so much ice was melting in so many of us, a massive wave was created that would carry thousands so far from home, many never made it back.

After my acoustic epiphany, on one of my visits to Meanwood Psychiatric Hospital, to find the phenomenological meaning in the psychotic ramblings of patients in straitjackets, locked in padded cells, I tried to explain to the psychiatrists that if they would play rock music to their patients through headphones, then those vibrations might do what no lobotomy or leucotomy could. But I hadn't yet got grant money from the Medical Research Council to prove it scientifically and so this contribution to psychiatry never came to anything. Neither did my potentially Nobel Peace prize winning suggestion that each United States senator should hold a Vietnamese baby in his arms for fifteen minutes, then change its nappy.

While Steve, Neal and I discussed what the latest Captain Beefheart lyrics might mean, Winnicott chatted with Professor Kay discussing, I am sure, very different topics. Eventually we were invited in to meet the man. We walked in and he stood up to shake our hands. He laughed.

'Should I say love and peace man?'

He turned first to Neal smiling. 'How do you do?'

'Fine thanks' said Neal.'

Again to Steve, 'How are you?'

'Good thanks, how are you?' said Steve. This man has such good vibes, we are all smiling now. It is my turn.

'And how are you?' he said, grasping my hand, holding it rather than shaking it.

He looked into my eyes as he spoke. Just those four words, each one said with a warmth that seeped right into my bones. I could not speak. He smiled into my eyes with, and there is no other way to describe it, pure love. I was shocked, no one had ever looked at me in this way before. This was utterly different from the intrusive eyes of my childhood that had stared into my soul looking for the stains and devils in there. In Winnicott's eyes I gazed into a soul. And was struck dumb.

Now I am sure if you scraped away at the details of Winnicott's life on a wet Monday morning in February when he had a cold and couldn't find his reading glasses then stubbed his toe, Winnicott would look very different from the channel for love and wisdom that I met. But of course. He was human. And it was his very humanity that spoke to me.

He sensed I had been touched somewhere I had never been touched before and held my hand for longer than he needed, gently reassuring me with the pressure of his fingers that he understood.

'Come sit next to me' he said, patting the chair to his left.

I sat down and smiled. I dare not speak. Tears were welling up inside me, and if I had spoken I think I could not have restrained my weeping. Ancient ice in my heart was melting. There was nothing to say. He held my hand and talked with the others but I have no memory of what was said. All the communication between us was in silence.

The way in which Winnicott looked at me has stayed with me all my life. He had seen so much suffering. He had seen children in so much pain, confusion and despair they were terrified to do what children do even in the dust of poverty – play, kick a ball, pretend to ride a horse, fight and laugh with friends. He had met children too broken to even move, frozen children, terrified out of any spontaneity into a petrified goodness. He had talked with mothers who were as lost and as anxious as their children, who had hurt their babies as much as they themselves had been hurt. Yet his eyes spoke of something else, something more than all this desolation and pain.

Winnicott would say again and again in his books, on the radio, to his clients, to his students, to whoever would listen, that we do not need to be perfect, none of us, all we need is to be 'good enough'. No one had ever told me that. I had got the message I had to be perfect and, naturally, was failing, left and right, up and down, in all directions of that stalking cross.

That night I didn't go out to party. I walked home by the longer path through Endcliffe Park. It was a clear night and through the bare branches of oak and beech trees I could see the moon. The hoot of an owl sounded to my left. I walked alone through the empty peace of the night, with just foxes, owls and sleeping birds for company, for the first time hearing the sounds of silence. I pondered what had happened with Winnicott.

You have to suffer a lot before you can look at people in the way Winnicott looked at me. He seemed to know that even in our most terrible failures and despairs, our bitter rages and devastating loss, there is a redemptive love possible that can heal us. And, what's more, this love can happen between people anywhere. All we have to do is be vulnerable. Yet the word 'vulnerable' literally means 'able to be wounded' – take off your protective armour and it is likely that you will. The first law of the jungle is 'eat or be eaten' after all. Yet if we are not vulnerable to love, what chance have any of us got?

I wandered through the trees by the light of the moon. Winnicott seemed to know both the joys and the heartbreaks of human life, and to have seen through both. I hoped one day I might have such wisdom; then I too could look at someone frozen in fear, and the ice in his or her heart might thaw and melt a little. Perhaps then I could look in the mirror and fulfil an earlier promise to become that for myself. Yet you do not have eyes like Winnicott's only when you read and observe pain, you have to have suffered yourself. Winnicott must have suffered the truth of all that innocent pain he had worked with. Is that how he knew there were hidden wounds in me? Because he had met pain so often he had developed a sixth sense for it? I had always believed pain should be eradicated, but should suffering also be experienced? So we can learn from it and uncover its meaning?

I sat down on a park bench. My whole life had been dedicated to trying to ease suffering. The suffering in my family, the souls in purgatory, the working class, the Vietnamese peasants, the suffering of the whole world. Even my own suffering came in here somewhere. But are there different kinds of suffering, some to be healed, some to be experienced? Was I wrong to imagine life was about having a good time, being happy, getting high? Is life about something else? If so what?

I reached home and undressed in the dark. I climbed into bed. The rain tapped gently on the window, the only sound as I fell slowly towards the silence of sleep.

In the morning, I woke without my familiar despair. My morning demons were silent. I lay, not plagued by dread and anxiety, but contemplating what had happened with Winnicott. He had shown me how much can happen in silence, without words, without doing. He had not spoken to me, but held my hand and it had all happened; a deep unfolding in my heart had struck me dumb with feeling.

Silence was not something I had met a lot in those days of heady revolutionary talk and intense intellectual dialogue, yet although 'dumb' has come to mean stupid, when confronted by the deepest realities of all, there is, quite simply, nothing to say. Communities all over the world, honour victims of terrorism, memories of war, tragedies, and death with silence, because anything said will always be less than what has happened. Yet my friends and I were rarely at a loss for words. There was always so much to discuss and argue about in the excitement of revolutions and cosmic consciousness just around the corner. Things were about to change.

A group of us went to see the first performance of the film 'Easy Rider' at the Sheffield Odeon. Having heard what a great movie it was, we had planned a party afterwards with that wonderful west coast road music. We did not know the film ended with the death of exactly the same innocent freedom we were so much enjoying.

We walked out the cinema, sixteen of us, devastated. In total silence. Shocked because we already knew in our heart of hearts that the same profound darkness was creeping its way toward us.

March, the year I graduated, U.S. planes bombed the Ho Chi Minh Trail in East Laos. In April US troops moved into Cambodia. In May, four student anti war protesters were shot dead at Kent State University, Ohio. In June, the Conservatives won the general election and authorised the first use of rubber bullets on protesters in Northern Ireland. Hell's Angels killed someone during the Stones concert at Altamont. Jimi Hendrix died on his own vomit in a drug overdose. Sid Barrett from Pink Floyd went crazy. So did Brian Wilson, the genius behind the Beach Boys. Marvin Gaye was shot dead by his father. Deaths and rumours of death from 'the dark side of the moon' were arriving.

What the demons lying in our human soul had shown Winnicott, was slowly finding its way through to me. As it does to us all. Perhaps to destroy us. Perhaps to frighten us to death.

Or perhaps to teach us we must look so deeply into our human darkness, including our own, we reach the painful wisdom that knows we are not paddling our own canoe as we may have imagined, we are all in the same boat. In which to be or not to be are equally unbearable.

Chapter 5

Learning Nushu

In the 1960s, we – the sisters in the underground counter-culture and radical left politics – had the choice of several roles. We could waft gracefully in gossamer kaftans, some important bloke's girlfriend, silent, smiling, mysterious, though as this required long straight hair that hid your face mysteriously and wafted as gracefully as you did, not for me. Another option was to be an honorary bloke in the class struggle, freeing the working man from his alienation from the means of production – been there, done that, got the protective clothing. Another possibility involved training with weighty books to become an intellectual who 'thought like a man'. Or you could be Janis Joplin.

For a while I was the singer in a rock band. I had the hair and the moves but not the magic howl. I croaked. But when you are singing hauntingly of that 'needle of death' or in soulful rapport with the anguish of black convict railroad workers, you don't want your audience ro rush forward with throat lozenges. I'd like to tell you we disbanded because the band forgot we were not multi-millionaire rock gods who could buy new gear no problem, and in an orgasmic frenzy smashed the guitars to pieces, but I can't. Eventually, even we realised we were not the Grateful Dead, and never would be. We wandered off like those album tracks that end in an inglorious fade because no one knows how else to end them. Other doors closed to me, I became an intellectual.

For this you had to spend a lot of time reading impenetrable French stuff about Lacanian mirrors and the penis being the signifier, but at least your hair was free to go its own way and you could say what you wanted even if it was incomprehensible. Though that was OK, we were going beyond the frontiers of the mind anyway.

We had happily got on with the business of being sisters, girl-friends, mothers, daughters, muses, honorary blokes, one of the guys, until somewhere about this time the glaring absence revealed itself. We also noticed in all the talk of making love not war, there was rarely mention of children. On the one hand birth control and abortion opened up sexual choice and liberated us from traditional responsibilities, on the other it appeared to relieve men from recognition of their own sexual responsibility. Mmmm. There can be no denying, some of us were changing or maybe we just stopped trying. Certainly, en masse, we were about to stop faking it.

We stood up and breathed more deeply. We put aside Jean Paul Sartre and picked up Simone de Beauvoir. We looked around and heard new female voices coming from America. Gloria Steinem. Shulamith Firestone. Kate Millet. We noticed the radical press was mostly written by men, for men, about men. And when we looked into that Lacanian mirror we found the significance of having no penis was, wow, having a vagina! Penis envy suddenly seemed relatively insignificant compared to womb phobia.

Other women, more intelligent than clever, jumped off the whole intellectual table and re-defined culture itself. They trusted their intuition and gut instincts more than the patriarchal conditioned intellectual mind and read tarot cards, practised martial arts, dangled pendulums, worshipped the goddess.

It began for me one night in a pub after a meeting about what to write on the banners for the next anti-Vietnam War demo and whether libertarian anarchy means you can drive on whichever side of the road you feel to. These post meeting booze ups were where we got on with other business – non-revolutionary gossip such as where to score the best weed, which party to go to Saturday night, and of course the hidden agenda behind even the most fervent slogan chanting, getting up close and personal with the one you fancied.

More and more frequently these post-meeting meetings found us female comrades huddled in the loo, swapping make-up and laughing at tales not for our male comrades' ears. Ladies' Toilets are exclusive clubs but without the applications for membership that apply in similar establishments for men, and certainly there's none of the antler wearing, one trouser leg rolled up antics some of those go in for. Many a life changing deal has been sealed in women's lavatories, and I don't just mean various kinds of powder sharing. Possibly women's toilets were the crucible everywhere for what was to follow. Not so surprising, many other places were hostile to us.

That evening we were told that this particular pub did not serve women. Neither were we allowed to consume the drinks bought for us by our male comrades in this bar, we had to go next door to sip them in the lounge. The brothers swaggered around, waving their roll ups, offering to buy us ladies Babychams. They thought it was funny, just like most people thought Stokely Carmichael was funny when asked about the position of women in the Black Power Movement and he answered – 'on their backs!' We didn't. We walked out and began our own meetings.

The comrades were not pleased. They tried to talk us out of our bourgeois individualism and told us feminism was a divisive capitalist plot to undermine the solidarity needed for the class struggle. But we just stared at them with a new look, one eyebrow raised, a knowing smile and fuck-you drags on the fags.

'Back up boys, you're breathing our air!'

They soon came round. Most of them anyway realised pretty quickly, if they wanted to get up close and personal with any female comrade in future, they had to take feminism seriously. Apart from the hard left, that is, who still practiced manoeuvres in the dark around corners in Broomspring Lane so that they could do their bit in the guerrilla war that was about to break out on the streets of Sheffield. But as they tended to be the guys who never sighed when making love, just grunted, this was no great loss.

We arranged to meet the following Wednesday at Mary's house. A student of English Literature and a fan of Virginia Woolf, Mary had insisted on a room of her own long before the rest of us had even thought about it. Twelve of us gathered there for our first ever women's meeting. The last time I had been in a room full of only women had been in the Loreto Convent, and that was probably only to wait for a priest, here we were waiting for neither God nor man. Actually we were not sure what we were waiting for. Nor whether we should sit as in a meeting, or move round the room as at a party.

We knew we were not meeting for make up tips, Tupperware and fashion gossip, but would we fall into factions and argue all the time as per usual in the left, or would we be friendly and girly, or what? All I knew was an imperative feeling of urgency had forced me here. I had even turned down the chance of a curry cooked by an Indian friend, a great sacrifice as there were no Indian Restaurants in Sheffield then; if we fancied a curry, it was stew with a few sultanas added or the dried powdery prawns rattling around in Vesta packets.

Mary puzzled me. She was sexy, smart, intelligent – a real foxy lady in every way, including long straight hair that wafted. That wasn't what puzzled me.

'How come you're so together when you were brought up a Catholic?' I asked her.

'But you were a Catholic, and you're cool as well as together.'

What! I was dumfounded. But did she really see in me what I saw in her, or had she been taken in by my flawless act? I tended towards the latter as I certainly had a good act together if nothing else. Though could it be that getting your act together is the real thing anyway, as isn't being unreal the reality of being really human? My head is spinning and I am only in the kitchen making tea *before* the meeting. Clearly we will be discussing very different things from the Marxist, Leninist, Trotskyite debates that went on in those smoky rooms off the union bar. Or even from the Marcusian, Levi Straussian, Lacanian semiotics we went in for before we got too stoned to pronounce the words.

We sat on cushions and chairs around the room at different heights, as were our skirts, some mini, some midi, some to the floor, though most of us, still in honorary bloke mode, wore Levis. Balancing mugs of coffee and tea on our knees, we completed the hellos and 'how are you?' gossip that settles a tribe before the real business can begin. We gazed around. None of us spoke. The silence told us we were here for something more profound and mysterious than we had anticipated. Perched on the rock face of a sheer cliff, we looked down into the ocean, where, beneath the waves, we could make out obscure shapes in the dark. Our breathing quickened. Our hearts beat faster.

'This feels strange, just us. Just women I mean.'

'What's even weirder is it feels somehow wrong, as if we shouldn't be here, yet I like it, I really like it.'

'That's exactly how I feel!'

'Me too!'

We sit looking at each other. We have no agenda. No minutes. No chairman. No hierarchy – not yet anyway. And no idea what we were going to talk about. This is absolutely not like the meetings we are used to.

'I suggest we start by talking about what brought us here.' This was from Mary. No way was I as together as her, whatever she said.

We began to share concerns that we hadn't realised were bothering us because the context hadn't been there to recognise them. Like the first time we'd heard The Velvet Underground's 'White Light, White Heat', we hadn't known whether we liked it or not because there was no way of knowing – the music itself taught us how to listen. And that's what we were doing – teaching ourselves to listen to the new sounds of women talking about themselves, for themselves, to themselves. A Chinese woman died a few years ago, the last speaker of Nushu, a centuries old language known only by women, taught to girls in secret, to express their inner feelings, to articulate their hurts and angers that could not be spoken elsewhere. We were learning a new language – our version of Nushu.

'I can't stand the way men dominate every meeting I have ever been in.' Suddenly it occurs to us that this has always been our experience too.

'And even worse is the way they put you down by turning you into a sex object!'

'Wow, that is so how it is!' we chorus.

'Yes. And we're expected to be supportive, available, sensitive, in the background, caring but *never* powerful, authoritative or angry.' This is so clearly the case, why have we never noticed this before? We shake our heads in disbelief while nodding in absolute agreement – a knack very useful in such meetings.

'Sexual roles are learned through culture not biological instincts.'

'Marriage and the nuclear family are ways to keep women in bondage both psychologically and materially.'

'Women's bodies are seen as machines by the capitalist system that has to control the means of production so has to control us.'

'Men are so afraid of the power of women they keep them oppressed in every culture.'

'Patriarchy, the rule of the father, has its roots in fear and hatred of the power of the woman and the mother.'

'The oppressive inequality of sexual relationships manifests in every intimate relationship between a woman and a man.'

The insights are coming thick and fast, and we know they are true even if we haven't yet worked out the theory of why or how. But we will, we will.

'Yeah! Even language is patriarchal, man … shit! See what I mean?'

Yes we do, sister!

What stunned us most was as soon as someone shared their experience suddenly we realised this was our experience too, but had not known it. It wasn't scales falling from our eyes; it was steel shutters crashing down. We had not seen all this before because Patriarchy, the rule of the father, is so intrinsic to society, culture, language and thought, we had taken for granted that this is the way things are and always will be. Like the very air we breathe and the atmosphere in which we had grown, it never occurred to us that reality could be different. Not really. Though when I thought about it, I did remember being up in arms that my brother had the job of cleaning shoes which only happened once a week, while my sisters and I had to share the ironing, cooking, dusting, washing up, drying and shopping, and that had to be done everyday.

It didn't take long for a whole new set of graffiti to emerge, naturally as I've explained, first appearing in women's toilets, but later on walls throughout the city.

'The personal is political!'

'A woman without a man is like a fish without a bicycle.'

'Sisters are doing it for themselves.'

'Don't fuck in the missionary position – fuck the missionary!'

'If men had periods, menstrual blood would be sacred.'

And the more prosaic 'I like dykes.'

We learned fast. After a few meetings we were quoting Heather Booth, Evie Goldfield, Sue Munaker, Kathie Amatniek, Marge Piercy and a whole host of women who had begun to write about Women's Liberation. In just months we were fluent in the Nushu of the Women's Movement with the ease of native speakers – which of course we were.

Suddenly lesbians and gay guys sprang up everywhere. Where had they been? Hiding of course. Surely I should have understood that as well as anyone. Denise came out and told me she loved me. Well I loved her too but not in that way. It was cool though as I introduced her to Angie and they fell in love. They cut each other's hair, went shopping for dungarees, and wore home made badges proclaiming 'A dyke without a bloke is like a bike without a choke!'

We all went in for rather surreal badges, you understand, as back then, we were hacking through the undergrowth of centuries, creating the footpaths that have now become motorways, and there was no political IKEA with pre-packaged stylish slogans, we had to construct our own. As well as our own music. Fortunately no one now cared that I croaked, and anyway how else would a woman sing having been gagged and in chains for centuries of Patriarchy?

In cities all over the US and Europe groups of women like us were coming together to discover that Patriarchy had set sisters against sisters, divided us from each other in order to rule over us, but now we could befriend and love each other. We discovered that the sisterhood was the tribe we had longed for all our life but so profound had been our exile, we had not known it.

Coming home to this land of milk and honey and all the gossip you could wish for, had in it a poignancy all the sweeter for being the realization of a hope kept alive through the injustice and suffering of countless generations of women. A secret promise passed between mother and daughters through millennia, was at last being fulfilled and our mothers and grandmothers rejoiced right back through the generations.

We packed into four cars and went to Oxford for the inaugural Women's Liberation conference in 1970. Glorious confusion reigned. Anyone who wanted to stuck up sheets of papers offering workshops on 'Socialist Feminism', 'The Politics of Sexuality', 'Lesbian Liberation', 'Wages for Housework', 'Love and the Nuclear Family', 'The Body Politic and the Politics of the Body', 'Radical Separatist Feminism and Cooking', 'Anyone Wanting a Lift Back to Liverpool'. And you signed up for whatever took your fancy.

Women sitting in circles to gossip, listen, offer advice, to support and take care of each other, is an ancient ritual. We could have been shelling peas into wide skirts, squatted on mud floors grinding spices, or making coil pots outside a cave. In these circles, we were taking the shells off ourselves, coiling a different kind of pot, and weaving potent new spells. I had a great time, we all did, including the kids in the 'Men Against Sexism' crèche. We drove home with a new freedom in our hearts to love each other – and ourselves. From now on, the sisters were doing it for themselves.

In the same DIY spirit of the times, I came up with my own graffiti – 'When God returns to Earth, She'll come back as a group of women.' Not catchy, but deep. At least I thought so. Someone else must have thought so too as less than a year later a friend told me she had seen it in a women's toilet in Chicago. We really were gossiping in a global village, either that or I had a soul sister out there somewhere.

Not long after our great seminal coming together in Oxford, where, high on the sisterhood, we had proclaimed to the world the necessity of breaking down Patriarchal structures such as the nuclear family, I got married. I was not only a divided self, I was a fragmented self. And some of the fragments clearly did not know what other of the fragments were up to.

I married Pete of the black Levis. I however wore white when we got married in St Teresa's Catholic Church, where my father gave me away and hymns were sung in a nuptial mass.

Pete and I had been living together for over a year after he had switched from Nottingham University to Sheffield for the final two years of his architecture degree. We were lovers and comrades, and in my plan, were to become the Simone and Jean Paul of the cool feminist counter culture. Except that I was terrified my parents would find out we were living together. Rather a stumbling block should we ever go public.

My parents came to visit me once. I cleared out every sign of Pete's presence, drafted in my best friend Alison as flat-mate and sprinkled a few of her cardigans and dresses around the place. I spent their visit smiling frantically while offering random and rather manic suggestions about what they might like to do in Sheffield to distract them from all the details I kept noticing I'd missed – shaving cream, a black leather man's jacket, size 10 shoes, architecture books. I knew I was terrified but not really aware of what exactly it was that frightened me.

I suffered regular panic attacks that I might die in a traffic accident. I wrote my first novel which abruptly ended with the heroine killed in a car crash. I was convinced that paper bags lying by the road were animals writhing in prolonged agony having been run over and left to die. I even wondered if the Church had been right all along and these fears were my punishment for living in sin. My doctor gave me muscle relaxants but I only took them once. The unfamiliar relaxation felt like depression and I preferred the intensity of my tension. Pete suggested we get married; perhaps this would put my demons to rest.

I discussed it in my women's group. We were still in the exploratory phase where every question and cultural dynamic had so many unknowns we hung loose with them all, not yet sure what was the correct ideological line. Should we, for example, refuse to pander to male definitions of beauty, chuck our lipsticks in the bin and go forth pale lipped, or should we proclaim ownership of our own lips by painting them any colour we fancied? There were those who advocated lipstick guerrilla warfare, waiting in dark corners with Revlon's 'Shocking Pink Sizzler' and Rimmel's 'Luscious Crimson' ready to leap out and mark random male chauvinist pigs passing by. Hopefully not the same corners where the hard left practiced their guerrilla tactics, a lipstick-gun shoot out would lead to only one sudden death. And if all else failed there was always the semiotic analysis of that phallic red stick emerging glistening from its protective sheath.

We explored the personal, cultural and political dimensions of my getting married.

'Perhaps you should think about what you want and not what your parents want?' suggested Jill.

A good suggestion yet that was my dilemma – I didn't know what I wanted.

'Maybe you get married but keep your own name and refuse to wear a wedding ring' Janet pondered.

Wouldn't that just confuse further a person already confused?

Rosie was adamant.

'If you marry you are pandering to patriarchy, and become property not a person.'

Surely there's a slogan in there, somewhere.

'Whatever we say, no one knows better than you what is right for you.' This was Mary, like I said, a foxy lady.

One fragment of me was a feminist committed to redefining the politics of sexual intimacy. Another fragment was stylish and cool – not so cool I could freeze hell, but I was working on it. Yet another was walking up the aisle of a Catholic Church dressed in a long white dress, with the organ playing here comes the bride. And when Pete and I went back to our flat in Sheffield that night, one of my fragments could not get over the fact that making love from now on, at least with this man, was NOT A SIN! My demons whispered this was more than ordinary schizophrenia, it was a multi-faceted-compound-fractured psychosis.

Pete and I went on our honeymoon to Venice, where to appease the goddess I read the Second Sex all over again, as well as Tolkien's *Lord of the Rings*. Pete, to keep his gods happy, read Trotsky's letters to Lenin. While we were there a tornado blew down a tree onto the tent next to ours. Two people were killed. Maybe it is not so easy to appease a goddess.

The most successful revolutions are ones where no one looks back to the good old days and the next generation have no idea what it was like before. The Women's' Movement of the seventies was so successful young women today have no idea how bad it was before. That's good – because it was pretty dreadful. And our Women's Movement was a revolution of the spirit, as well as of hearts and minds.

As well as creating a new future, we reclaimed out history. We unearthed the truth of women's power that had been buried and wiped from record. We turned our backs on the Patriarchal God to find the spirituality of the Earth, the sacred that is in this life, not an after-life. We called out to the goddess and She came back down from the mountains and the hills, emerged from the forests, the oceans and the wilderness. She returned from where She had been living with the birds and the beasts, banished by a Patriarchy that was afraid of her.

The Goddess returned from her exile, bringing with her a lot more than healing and light. If you have been repressed, attacked and incarcerated for millennia, confined to the dark dungeons of the collective unconscious for centuries of Patriarchy, when freed, you are unlikely to emerge with just a sweet smile. As any goddess worth her salt will tell you, she is as destructive as she is creative, as raging as she is compassionate. Even sex goddesses. Marilyn Monroe would glide up the aisle of cathedrals, so luminously beautiful, so gloriously sexual, everyone would turn and stare. 'See' she'd say, 'the power of the goddess is even greater than the god in his church!'

Yet at last the Goddess was coming home. She came home to us. And those she loved would be the ones she burned the most intensely in her transformational fire.

But then those whom the goddesses loves, die old. And very wise.

Chapter 6

A Dark River Runs Through

After our honeymoon, Pete and I returned to Sheffield. I began my Ph.D., Pete his Diploma in Town Planning. I told everyone my research explored the interdependency of the body and the mind, rather a grand spin on actual reality where I sat in a room and filmed children of different ages as they tidied a messy desk. I analysed every tenth frame, made holes in ticker tape which I fed into a vast Elliot 903 computer that took up the whole of one room, to arrive at the stunning discovery, children of different ages tidy desks differently. While I added to the list of articles in academic journals, 95% of which never quoted again except by the author, Pete, more usefully, designed cheap eco-housing for the council. We moved to begin our new life in a coal-mining village outside Sheffield and our little cottage in its walled garden with an acre of orchard and flowerbeds became the first home I loved.

I suddenly discovered interior design, though then it was called 'decorating'. Pete designed interactive art – paintings and mobiles with dangling bits you could move around to suit your mood. I made cushions in the shapes of liquorice allsorts and bought bright non-matching crockery from the local market. New winds were blowing through the design world and Habitat had just opened in London. We made the pilgrimage and brought back what may have been one of the first round paper and bamboo lampshades to hang in Sheffield. It was an object of wonder dangling in the middle of our living room for a few weeks, until everyone got one.

We learned to cook 'foreign food' from Elizabeth David's recipes from around the world. These used garlic, peppers, sour cream, and even live herbs. Amazing. Though I think around this time everything became 'incredible'.

If you are lost to yourself, however, whatever house you inhabit, you are not at home. Even in the excitement of expanded horizons in all directions, there were times I felt I did not belong anywhere, rather more bewildered in the wide-open space around me. Whatever had been my original hopes, academic psychology had not helped me understand myself. My internal world, with all its contradictions and confusions, was so baffling I thought it would drive even one of Maslow's self-actualised beings to despair.

I had first heard of these exotic creatures in a psychology seminar where we had drawn a diagram of the hierarchy of needs, showing preoccupations with survival meant you could not focus on the higher things in life. Only when all our basic survival, personal and social needs are met can you become 'self actualised', the psychological equivalent of the Holy Grail. Ever since then I had been trying to make it as a self-actualised individual. I well knew being high was better than being low.

'Weed of the week' for the week of the seminar was pure THC, the active ingredient in cannabis, which has a particularly smooth full-bodied high. The lecturer attempted to describe the 'peak experiences', signs of 'self actualisation' and, remembering our peak experiences from the night before, several of us laughed. He asked what we thought was so amusing. I told him he sounded like he was on drugs. He smiled, pleased to be thought 'with-it'. Why is it people often want to be cool and charismatic, but condemn the experiences inherent in that? No way could you be cool and charismatic, at least to our generation, without the hallucinogens, the weed and at least 12-inch flares on your loons.

What really struck me however was not the condemnation of our highs by lecturers who brewed beer in the attic of the psychology department in vast quantities, then spent hours up there quaffing it by the gallon – though it did occur to me there was a Ph.D. to be had in videoing them and comparing the rate of stagger before and after their visits to the attic. You wouldn't have to analyse every tenth frame, simply threaten to show it to the Vice Chancellor. No, what impressed me was if self actualised, you hit your highs without any pharmaceutical help whatsoever. You might be cleaning the sink or shopping and suddenly find yourself sky high, overwhelmed with wonder at the cosmos, before gently drifting back to ground. No side effects, no come downs, no post trip lows, no crashing back to planet Earth with awful realizations of your true insignificance in the greater cosmic scheme of things. Sounded good to me. The only down side seemed to be that during these peak moments you experienced reality with a type A perception. This meant if a tiger leaped out at you, you would just stand there, amazed and in awe of its beauty, whereas in normal type B mode, you'd scream and run away.

Most impressive of all however, was that when you lived at this higher level, you always did your own thing whatever others thought. This was definitely appealing to someone caught between keeping everyone happy and being drop dead cool. Saying 'Oh really?' with a friendly smile when someone tells you their favourite singer is Val Doonican when, in truth, you dare not breathe in case some of their dreadful un-coolness attaches itself to you, is a double bind would create a divided self in anyone.

For some time, therefore, I had been trying to rise above my need to be liked, my need to belong, my need to be seen in only the most trendy gear, and other ''lower' level needs, in order to achieve the heights of self actualisation. After many shakes of the dice I'd get there, 99 on the snakes and ladders board of life. For a few glorious moments I needed nothing and no one. Then my hair would frizz or I'd make a witty remark no one noticed and I'd hit that snake, my old adversary from Eden days, slip right back to '1', and have to start all over again. Sometimes I'd fall right off the board into the regions below – there wasn't a category in my diagram for those who needed so much so desperately, they tried not to need anything at all.

Hoping to get a few tips on how to rise up the needs hierarchy, I asked one of the lecturers whether self actualised people were alike and so less uniquely themselves, or whether they were more uniquely themselves and so all very different. He referred me to a paper linking the hierarchy of needs statistically to recovery after a heart attack. What did I expect from the logical positivist behaviourism of academic psychologists who thought psychodynamic psychoanalysis was unscientifically introspective? And try saying that when you're peaking on some high.

Half of me recognised that of course humans need each other, I was simply afraid of the vulnerability of that need. The other half was convinced that not needing anyone was the ultimate liberation to strive for. Thank goodness no one was videoing me and analysing every tenth frame. Reality TV for us was the blue sky and green leaves that had recently appeared rather than the shades of grey we had grown up with. Anyway, how would you analyse someone who one moment swept into parties turning heads with a star-like leader of the pack cool, only to be seen a few drinks later confessing to such a lack of self worth she was probably breathing oxygen that would be put to better use by a rat in a psychology department?

Each day Pete and I, plus whoever was crashing with us, drove the six miles into Sheffield in our ancient Morris Minor, frequently stopped by police. Not surprisingly, a bunch of longhaired hippy types in mangy fur coats in a coal-mining village looked suspicious. We were always calm, having what we considered a foolproof hiding place for our dope inside the car door. Seeing that we were friendly, they were friendly too and usually just asked to see licenses, log book and insurance. We might even joke, though their jokes seemed funnier than ours. Or was it just our laughs had an edge of slight hysteria because best quality Class A and Class C stuff was in that door they were leaning on?

One of my best friends was Barbara, a soul sister from New York. She was over here with her husband who had a Fellowship in the Psychology Department. Beautiful, intelligent, funny, another woman of many parts, she seemed to orchestrate their collective existence more easily than I did. We spent many evenings meandering through hip counter-culture raps, feminism, smoking the weed, listening to Joni Mitchell and The Doobie Brothers, dancing on the lawn. The first woman I really opened my heart to, apart from my sisters and I loved her just as she loved me. Nearly forty years later and living on opposite sides of the globe, we still do.

Friday evenings, friends would gather at our house for a psychedelic weekend in the country. After eating the latest cookery experiment and sharing recent feminist-cosmic-politico gossip on who was making love and/or war with whom, we'd drop the acid. You know the kind of thing, deep esoteric meaning in a tea leaf, going back to your roots as a plant, realizing you hadn't realised that you've never realised what was really going on, and so on.

Opening such ancient Pandora's boxes, we released the most ravishing and beautiful creatures with translucent wings the colours of rainbows that flew and sang and laughed. We also released ugly slimy creepy crawlies that slid menacingly across the floor to sit at our feet and stare accusingly up at us. Despite studying for a Ph.D. in Psychology I did not have the language to talk more intimately with Pete about my inner world. I could talk *about* my depressions, anxieties, unnamed fears and dreads. I could *analyze* them, I could even *explain* them in terms of various social and cultural contexts, but I was not ready to *experience* them and therefore learn about them directly. So when my familiar demons came to visit me, thousands of eyes protruding from every orifice, mouths full of snakes, I would simply go to bed where they spewed their entrails all over me, peered into my soul, and told me I was so worthless it would be better if I'd never existed, until either they or I would fall asleep exhausted. Eventually I would get up, able once more to smile and sing under all difficulties.

When these nameless familiars judged and condemned me, Pete tried to help by cooking my favourite meals, buying me flowers, suggesting we relax and smoke a joint. He was as helpless as I was in the face of these entities that hung on my soul and sucked on my life force. The Church had told me witches feed devils with black milk. This must be me. I feed these demons with the dark river that ran through my soul. I have one breast flowing with the milk and honey of love, the other with the poisonous black milk of evil.

A deeply divided country will eventually find itself at war – and civil wars are the worst. Friends turn into enemies and sisters kill sisters. After rushing through space like a bunch of satellites desperately focused on a particular spot on planet Earth, some of the fragments that made up 'me', began to spiral out of control. Some were leaving the gravitational pull of the group; others were set on a collision course. My first disintegration began.

Our 'very, very, very fine house, with two cats in the yard', began to look like a prison. I had a beautiful home, a loving husband, friends, and a successful career. I was living in exciting times and had just bought the Rolling Stones 'Sticky Fingers' album with its killingly cool Andy Warhol cover. And all the while monsters were encircling me with their threatening menace. They were the real prison, but I hadn't realised it yet; and a few fragments of myself wandered off to find what I was looking for somewhere else. I fell in love with another man.

Pete and I were equally bewildered. I tried to bring my warring fragments back into some semblance of coherence, but failed. I was hooked on the greatest poison and medicine of them. And while I did my best to turn away from its seductive embrace, I kept falling and falling and falling into its deadly sweetness. I could perhaps have had a secret affair, but I could not lie to Pete. This was the man with whom I had shared dreams, even more significantly I had entrusted with my nightmares. I could not now betray him with a lie.

Pete and I lay in our bed and started at a ceiling that had watched over many nights of our loving. We no longer knew what to say. It was not the alienation of years of accumulated resentments that silenced us, more an incomprehensible devastation. We held hands and wept as the losses washed over us.

'I'm so, so sorry' I repeated, 'please forgive me.'

No act of contrition could have been more heartfelt or accompanied by more remorse. Pete squeezed my hand even tighter and our hearts broke in unison.

Memories of dancing all night and climbing into trees at dawn, running along cliff tops before swimming in a warm sea, travelling on trains to unknown destinations, sharing secrets, planning homes, memories of our comradeship, our friendship, our laughter and our love through the struggles and surrenders of years, gathered into a storm cloud that built layer upon layer, deepening and darkening until it broke over us. We drowned in the deluge of our grief. I stood on one bank, he on the other, of a great flooding river.

Pete and I wiped away each other's tears with a tenderness that spoke of all our years of love and said good-bye.

There were plenty waiting in the wings, ready to hold Pete's hand; the most beautiful was Bonnie. She took him back with her when she returned to the USA and just before they left she gave me a pair of earrings she had made, two clouds, one with the sun, the other with rain.

It is a mortal sin to leave your husband. My mother and father, afraid for my soul, had masses said to St Jude, the patron saint of hopeless cases. My friends were shocked and could not understand what I was doing. I couldn't explain because didn't know myself. They tried to help, but I was beyond their reach. I was lost – alone. Frightened, guilty and ashamed. My dreams lay shattered around me, sharp shards of glass. Wriggling splinters of myself blindly ran from each other, from themselves, from me. I moved to Edinburgh to live with this other man. Then just as abruptly left and drove back to the Northumberland coast. Then inland across the Pennines. Then I didn't know where. I ran all over the UK trying to escape my demons until only my Motoring Atlas knew where I was. And I went to hell anyway.

Hoping to open my third eye to a more benign reality than this cold unforgiving terrain, I took some LSD and tripped to the bottom of a dark well. I lay on the floor frozen stiff as a circular saw came up between my legs and slowly sliced its way through me. It moved up between my legs, through my vagina, my womb, my stomach, my heart, my face, my brain – dividing everything. When the job was done, I lay there in agony, unable to move. Utterly divided in two, split down the middle forever, a chasm lay between one part of me and another.

Each eye wept for the other.

My friends, Barbara and Danny, found me. They took me into their bed and held me while I sobbed deep choking tears and told them, last night

I'd dreamed I was a person with a life; now awake, I'd discovered I was a piece of rubbish having a schizophrenic breakdown in the gutter. Once more my future stretched before me in chilling, remorseless detail. Incarcerated in a mental hospital, institutionalised and chlorpromazined out of all hope, I would shuffle endlessly in slippers along bleak, tiled, corridors that echoed back to me my alienation and despair. Driven insane with my heart utterly and irrevocably broken in two. Divided so completely, each side would be lost forever in unrequited longing for the other.

In the morning, surrounding by the debris of what had once been my life, the demons and I looked at each other. When devils have done their worst, however, they have lost their most potent weapon, the terror they strike in your own heart. I was still afraid of them, but no longer quite as terrified, and that morning, invited them to stay for breakfast. They argued about whether to have their muesli with white or black milk, and then laughed. But with me this time, not at me.

And why, if I squinted at them sideways, did some of them look like fragments of myself?

I returned to my Ph.D. and the videos of children tidying desks, to discover children may be uniformly 'messy', but that each child is tidy in their own unique way. Any parent could have told me that. I also learned that what we might consider messy has its own logic, hidden to us but obvious to the child. Of course the blue-tack must be wrapped around the green pencil then stuck on the cover of the red book – they felt lonely and liked each other. My most significant discovery, however, was that I preferred the company of children to that of academics, and as a consequence left the ivory tower, or rather the ivory Portakabin in the case of the MRC Unit, to work with children directly.

I lived now in a terraced house in Filey Street I had bought with two friends, Mike and Alan, near the university where we worked as researchers and lecturers. We spent the summer painting, decorating, re-wiring and making it generally habitable as even in the early seventies you could not buy what estate agents were beginning to call 'desirable residences' for the £360 we had each paid out. Homes were still places that kept the rain off and where you relaxed, not objects of desire that must have the perfect window dressing before you put your feet up, and we kept it simple. We covered the living room floor wall-to-wall with mattresses and lounged around in this large bed listening to the Byrds' 'Eight Miles High', as high ourselves. Friends and acquaintances would join us, to smoke, gossip, sleep, drink Laphroaig single-malt whiskey, Southern

Comfort or tequila – all of which we believed were hallucinogenic. I don't know if they are but when you're eight miles high, you don't care about the pharmaceutical subtleties.

Throughout a long summer many came for 'a trip on the magic swirling ship' of our giant bed, where we lounged and gossiped 'out of the twisted reach of crazy sorrow'. And we did not care that 'below us was a bottomless canyon', we danced to the music and laughed. My demons would have to travel a wide meandering route to reach me now.

John came to do the re-wiring looking exactly like one of the Byrds with his hat, his moustache and his cool unsmiling stare. His day job was research into artificial intelligence, and though he himself was very intelligent, he was not at all artificial. In fact he was brutally honest. He did not like Alan who, one day, mentioned he did not feel well.

'Perhaps you are sickening', John offered with a smile. I kicked him under the table and we fell in love.

His wicked one-liners had a cutting edge, a useful weapon in a long survival strategy. His father had died when he was four, his mother killed herself when he was 10, he went to live with his grandparents, and a year later his grandmother died, the next year, his grandfather. He then went to live with an aunt who died the following year and finally ended up with an uncle and aunt who were cruel and mean and did not die however much he wished they would. He knew what the rest of us neither knew nor wanted to know – that however many sleep in the same bed, we are born alone, die alone and in between we live alone. Perhaps that was why he was the only person I've ever met who could decipher the lyrics of Frank Zappa and the Mothers of Invention. He even understood Captain Beefheart, and you can't get more intelligent than that.

The way that young lovers do, we dreamed we were the way we wanted to be, and I suddenly found I was an even greater expert on what was cool in the music scene, because John, for example, knew all about Ziggy Stardust and the Spiders from Mars before the album was released. I may have been the first person in Yorkshire to sing the words to Lou Reed's 'Perfect Day' – apart from John that is, but he couldn't sing, while my croak suited Lou Reed's heroin wrecked voice. Our love 'made me forget myself and for a while thought I was someone else, someone good'.

One evening, in between swigging the Tequila and arguing over who got the worm, Mike's girlfriend told me that North Yorkshire was the only Local Authority still employing Educational Psychologists without teaching experience. I wrote to ask if they had any openings and, after an interview at Northallerton County Hall, in which I gave the airbrushed version of my research, I was offered a job at The Child Guidance Clinic, 2 Dragon Parade, Harrogate. There would be more fun in a city than in the fading splendour of genteel Harrogate, so I moved to Leeds to begin my new life as a psychologist by day, a feminist revolutionary by night.

Several months later John moved up to Leeds to join me. We moved into a flat in Headingley with Lee, another John, and their daughter Alexis. Lee and I, together with the two Johns, tried to integrate feminist theory on sexual politics with the practical politics of sexual intimacy. Like many others, we encountered turbulence as the psycho-sexual political climate warmed up. Alexis, a lively three year old, seemed to be working through her turbulence rather better than we were, integrating her fantasies and reality through her play with whatever came to hand. She especially enjoyed the tests I practiced on her as they seemed games that she won and I lost.

'You are not very clever are you?' she'd laugh, 'but I am! Let's play some more!'

She taught me how much children love to play with adults, and how much more they learn through play than when we formally teach them.

Living with Lee ratcheted up my feminist consciousness by several notches. She had a knack of expressing complex sexual politics in succinct sentences that hit our socialist-feminist chakras exactly on the collective G-spot to raise our political Kundalini. Yes, various fragments continued to pursue their widely varying paths in me.

There was the socialist feminist who thought the dialectical materialism of the class struggle was integral to women's liberation. There was the radical feminist who explored the politics of intimate sexuality. Another fragment was attuned to cosmic consciousness and, with the help of lurid and garish Hindu posters, was having its Kundalini raised. There was now also a child psychologist next to the confused fragment, whose subterranean homesick blues continued to lay me up in bed periodically, with just my demons for company.

It was getting crowded in here.

My day job involved driving the twelve miles to Harrogate in a car that had just come on the market from Czechoslovakia – a Skoda. I didn't care that it slid rather than drove round corners, that it made strange tinny noises above 40 mph, because I had fitted a state of the art sound system. Rovers and Jaguars would speed by me, metallic blurs of purring engines and leather seats, but I would simply smile. They were not being blasted by Bob Marley at decibel levels that meant there was no engine noise anyway.

I'd sit in my car in the car park, waiting for the track to end: 'If you knew what life was worth, you would look for yours on Earth. Stand up for you rights, don't give up the fight! Yeah movement of Jah people!' I would then emerge dressed in my smart clothes, trying, but failing, to smooth my hair, and walk sedately into the Child Guidance Clinic.

I learned on the job how to diagnose and work with the children who came to us, but what I did not have to learn, because it came immediately and naturally, was how to communicate with hurt, frightened, insecure, anxious, depressed and angry children. I could enter their world, put myself in their shoes, see through their eyes and communicate with them. Sometimes they acted out their distress in rages and furies, sometimes they acted it in with depressions and a frozen obedience. I could also see what many could not, the frozen good ones were often the most terrified and traumatised. I could even connect with the autistic children who lived in severe isolation unable to communicate except through their own behavioural languages. I was asked to give talks and explain the methods I used to get the children to open up, communicate, even laugh with me. People asked me how I did it. But I did not know what worked, other than hidden inside me was a fragility and vulnerability the same as the children's.

I would get on the floor, lie down and look at the ceiling. For half an hour I might raise and lower a blanket, my eyes appearing and then hiding. I wandered around touching objects as gently and lovingly as I hoped later to be able to touch their hurt and bruised hearts. I allowed children with the crazy hyperactivity of deep anxiety and rage to stare at me and yell their worst insults until they laughed when I fell over at their power, or pretended to pretend to pretend to be shocked by their outpouring. With the frozen little angels, who never caused any trouble except for their nightmares, wetting of the bed and panic attacks, I let them see into my soul, where the devils there said hell-o, with smiles in their eyes. And then we'd simply play together.

Those little sweet innocent angels with large eyes would take a while to warm up but then they would play the coldest, meanest most hurtful games. They would stick pins into mother figures with voodoo like precision, they would shove the father doll to the back of the cupboard and try and make me promise never to bring him out. They would look sideways at me as they slyly pinched me – hard, with their finger nails, drawing blood – but that was only after many months, when they had learned to trust me. And still I smiled. I understood them, you see.

Trying to find out why could I be myself with children so much more easily than with adults, I went to see a Kleinian psychoanalyst. She was of the classic school. She said nothing after our first session, not even hello or a smile of welcome. I was not allowed to see her from behind and had to go up the stairs before her into an austere, sparsely furnished room where I lay down on a couch and stared at her ceiling. She sat behind my head, where I could not see her, and said nothing. Neither did I. What did she want me to do? What was I supposed to say? I lay there, week after week, feeling an inadequate failure and too ashamed and afraid to voice this to the impersonal presence behind me. I could not even climb into the boat to set off on the voyage that so many of the children had had the courage to take with me. Eventually I realised that either I was not ready for this or it was not what I needed. The first complete sentence I spoke was my last. 'I don't think this is right for me, either I'm not ready or this is not what I need.'

I lay in John's arms that night and told him what I had not been able to voice in that cold impersonal room – that I felt lost and in fragments, ashamed and fearful, but of what I did not know. In the warmth of John's arms, where the currency of modern intimacy is exactly those forbidden secrets, I was able to share the confidences I could not tell elsewhere.

Far more has happened for me in a bed than has ever happened in a confessional, or on a couch. What has healed my childhood wounds has not been the clinical professionalism of psychoanalysis, but whispers with a lover in the dark, naked meetings between the sheets, shared secrets with a lover. In the arms of my lovers I have been able to whisper the raw need and incomprehensible inadequacies that would have me tongue tied elsewhere. And in the sexual intimacy was made the love I so much needed.

Back in the real world, I was getting confused about what was the real world – the playing or the reality. My school report when I was twelve had said: 'Anne still has not learned that work and play do not mix!' Yet by day I worked playing with wounded children and by night I played working for the revolution. I knew the personal was political and the political, personal, but which was more important, for a child to have good food, interesting toys and a comfortable home, or to be listened to, to feel loved and understood? Which mattered most, equal pay, wages for housework, fairer divorce settlements, or liberation from depression, helplessness and fear?

Hoping one night, to find a path through the middle of these contradictions, I walked in the empty parks and overgrown cemeteries of the sleeping city. I often walked at night when I could more easily hear the frail and uncertain songs of myself and, despite the warnings of friends, only ever met foxes, who sniffed in the undergrowth before padding on to enjoy urban dustbins. I wandered down towards the lake where willow trees shivered in the night breeze. Owls hooted from the darker more obscure regions of oak and beech trees. The air was crisp with an early autumn frost and I could see my breath. I hugged my coat around me. My body, shivering with cold, welcomed the warmth of my coat. Suddenly it struck me, hot and cold, in and out, you and me, everything meets and touches right here, in the body. It all meets in us. In our mysteriously expanding omni-centric universe, where each point is the centre, our bodies lie breathing and feeling at the heart of a whole cosmos. We ourselves are the bridge between the worlds.

I had reached the lake. A sharp moon rose in the east from behind a bank of dark clouds. I gazed down at the moon's reflection and waited, a single point at the centre of this vast event, the universe. A breeze ruffled the water. The moon dissolved into a thousand pieces.

The visible is born from the invisible and in between breaths, in the crack between myself and not-myself, formed the longing for a child.

The waters stilled. In the water was the moon again.

Chapter 7
The Rise and Fall of a
Feminist Consciousness

No self-respecting city could continue to be on the map in the early seventies, excluding the Ordnance Survey Motoring Atlas, without a collection of Consciousness Raising groups dotted about the suburbs. In Leeds, the Marxist Feminists, the Radical Feminists, the Socialist Feminists and the Alternative Libertarian Anarchist Feminist Separatists, rarely got together, except to argue about which was worse, Patriarchy, Capitalism or Racism, until one evening about a hundred of us, the whole feminist contingent at the time, representing all shades of feminist theory and practice, even the Bradford Lesbians, an elemental force rather than a movement, congregated in a church hall to organise ourselves into consciousness-raising (CR) groups.

The idea was not just to hang out with friends and sound off about men being bastards – we did that anyway. Each time one of us was hurt by one of them, we'd be round with our tea and sympathy, coming up with the latest feminist explanation of why men are such arseholes. In this meeting, we were to link up with sisters whose experiences of the politics of experience were different, so that we could raise each other's consciousness as well as our collective consciousness.

We sat in a large circle. Most of us knew each other to some extent having already dialectically struggled with the dialectical struggle and who had eaten our organic hummus in the communal fridge, but we went round anyway, each saying our name. We then tried to non-patriarchally organise ourselves into mixed groups of six. But the Marxists were definitely avoiding the radical separatists, and lesbian lovers eyed each other jealously before making a beeline for the same group. I thought too, the intellectual mob was drifting en masse into a different corner from the goddess crew. The structurelessness of these meetings was not yet tyrannical but it was certainly chaotic.

Someone had the bright idea of forming groups based on where we lived. We re-convened and gathered this time according to geography rather than ideology. Many of us lived in Headingley, trendy, near the university and cricket ground, so the Headingley Massive, cool intellectuals who played fair obviously, splintered still further.

I linked up with six others and we arranged to meet on Monday at Margaret's, because she had a large living room and, something I had never encountered before, *two* sofas. Then we all went dancing.

A hundred women hit an unsuspecting club in down-town Leeds on what would normally be an empty Thursday. The DJ rifled desperately through his collection as we demanded only women's music, especially of course, Joan Armatrading. And then we took to the dance floor and 'really moved, really danced, to the limit here we go, from the bottom to the top'.

Apart from a skirmish between a Goddess Worshipper in a 'Wages for Housework' T-shirt, and a 'Reclaim the Night-er' in a 'Vaginas With Attitude' T-shirt, there was love and affection all round. Though it might have been 'Vaginas with Altitude' as getting high did not conflict with feminism that I was aware of, but I couldn't see too well because of the smoke. Whatever our faction, most of us still kept faith with our old friend nicotine, the most familiar and intimate drug of them all. Apart from love, that is. Before mobile phones, you were only 'never alone' with a fag in your hand. However dark it got, in or out, when you lit up there was a light in that darkness, a glowing red tip to keep you company.

Apparently nicotine is an ancient friend of humanity, it is the only drug that when you are high helps calm you down and when you are down helps bring you up. It interacts with our human metabolism so synergistically that some scientists have suggested it evolved in conjunction with us, not separately. Rather like dogs are supposed to have done – though that does not explain why they love us and we treat them like ... well ... dogs. Gurdjieff said it was because dogs, along with horses and elephants, know that we know something they don't. Though I'd like to know what that is.

I have no idea what happened to the other groups, but our consciousness-raising group met each Monday for the next five years. Those two sofas held us through many risings and fallings of consciousnesses, hemlines and hopes. Perhaps MFI's single most significant contribution to the raising of the collective consciousness lay in the manufacture of those steadfast sofas.

They did not shift, even when we threw ourselves about in the dramatic throes of sharing the wounds caused by patriarchy's brutal oppression and those bastard Marxist men we'd tried to turn on with our sexy dancing but who would insist on seeing us as sex objects, so we had to turn them down. Sigh. It wasn't all bread and roses you know, being a hard-core feminist in those pioneer days.

In our group, we even had a virgin, and I bet not many CR groups could boast that. But as she used to have orgasms on the top decks of buses as they jerkily lurched through Leeds city centre, I'm not sure she could be described as truly virginal. Some were mothers and struggled every week with the complex dynamics of being a woman, a cook, a taxi driver, a night-nurse, a story teller, a washer of nappies, a singer of nursery rhymes, a referee of squabbles, a kisser better of bashed knees, a hamster cage cleaner, a walker in the park, etc. As well as a self-determining sexual being struggling for liberation from the oppressions of patriarchy – plus the day job.

We began each meeting sharing anything significant that had happened that week. When one of us was in a crisis such as a broken heart, homeless, no money, or the terrible realization that we would never again be a size 10, then we would of course focus on that. Otherwise we'd explore particular subjects we had planned in advance. Hot topics were naturally – sexuality, motherhood, and what on Earth has this thing called love got to do with anything except that it seemed to have something to do with everything. And there is more than one kind of love.

I was in love with John; I was also in love with Lee. Feminist consciousness, like all labours to give birth, did not arrive painlessly. I heard Lee and the other John struggling just as they heard John and me. Perhaps the two Johns comforted each other, as did Lee and I, when we moved out into a house with friends five minutes away. Alexis spent half her time with us and half with John and John.

The first evening in my new room, I was anxious my demons, finding me alone, would rush in to keep me company. I had my Benson and Hedge, my Rizlas and my weed, ready to do combat should the need arise. It had never occurred to me an evening alone could be pleasurable. Staying at home alone was what the sad, unbeautiful people not invited to the parties did, the uncool equivalent of 'lying in a burned out basement thinking about what a friend had said and hoping it was a lie'. I curled up on the sofa and tried to read, but I knew I was really waiting for my uninvited guests to arrive.

I fiddled with the bits and pieces on the mantelpiece. I contemplated which combination of posters would make me appear most fascinating. I thought about putting my books in some kind of order – should they be arranged by author, title or subject matter? Perhaps it would be better to put the heavy classics and latest feminist imports from the US on the eye level shelf where people could more easily notice my intellectual depth and with-it connection with the Zeitgeist. Or would it actually be more cool to leave the whole lot shoved in as randomly as I had unpacked them, not caring because my mind was on higher things. I made a mental note to respect librarians more in future and shifted position on the sofa to read a P. G. Wodehouse.

Suddenly it is midnight. What has happened? I am alone and enjoying myself, just myself, no one else, and not a demon in sight. I listen to an unfamiliar silence. The room is empty of the relentless static of unspoken need, judgments and disappointments normally crowding the airwaves with an invisible human unhappiness that colonises my inner world and demands my attention. I yawn and stretch. I scratch my armpit. I mess up my hair. I try out a few dance moves. I can lie on the floor and do nothing at all if I feel like it. For the first time in my life I am not considering another being in any way whatsoever. The only one here is me.

I lay back on the sofa. In this spacious silence that allowed me everything, a tear escaped down my cheek. I had dreaded being alone and yet solitude had brought me what I'd longed for. Not for the last time, what I most needed had been hidden behind what I least wanted.

There must be a stronger magic than I realised in the interior of that Dark Continent, the body, because while I was discovering the joys of solitude, the cauldron of my womb was cooking up a different spell and my longing for a child grew stronger. And wombs do not argue. Wombs are so potent, not only are we supposed to long to get back to them, we are also apparently terrified of being consumed by them. Though I think men must have said that, because when the subject of our wombs came up in our CR group, which was frequently, I didn't notice any of us feeling particularly full of either longing or terror.

One essential element without which no womb can create anything is of course a man. It occurred to us one Monday, without that small, but ever so significant detail, the wriggly sperm, we would quite simply be merely reproductions of our mothers. That stopped us in our tracks. Then Jan remembered that last Friday Michael had automatically assumed she would iron his shirts and we were off again.

I asked John if he would be willing to have a child with me. After all, I loved him and he loved me, it was just that the psycho-political implications of sexual love had made living together more difficult than living apart. Especially if like me, you are at war within yourself, then you tend to find yourself in a projected war with your partner. John said 'no'. A week later he said 'yes.' So I stopped taking the pill and within two months was pregnant.

I tell my CR group I am pregnant. Their eyes widen. It's clearly going to be motherhood tonight. And that of course will include sexuality and love. Business as usual.

The first to speak are those who do not have children. Perhaps it's simpler for them.

Angie says sternly, 'You do realise, Anne, that once you are a mother you will no longer have the same freedom as before. You have to put your child first, after all they're more important than your husband or lover.'

'We-e-e-e-ll' says Jan, one of the mothers, 'it's not quite as simple as that. All mothers are first a woman, else how the hell do you get a man to make love with you? And without that there's no child is there?' She doesn't wait for an answer. 'The mother is born out of the woman not the other way round. I am myself first, a mother second. My kids may not like it that way, but there it is.'

This strikes me as a stark truth and shakes up my conditioning that to be a 'good' mother is more important than even being myself.

'I wish my mother had thought more about it before she had me. I think if you have any doubt you shouldn't have a child. You will regret it when you've got it and then it'll be too late.' Karen's mother left her when she was six.

'But don't mothers always love their children!' cries Dawn. She looks around the mothers in the group anxiously.

Jenny sighs. 'Yes, but, Dawn it's very complex.' Jenny has five children.

In those first days of the glorious feminist revolution, nothing was sacred. We were willing to look into the hidden underbelly of society and question everything with a ruthless honesty that turned away from platitudes, easy sentimentality and escapist fantasies. Topping the bill for analysis tonight is clearly the 'good mother – myth or reality?'

The mothers look at each other remembering long nights with a screaming baby, anxious days over a sick child, tantrums in the supermarket, the restrictions, the expense, the tiredness, the exhaustion, the constant demands 24/7/52/18 and more.

'It's very hard to admit' says Jan quietly, 'but sometimes I regret I had a child and am jealous of those who don't.' She takes a deep breath. 'There. I've said it. It's true.'

Jan has just voiced not only the un-sayable, but the unthinkable. We sit there open mouthed on the MFI sofas, staring at what we have been conditioned into thinking is the ultimate criminal – the 'bad mother'.

Suddenly we crack up and cannot stop laughing. Tears run down our cheeks. We can hardly breathe and still we are bent over each other weeping and crying with gulps of laughter. It is so, so funny. We laugh because it's the funniest thing in the world to try so hard to be what is absolutely impossible – someone who loves unconditionally, unfailingly, every moment, for all time, these little creatures that cause so much disruption and chaos. The truth we all knew, but had never faced, that had been as true for our mothers and grandmothers as for us, was revealed as one of the funniest jokes in existence. At least that is how it appeared to us then.

We began to unravel the hidden truth that all mothers are sometimes 'bad' mothers, the ones who don't know this perhaps the worst of all. If we are perfect mothers then the anguish and struggle our children experience is absolutely completely their own fault, plus, in comparison to our perfection they are doubly messing up, as well as having no one to blame. How mean can you get? We all need someone to blame on. And anyway what kind of monster would a perfect mother create? A narcissistic creature who thinks the world is designed around him or her?

I remembered my Kleinian good breast and its evil twin – the bad one. Surely all mothers do their worst to their children, just as much as they all do their best. Isn't it always this way?

Many years later I met Jenny. She told me, ever since that evening she had felt less guilty and more accepting of her less than perfect mothering and this had made a massive difference to her life. Maybe for me too. I like to think in an old womb magic, that laughter when my son was just a bunch of furiously multiplying cells, lay like a homeopathic remedy in my womb, so that when I did my worst to him, we could still love each other enough to redeem it all.

I was determined to reclaim the sacred mysteries of childbirth from the male dominated medical profession. Anyway, soft music, familiar smells, massage and warm baths were far more appealing than steel speculums, bright lights and alien hospital beds. I had to fight hard for a home birth, however, as I was an 'elderly primagravida', over 25 having my first baby. Plus I had red hair. Red haired women tend to bleed more when giving birth so I did not mention my red-haired grandmother had died giving birth to my father.

My GP would quiz me during my pre-natal check-ups. While I lay supine under bright lights, on the examining couch with a steel speculum inside me he would order me,

'Remind me again; why do you want a home birth?'

Having a set of fractured selves occasionally comes in handy and in this case, one fragment was able to detach itself and speak with clarity and precision about the body politics of a patriarchy that had to control, like Capitalism, the means of production. He just grunted in reply.

My midwife, Grace, was a large black woman from Jamaica.

'Now don' you go worryin' about him, dat's a good girl. He's a good doctor,' she went on 'but he's not a midwife, you unnerstan'?'

A month before I was due, Grace went away on holiday.

'Now don' you even tink about dat baby commin' into dis worl' while I am away!' She wagged her finger at me.

Neither I, nor the baby, would have dared to even dream of it.

Lee and I now lived in a Victorian house we'd bought, with four bedrooms. Feminist Books took over one room and we lived in splendour in the rest, a mini-feminist community with friends in and out to help unpack boxes full of Lee's *Wedlocked Women*. We took review copies in person to the Fleet Street offices of the press, smoke filled caverns of typewriters and dangling neon lights, coughing men with beer guts, crap jokes about how liberated women just needed a good shag to put them right. Unbelievable.

Six months into my pregnancy, however, I put the cat among the pigeons, or rather the pigeon among the cats. John had been spending more time with me and deep in my unreconstructed pre-feminist psyche I found I wanted to make a home with him and for us to live as a family with this baby. I felt strange new vulnerabilities and once burst into tears for no reason. Heavy duty, radical-socialist-feminists do not do that except in consciousness raising groups, but this was in Safeway's car park when I dropped the car keys down a drain.

The feminist fragment committed to the women's movement spun away in disgust from the soon-to-be-a-mother fragment that wanted to make a home with a man. Ideology, however, gave way to the more persuasive arguments of instinct; I bought Lee's share of the house and John moved in.

More bourgeois tendencies revealed themselves. I bought a duo-controlled electric blanket that you could keep on all night. John and I connected it up and I looked forward to a night luxuriating in toasty warmth. It didn't work, I kept waking up cold. I turned up the controls each time until they were on the highest 9, but still I was cold. In the morning I complained to John how disappointed I was that it didn't work. He agreed. It was useless. He kept turning it down all night and the thing just got hotter and hotter.

During the last weeks of my pregnancy a driving motor in me stopped. At first I thought there was something wrong when I woke up not knowing what I would do that day, perhaps pick a few flowers, dust a few surfaces, flick through back copies of Spare Rib, but I soon slipped into the luxury of empty days and before long was completely at home in this pleasurable lightness of being. I had an excuse – my body was working hard so I didn't have to.

Like so many mothers before and after me, I had no idea of what was about to rush into my life and blow it to pieces. I lazed around arranging flowers, never done that before. I wiped picture frames, never done that before either. I cleaned in places I had not known existed, like behind taps and the back of the airing cupboard. I even attempted to knit some baby clothes. But then I would have to lie down and read yet another Agatha Christie or watch Coronation Street. My collection of weighty books gathered dust even if the shelves did not.

I felt the first contractions of labour while walking sedately through a flower show, my last aimless meander before the tornado of motherhood crashed into me. A while later I was in our bedroom sweating, breathing deeply and swearing. Three hours of hard deep breathing with John on one side of me and my friend Christine on the other, there came the point of transition.

'Stop!' I called out to anyone who would listen, 'I've changed my mind!'

Grace patted my hand,

'Dere now honey, it'll soon be orl over and you'll be holdin' a new babe in your arms and lovin' it's little lovely self.'

'No baby! Don't want one!' I gasped.

But no one paid me any attention. I was swept aside anyway by an ancient elemental force that rushed into me and began waves of pushing.

A baby's head appeared between my legs.

'Look, a baby!' I cry, astonished. I'm not sure what I was expecting but the living reality of a baby surprised me.

I reached down and touched this delicate, blue, slippery, velvet head. I panted to stop the pushing as Grace tried to hook the umbilical cord over the baby's head, but it was wound twice around his neck so tightly she had to cut it while he was still being born. The shock of this meant he did not breathe. He turned blue. Eventually he yelled but the doctor, who arrived half an hour later, told me, had he been born in hospital, he would have been put into an incubator because of his shock. He told us we must leave him alone for the night, until they returned in the morning.

How could it be right to leave this tiny creature lying in his cot on the other side of the room, alone, so far from the familiar smells and sounds he had known in the womb, without the breathing warmth of a human body close to him? As soon as they had left I nudged John.

'Bring him here.'

I looked down at his little helpless body, his small fingers moving like bits of seaweed groping for his first home, the salt seawater of the womb. He opened his eyes. I looked into them and was surprised. They were clearly those of another being, a 'not-me' that had come out of me.

Is it the first breath that holds the primal shock of arrival on this planet, with its strange air element that rushes in and rushes out, doesn't hold us, doesn't support us, doesn't cushion any of the blows that come at us? Or is it the eyes, as they open onto a strange world of angles and edges, of movements not just around us and towards us, but away from us, leaving us lonely for the first time?

I looked down at this utterly defenceless baby and broke out in a sweat. If we come to know ourselves in the gaze of others, then there is a dreadful power in a mother's eyes. I stroked his fragile little head, still damp from the womb and wished with all my heart to protect this utterly defenceless creature from the bitter winds of circumstance, praying he would be safe from harm. But who can protect you from your protector? Not even God can protect you from your mother. As I well knew, it is mothers, not daughters, who do the most violent harms. And they have done them long before we get old.

Blissfully unaware of his mother's turmoil, this little living breathing creature yawned. His open mouth tried to find my breast, searching blindly in a vast new world. I placed my nipple between his tiny lips and he fastened on and sucked. A tide turned. His determined sucking called out of me the milk he needed, and the vulnerability that had overwhelmed me, now elicited tenderness. A nameless love welled up in me for this nameless being that belonged to me yet, as I had so clearly seen, belonged primarily to himself.

My first lesson of motherhood – the power of vulnerability is as great as the vulnerability of power.

It was nearly midnight. The three of us slept.

In the morning I woke, for a moment oblivious, then surprised all over again at the raw reality of this baby, stirring and mewing on my belly. I lay on my back and stroked him on this his first morning. A new life for me too was beginning.

As Tim grew, he thrived, smiled, burped and did all that babies are supposed to do, but he did not drift off into sleep peacefully like the babies of my friends. He would scream and fight before finally dropping off exhausted. I thought maybe the shock of having the umbilical cord cut too soon had put into him a fear of falling into the dark unconsciousness of sleep; that first cut must surely be the deepest. Perhaps they were primal screams at his abrupt thrust into existential aloneness. It must feel a betrayal when what has nourished you, suddenly starts to strangle you. Maybe he was struggling with the dilemma that to be born means you also die. My demons told me it was all my fault. The district nurse just told me 'Don't worry, my dear, he'll grow out of it.' But Tim's screams did worry me.

I felt he was angry with me, protesting furiously at my deep inadequacies. His howls were signs I was doing something dreadfully wrong, though I had no idea what. Perhaps my profound fucked-up-ness was coming through in the breast milk and my old fears returned to haunt me. I had one breast full of nourishing milk, the other full of the poisonous black milk of demons. In a deadly spiral I began to get anxious, and then anxious that I was anxious, and then anxious that I was anxious that I was anxious. I peered over and into another deep, dark well. Then one morning I put Tim in the pram to walk to the shops.

It was hot. I fixed the sunshade to the pram. I paused. Maybe he needed the sun on his face. So I took it down. Then I thought he would overheat and burn so I put it back up. Then I thought it's early morning, the sun won't be hot yet. So I took it down. Then I thought why take the risk, better to be safe with the shade, so I put it back on. Then I remembered babies need sun for Vitamin D, so I took it off again.

I stood in the hallway indecisively swinging from one option to the other, afraid a catastrophic disaster would ensue if I got this wrong. I had to get it right – sun or shade. The quality and worth of my whole mothering hung in the balance.

Two hours later I was still in the hallway, in tears and panic because I could not decide.

John did his best but was puzzled by my fears and worries about Tim, about myself, about my mothering. He tried to point out what was clear to him, Tim was a happy thriving baby, and I was a caring and sensitive mother. He became frustrated when his common sense did not ease my irrational anxieties. When we tried to talk, he felt helpless and impatient and I withdrew feeling misunderstood. It did not occur to me that I was suffering from post-natal depression, I just assumed, as usual, that there was something shamefully wrong with me.

Eventually I went to see a therapist who told me that I was asking too many questions and would go mad if I continued to turn over every stone to find out what lay beneath it. As one of my fears was I was already mad, this did not help. I tried another who told me I felt so guilty about existing, I hardly dared breathe in case I took oxygen from someone else. I could have told her that. Yet another told me that to get rid of my anger I must beat cushions either for twenty minutes every day for forty years, or forty minutes every day for twenty years. I gave up on him too. Instead of psychoanalytic psychotherapy or reading my books on existential psychology, I decided more experiential forms of therapy might help me.

I found a leaflet in the local library describing co-counselling, a process that teaches people to be therapists for each other, rather than one being the knowledgeable expert, the other the vulnerable client, with its inherent imbalance of power. I read 'When we have been hurt, we pull away from people and situations to avoid being hurt again. To come fully alive we must release these unconscious holding patterns.' Perhaps this would work, I was sure I had a lot of 'unconscious holding patterns'.

I went along to the church hall where the meetings were held. We sat around on folding chairs, among Sunday school drawings of nativity scenes and angels, while the teacher told us we had to release the accumulated hurts and memories we held in our bodies.

We sat facing a partner, held hands and for twenty minutes one of us spoke while the other listened with encouragement but no analysis or advice; then we swapped over. We were to talk about the repeating patterns of our sexual relationships. In at the deep end then. I had a lot to say. I was funny, entertaining, honest, insightful, full of interesting stories and deep realisations. All around me people were crying, weeping, expressing anger and rage. I obviously had a lot more to say than anyone else, I must be the most fascinating person here.

Our teacher gathered us back together into a circle and praised everyone for being so emotionally expressive. I sat there, the only one with dry eyes. From imagining I was top of the class I suddenly realised I was at the bottom. The teacher explained it might take a while for the emotions to flow, and until that happened he would help me with some private tuition. That was fine by me. He had a motorbike and also taught Tai Chi – a rare combination of sexy talents in the mid seventies.

We went for rides on his motorbike where leaning into the curves of the roads despite my fear, was a teaching in how to let go. That's what we told each other anyway. We did not go further with the private tuition because after several hours my breasts would leak milk, a sign for me to return home.

It's hard when you are a breast-feeding mother to remain sexy for very long – or spiritual either for that matter. I've heard it said men only invented meditation because they couldn't breast feed, and certainly the sensual bliss of simply being when breast-feeding is unlike anything else I have experienced. As well as being so convenient. You just pull up your T-shirt and are away. Besides, eating for two, including that second piece of chocolate cake, is far more fun than fiddling with the paraphernalia of bottles, saucepans and dried milk mix.

Meanwhile back in my consciousness raising group we sipped our teas, scratched our heads, shifted around on those glorious sofas, as we struggled each Monday with our anxieties, frustrations, self doubt and waistlines, only to discover again and again that what we thought were our personal inadequacies had their roots in the politics of society. Even fat was a feminist issue. Though when we tried to argue eating chocolate was therefore an imperative political act, the dialectics didn't work out. But we ate it anyway. Experience always precedes theory.

We challenged and questioned cultural ideas of what was a woman and every time came to the same conclusion: a woman was anything we said she was – because we were women. It was obvious after we'd said it.

We incorporated some of the therapeutic techniques I was learning and our explorations took on another dimension. We began to show some emotion, weep and express anger in our meetings rather than just talk about our feelings. We drew pictures, free associated, exaggerated unconscious body movements, repeated emotional phrases and then their opposites – 'I love chocolate and hate men!', 'I hate chocolate and love men!'

Sometimes this would dissolve us into laughter, sometimes reduce us to tears, but it took us into more dangerous territory than just our anger with men. Though we tiptoed around our jealousies and competitiveness, our judgements and fears of each other. After all, you do not want the shoulder you have cried on about your bloke's insensitivity to suddenly become the insensitivity you cry on your bloke's shoulder about.

Very carefully we opened the lid, just a crack, to yet another Pandora's box and found rather than liberating ourselves and each other to be whomsoever and whatever we were, we had created a new feminist version of how we should be as women. Especially how we should be as mothers.

The taboo against the mother who leaves her children, the mother who decides she has to find something of herself before she can give her children what they need, the mother who even concludes her children are better off with someone else, these taboos were too deep in our psyche for us to challenge them directly. Though we did find out we had created new ideas of what is a 'good' mother, nearly as tyrannical as the old. We should breast feed without embarrassment anywhere, anytime in our manifestation of the Earth mother goddess, while destroying patriarchy in all its forms in our manifestation of Kali the goddess of destruction, and we must define and experience our own sexuality our own way, which I think is another goddess. Though trying to be a goddess is not a liberation, more a recipe for feeling inadequate.

Despite our failings we managed to discover that many ideas of what is a good mother have their roots in a patriarchy that controls women's sexuality. After all if a man does not know whether his sons are his sons, how can he lay claim to any ancestry and future line? Who inherits his wealth? Patriarchy, literally means the rule of the father, and when women are sexually free no man knows for sure who are his sons, or even whether he is a father at all. Women's sexual freedom threatens patriarchy at its roots, sexual mothers with attitude blow it apart completely. Clearly my post-natal depression had many more levels to it than just an imbalance of hormones.

I wrote an article about how the tools of humanistic psychology can help us explore the oppressive dynamics of patriarchy in our own psyches, as sometimes we women can be our own worst enemy. For a while I was the worst enemy for some sisters who were outraged at this, but others contacted me similarly struggling and a group of us organised a conference in Lauriston Hall in Scotland. When Tim was just over one year old I left him for the first time for this week in Scotland. Not for the last time, Tim stayed at home with John while I went to raise my consciousness and change the world.

Among the participants at this conference were two people dressed in orange, wearing beads and a locket with a picture of an Indian guru with a beard and flowing white hair. When we discussed the politics of experience, these two leaped up and shouted 'Get out of your heads and into your body!' When we talked about the unconscious patriarchal dimensions of sexuality, these wild orange people yelled: 'Who do you fancy? Follow your energy – don't just talk about it!'

I told them they were abdicating their political responsibility to the collective with their self indulgent, individualistic, unresolved Oedipal obsession with their own energy. They told me to fuck off.

Yet despite my rhetoric, I had already followed my energy. I was not in love at the beginning of the week but obviously open to persuasion, because by the end of it, I had let love take me by my hand and lead me where it will. I had fallen in love. Nigel had recently written a feminist critique of sociology, *Reconstructing Social Psychology*; but before any reconstruction must come the deconstruction. Our relationship was about to deconstruct both our worlds.

Chapter 8
The Politics of Experience

Nigel turned me onto new levels of sexual exploration and feeling in my body. I turned him onto acid, mushrooms and hallucinogenic explorations beyond the mind. Together we explored the hidden realms of the psyche using the new humanistic therapies – Jacob Moreno, Fritz Perls, Frank Lake, Carl Rogers and especially Wilhelm Reich, who had been hounded by the American authorities, imprisoned and his books burned. That made him a revolutionary hero as well as a psycho-spiritual guru.

Wilhelm Reich was the first person to link a lack of love in intimate relationships with the politics of fear and oppression in society. We can be cruel only when out of touch with our own life force; we can abuse others and our environment only when we no longer feel the sensations in the most intimate piece of Earth of them all, our own body. He told us the unconscious is not an abstract entity invented by Freud, vaguely dangling in the ether, it is a real living entity, the body.

According to Reich, although we have to learn to control the beast else no nursery would have us, the beast does not die, quite simply, because without the animal body we are dead. The beast lives on in the deep tension of our muscles, the tides of our hormones, in the workings of our organs and living tissue. To reclaim our lost animal vitality and achieve total orgasm, our holy grail at that time, we must first release the accumulated unconscious tensions in our bodies.

We found a book with diagrams of Reich's bio-energetic exercises. We angled our bodies in various 'stress' positions, breathed into our bellies and knuckled into each other's tight muscles, sheer agony, but no pain, no gain. After months of bending over the backs of chairs and bending over while standing on one leg, we got creative. I can't say I'd recommend releasing cellular memories by making love on acid while rebirthing through several past lives in an orgone generator, but then that's like looking back at a party the morning after; you see it in a different light from when you were having fun in the dark the night before. And we were rather in the dark back then. And I don't just mean between the sheets with the light out.

Every age is a dark age as much as an age of enlightenment, and I had seen how dark were the corners of our culture and society while working with children and families so crushed and powerless in every other arena, they took it out on each other. Nigel and I saw the anguish and pain we struggled with as more than just our personal concerns, they were manifestations of the oppressions and injustices embedded in society. In fact, to go for the total orgasm was a revolutionary duty as far as we were concerned.

Unfortunately you cannot fight civilisation's darkness on all fronts. John and I had drifted into different worlds. We dismantled our home and, in the painful tearing of all such separations, divided our possessions. The demolishing of a life built over years was no easier with John than it had been with Pete, and this time there was also a little boy, eighteen months old, who had known only this home with the two of us. Whatever were our own losses and regrets, John and I did our best to shield Tim from the pains of such an arrangement and agreed to share the care of Tim equally and as simply as possible, with whatever flexibility we each might need.

I packed Tim's bag with his favourite toys and John took him down the garden path to drive to his new flat. Tim waved good-bye to me and the cat, his red mittens dangling, full of smiles for the new adventure.

'Bye mummy. Bye Tabitha. Bye byeee! Goosey goosey gander...' showing off his new discovery of how to sing. His voice faded as they drove away.

Goodbye Tim. Goodbye John. Take care. Goodbye.

I forced a smile and waved. The car turned at the end of the street and I turned and went back into the silent house. I stood in a hallway empty of John and Tim. It was no longer a home. No family lived here any more. The absence pressed down on me, crushing me further into my loss. But far worse than my grief was the sense I had harmed Tim, had failed as a mother.

A friend found me weeping on the stairs. In between sobs I told her,

'I am a useless, worthless and a terrible mother. I have completely fucked up my whole life and Tim's as well.'

When a friend speaks like this, there's nothing to do but put your arm round them, pass the tissues, make a pot of tea, before both of you move onto the harder stuff.

My public face was completely at odds with my private grief. I was involved in a TV series on childhood, where as a feminist child psychologist, I said children were enriched when they could develop relationships with many adults, not just their two parents, and now the extended family had withered away, the nuclear family deprived children of this. I quoted research showing depression was endemic among mothers of young children, stuck at home alone. I talked about how each family unit with its individualised infrastructure of washing machines and ovens, was alienating women from each other while providing capitalism with a ready made ever expanding consumer market. The answer, I told them with conviction, was communal living. They wanted me back for another series but I refused. I felt a fraud, confidently sounding off in my assertions on TV and back home, feeling so cut up and guilty when Tim went off for his non-nuclear family experiences with John. Besides there was a revolution to attend to.

Inspired during our stay at Lauriston Hall, a plan for a commune organised on neo-Reichian socialist-feminist principles, where every decision was made by consensus, was evolving fast, despite the fact six of us had to agree about everything along the way. To break down bourgeois individualism, everything would be owned collectively. Even T-shirts and knickers would be kept in a communal drawer. We would write a manifesto to explain to the rest of humanity why what we were doing was better than what they were doing, and if they did it our way, they too could share toothbrushes and total orgasms.

I sold my house and we moved to Harehills, less trendy than Headingley where my, now our, money could buy a larger house. My solicitor tried to dissuade me from agreeing to all of us owning the house equally when my money was buying it, but I looked him in the eye and informed him, 'To each according to their needs, from each according to their abilities.' He looked at me with worldly compassion, shook his head and drew up the papers.

Consensual politics require everyone to have a lot of free time to decide what to do with their free time, apart from wandering around being free of course. Fortunately I now worked less intensely as I was studying for a M.Sc. in Clinical Psychology. I had decided it was the adults that needed fixing, not the kids. The wounded children I had worked and played with, were never the source of the problem, that always lay in the troubled dynamics of the family, especially in the parent's relationship. I came across a research study by Murray Bowen, which radically shifted my view of family dynamics.

He examined five different ways of dealing with children with psychiatric problems and young offenders – counselling for the child, family therapy, reward for good behaviour, punishment for bad behaviour, and doing nothing. His findings were stunning. He found that if either of the child's parents was more invested in being emotionally close to the child than to their partner, then nothing worked. The child's behaviour deteriorated whatever approach was used, and what's more, there was no significant difference whatsoever between any of these methods. He also found that if the parents were more emotionally invested in each other, even if that meant rows and fights, once again it made no difference what approach was used – every single child improved.

Here in black and white was what I have known all my life – let a child be and it will grow into itself, interfere with that, even with what you think is love, and you end up with heartbroken children who cannot be themselves. Heartbroken because, children love their parents and will give themselves body and soul to the work of making their parents happy. But they will fail. It was never designed to be this way. Adults are responsible for making their own love not relying on the ready made love of children who will distort their own growth in order to give them what they want. If adults turn to children to meet their psychological needs, like physical intimacy, this emotional closeness is deadly for the child.

I knew this failure intimately. Born into a family with a crack right through its heart meant I had a crack right through mine too. I had tried to love my family into wholeness, but when your heart is cracked, your love is too, and I had failed. Yet even though I had not been able to save my family, perhaps I could save the world. Our Feminist Alternative Socialist Commune would lead the way!

The light of revolutionary fervour shone so brightly in my eyes, I could not see what was lying in the shadows.

Hundreds of meetings later, after I had cut the labels off my designer gear, not wanting to be seen as a fascist fashionista when Dave told us the capitalist plot included the fashion business, apparently sequins were the new opium of the masses; and we had argued for four weeks whether to buy Kellog's cornflakes with the free superheroes the kids wanted, or the cheaper ones from the cash and carry, I walked away. We'd spent so much time arguing on beanbags in the living room or in the Orgone Pyramid in the garden, we hadn't even begun the manifesto informing everyone they too should be living like this. The loss of my money I chalked up to experience.

However expensive the lessons, I had not learned them all. I applied to join a neo-Marxist socialist-feminist commune. After an interview where I wore my badges of revolutionary slogans, dropped in the names of my most right-on mates, mentioned the conferences I'd attended, the barricades I'd fought at, I was in.

This was communal living how I liked it. For a start it was palatial with deep pile carpets and even a chandelier or two, though what Marxists are supposed to do with chandeliers escaped me – swing capitalists from them? Each of us had two rooms and our own bathroom. Neither the food nor the wine was from the cash and carry as the state we hoped would wither away soon, in the meantime, paid us all good salaries as university lecturers. Here too were far fewer meetings, and these took place not on beanbags or pyramids in the garden, but on stylish and more luxurious sofas than even those from MFI. Tim liked it here as well, there was a drum kit in the communal living room.

Another Clinical Psychologist on the course became a close friend. I recognised Barbara as a sister in the psycho-spiritual struggle for world peace in a seminar on bi-polar manic depression when she asked if anyone had tried re-birthing as a form of treatment. She explained her depression had lifted when she had re-lived her experience in the womb. I was glad she was at that seminar as I was on the verge of realizing that I was not only schizophrenic but possibly manic-depressive as well. I knew only too well those mood swings where you fly sky high, one of the stars one day, only to find yourself plummeting into a pit devoid of all meaning the next. Fortunately her re-birthing suggestion distracted me.

Jim, from our commune, liked her too and the three of us frequently got together to empirically research the politics of experience – Marxist-feminists are never off-duty. One evening we were lounging around in Jim's room high on psilocybin mushrooms. Or rather they may have been high, I was having my consciousness dramatically lowered, into the Earth.

Despite Reich, I had always assumed in the body politic, the head rules as monarch, the body being a subject of its consciousness. Here I was being told a very different story. What stands under us is what understands us. Wisdom arises from the ground, the body, it doesn't sink down from our heads.

I lay on my back with my eyes closed, arms by my side, not moving, a position I later learned in India is called the Corpse Posture, but my body was far from dead. It was discovering new dimensions of its life. The mushrooms, gown in the shit of cows, and you can't get more earthy than that, woke up the cellular memories of my body, because as I breathed I could feel my connection with the breathing of all living creatures, whether through lungs, gills or osmosis. I lay unmoving as nature showed me the greatest story ever told, was stored in my own DNA. How in the nine months of womb life, we travel millions of years, each of us making again the long march from a single cell into sea creatures, fish, reptiles, insects, birds and mammals.

Just as Reich had explained the unconscious is the body, the magic of these mushrooms revealed the collective unconscious is the body of all of us, all living creatures and plants. That we eat them and they eat us is the holy communion of life. Even disease is a inter-species dialogue. I opened my eyes and stared at the ceiling – yet another stick I had been holding at the wrong end my whole life.

In the typical insensitivity of people who have suddenly discovered one of the ultimate truths of the universe, I leaned over and interrupted the bodily embraces that Barbara and Jim are more wisely into.

'This is amazing! Wisdom comes up from the ground through your body and only hits the synapses of your brain at the very end!'

'Yes', laughed Barbara.

'You mean you already knew this!' I asked in astonishment.

'Yes' she smiled.

Must have been all that re-birthing.

But there is a time for wisdom and a time for experience and I left them to it, resisting the urge to proclaim this new message to the world. People struggling through the rain with the weekly shop from Safeway's, wanting to get home after a long week in the office, may not appreciate being hassled by my handing out leaflets telling them their sausages are manifestations of trans-species love. The mystic songs of one dimension do not translate easily into the language of the more mundane. So I sank back and listened to the singing in my ears, as the ancient Earth wisdom of the goddess taught me to read the unholy scriptures of the body.

As a clinical psychologist in the Psychiatric Units of St James' Hospital Leeds and Bradford Royal Infirmary, I continued my fight for justice and freedom. Still keen on the perspective, mental illness is a reflection of the insanity in society and major tranquillisers undermine the meaning of experience, I did not mention this on the unit. The staff had enough on without my suggestions to throw away the pills and syringes and try encounter groups and bodywork instead.

Psychiatry works at the raw end of life with some of the most dispossessed and marginalised people in our society. People with no power, status or self worth, and often no home, no possessions and no family or friends either. These are people who have fallen through the cracks in the safety net to catch the people who have fallen through the cracks. Some have fallen so completely, they no longer cry out for help. A grey devastation has become their home, they have forgotten any other life. I have not been inside a psychiatric unit since the seventies but some of the mental hospitals I visited were barren desolate places where the locked wards, the padded cells, the peeling paint, stained lino, barred windows without curtains, shabby torn vinyl armchairs, the snuffling and shuffling of muted human misery, even worse, the apathy and indifference in blank stares, were all signs this was the end of the road.

I tried to find the source of this desolation and despair, not just in the psyches of individuals, but also in the dynamics of society itself. Was there something intrinsic in the nature of being human that led to such suffering? The European psychoanalysts and existentialists, with the weariness of empires and several World Wars, seemed to say yes, the challenge is to live with the darkness not get rid of it. The effervescent vitality of America however, seemed to believe in a basic goodness in humanity and with the right conditions, our full potential will emerge naturally, the light vanquishing the dark. (Though precisely what are those conditions can become a source of conflict and war themselves. Western democracy? Material wealth? Fundamentalist Religion? A better sound system? Wars have been fought over less.)

Caught between the optimism of the New World and the more weary understandings of Old Europe, I decided to explore the wisdom of the East, but this time without the pharmaceutical help. I went to see Mick and Linda, friends who had recently become followers of Guru Maharaji, maybe they could throw some divine light on my confusion.

I rang the bell on a large Victorian Terrace. Mick opened the door.

'Hi!' he says stepping back to let me in.

I follow him up the stairs to their flat on the third floor. Slightly out of breath we arrive at their door. I walk in and stop dead. Everything has gone. There's no furniture, no carpets, no TV, nothing on the walls, and what really disturbs me, no sound system. There are just a couple of upturned orange boxes. Linda is on one and I lower myself gingerly onto another.

'What's happened?' I ask looking around in case their possessions are piled in a corner, maybe they're moving out. No. The whole place is cleared of all stuff except for these orange boxes. Not even an album cover left on which to roll a joint. This is serious. No one can live without music.

'We've seen the divine light' they explain with beatific smiles. They look at me gently with compassion. 'Would you like some lemon verbena tea?'

'Are you guys on something?' I ask. It's always good to know what level of consciousness you're dealing with when you talk with friends. It's no good using the lingua franca of everyday hassles if your mate is hanging out with beings from another galaxy.

'Yes. We are drunk with the pure bliss of being and walking in the garden, no longer trampling through its beauty with the elephant mind.'

'Oh, right, yeah, the elephant mind.' I say. I rapidly think with my elephant mind where to go from here.

'We don't drink or smoke now, not even home grown weed.'

Blimey! Maybe they are exactly who I need to talk to, then again maybe they are too far out even for me. Anyone who lives voluntarily without a sofa has clearly gone beyond where I've been – it's just I'm not sure I want to go there.

'It's like this.' I begin. 'I've done the anti-capitalist, anti-patriarchy, anti-racist, anti-organised religion, anti-psychiatry thing, but seem to have missed what it *is* about. Any ideas you guys?' They smile.

'You must open your ears to the sounds of eternal bliss, smell the aroma of divine honeysuckle, see the divine light of eternal compassion, taste the...'

'Sounds great but what's with the orange boxes?' I interrupt.

'We no longer need the illusion, the Maya of the material world because we now smell the aroma of divine honeysuckle, the eternal bliss of..'

But I want eternal bliss *and* a sofa.

They tell me about a talk being given in Manchester in a few weeks by the guru himself, the Maharaji. Maybe I'd like to go with them? They smile beatifically again.

About ten of us travelled across the Pennines, uncomfortably squashed in the back of a van. But I guess a few bruises here and there are nothing to write home about when you are sniffing eternal honeysuckle. We arrived at Manchester Poly to more beatific smiles. Lots of wafting hair. One of the organisers called us together, speaking into the microphone with a breathily sincere mid-Atlantic accent which perhaps he imagined was spiritually cool, but to the uninitiated marked him out as a flirty-fisher trying to love bomb us into disciple-hood.

The Maharaji arrives. I can only make out the odd word – 'peace', 'divine', 'bliss'… Yet even at the back among the less pious who shift about a bit, I feel warm and relaxed. Though that may have been the central heating after the freezing van. The main man left and another guy offered to answer questions. Despite being aware the elephantine dimensions of my mind were about to be revealed, I did what every feminist must do – I asked about the position of women in the movement. A beatific smile wafted my way. Apparently Maharaji had said women are closer to the divine because they are naturally more receptive and surrendered.

Not for me then. Anyway, the smell of eternal honeysuckle must get to you after a while.

Later that night I lie in bed and stare at the ceiling. My failures to bring liberation to the world parade mercilessly before me. Global capitalism obviously needs us to confuse consumer choice with freedom, so we stay chained to our desks marketing what we later buy with the money we make marketing it. Anyway who am I with my Smeg freezer to tell a family in Mumbai they can't have their cheap second hand refrigerator because it will deplete the ozone? And I was well aware transnational corporations couldn't care less that a bunch of weird lefties in Leeds denounced their soul-less materialism and rape of the environment – though our phone was tapped but what kind of victory is that? Neither do the world's religions want anyone to be free – who would sell their soul as an insurance policy against hell in an after-life if they are having fun in this one? I could even see Patriarchy has its place in the dialectics of history and arose in response to the overwhelming power of an earlier matriarchy – we all know what power tends to do whatever the sex of those who wield it.

The systems I had struggled with were just too powerful. I sighed. But if fighting these is not what it's about, what is?

Perhaps a walk through Woodhouse Moor would help me more than a long stare at the ceiling. I reached for my coat, pulled my hat over my ears, wrapped my scarf around me and wandered out into the night.

Maybe some divine light had worked its way into me after all. Halfway across the moor, it hit me. Organised religion had stolen my spirituality. And I wanted it back.

PART TWO

Playing Snakes and Buddhas

My second eye opens and
I see The Dream

Chapter 9
What the Id Did

The January of 1979 was freezing. Wrapped in a thick dressing gown after a bath, I relaxed by the fire with a bottle of Rioja. Tim was asleep next door. Barbara had lent me a tape of another guru, probably going on about divine bliss and eternal honeysuckle I supposed. Never one to turn away from an insight or two, however, I put it on. I leaned back in the warmth of the fire, closed my eyes and drifted into another world.

I heard the background noise of parrots and a train in the distance. The sounds settled, and from thousands of miles away, a voice, began to speak. Though not of what I'd expected. It spoke of fear, failure and despair.

The voice explained we can run from our demons but they remain always right behind us. We can run as far and as fast as possible away from them, through cities, fields, over mountains and across plains, until we stop exhausted, only to hear them move as we move, breathe as we breathe. In panic we get up and run again until we arrive at a tree. Our demons are still with us. We climb the tree. They follow us. We keep going until we reach the end of a branch that hangs over an abyss. But still we have not escaped. The demons are waiting where they always have, right behind us. When we realise there is nowhere left to run to or to hide, we can either jump and kill ourselves, or face what we have been running from all our life. If we turn and look straight into the face of our demons, we will find there is nothing there. There never was. We have been running from ourselves. We are the demons that make us so afraid. Demons 'R Us.

I sat transfixed, unable to move. This voice, speaking to me across a vast emptiness, seemed to know me in all my dark despair and told me exactly what I most needed to hear, about my most intimate struggle of all. I felt an ancient promise I didn't understand was about to be fulfilled as this man called me home, a home I had been exiled from my whole life. Yet I was afraid. I sensed I was about to fall into a darkness where there would be no light to guide me. Just the fall. And the darkness.

But it was too late. I had already fallen. This man must have named stars, sounded oceans, sung every song and spoken the trees and the wind, because his voice resonated through all the levels of my being and I felt myself falling in love with a man I had never met. I heard him promise to ease my anguish and heal all the wounds in my soul, and I believed him.

I fell into the river of my longing, and as the waters rose, the sorrow in my heart, broken with so many confused loves, broke over me and I wept. This man, Bhagwan Shree Rajneesh, welcomed me into his heart, killing me softly with his song, and a long, light years long, struggle ended. The war was over. In the sweetest of homecomings, I fell to his feet.

For the next two weeks I wept with a painful remorse as insights, sharp as icicles, sliced into me. I had been so afraid of death that I had become afraid of life. I had used my mind to have power over life rather than to serve life. I had been so lost, for so long, I had not known how lost I was. Again and again I heard this man inside my own heart say the words – 'You have come home'. My heart cracked open still more and I fell through the cracks and drowned.

I found an address on the tape for the ashram in Pune where this man, who spoke so eloquently of homecomings and demons, lived with his disciples. I wrote explaining his words had me drowning in an ocean of tears, and knew that once this letter was posted, I would have sealed my fate. So I kept it in my bag. Then one day I stood in front of the post box, pulled off my glove, reached into my bag felt for the edge of the envelope, and brought it out. I looked at the exotic Indian address in Maharastra, an address that even in the cold blizzards of Leeds conjured up mangoes, monkeys, incense and frangipani. I reached up to the post box and let the letter fall from my hands.

That night there was a ring at the door. I opened the door to a man with flowing locks and a beard, wearing orange clothes and a necklace of beads with a picture of the man with the golden voice.

'This is amazing!' I told him.

'Probably' he replied hugging his arms around him and stamping his feet, 'it usually is. And it's freezing out here. Can I come in?'

His name was a strange Pradeep. He had heard we were dismantling our commune and wondered if he could rent it for a meditation centre.

Wanting a break from collective, co-operative, communal living, I was buying a small house for just Tim and me. I explained the house was not for rent but perhaps he would like to buy it? He shrugged. I got the impression that such material concerns were ... well ... immaterial. I told him I had only that day posted a letter to the ashram in India.

'Goodness!' he leaped up. 'It is your birthday! We must go out and celebrate.'

I tried to explain it was not my birthday, that was over two months away, but he walked over to me in his flowing robes, abruptly took my hand and pulled me towards the door. He leaned in close and looked into my eyes.

'This is your true birthday, the start of a new life', he informed me with a meaningful stare.

We drove through the sleet and snow of the Leeds January to the main disco in town where I met three others similarly dressed in the orange and beads. They looked at me in my black sweater and blue jeans, the new kid on the block wearing the wrong kind of trainers. Or would that be more a virgin at a naked lunch?

We sat round a table facing the dance floor where another orange guy with wild eyes, long hair and a beard was dancing. This guy could really dance, an urban animal playing with the beat of seventies disco in moves so cool, you shivered. The black DJ smiled. He put on a long mix of Sly and the Family Stone, left his booth and crossed the dance floor. Slowly and deliberately, these two began to move. A murmur of respect ran through the crowd as the floor cleared for these black and white brothers, comrades and rivals, gearing up to play their combat. With the beauty of beasts, these shape-shifting urban witchdoctors moved through the fights and loves of animals, kings, friends and brothers as they danced a shamanic street medicine for us all. The track ended. They nodded a smile of respect to each other and the disco erupted with applause and cheers. The orange guy came over to our table and I met Sujan, the dancer with bright blue wilderness eyes.

Sujan had danced with Anna Halprin's dance company in San Francisco. They had worked in black neighbourhoods after the Watts riots, and when words and intellectual language had threatened to further divide the community, they had used dance as a form of self-expression and dialogue. Fluent in the language of the body, words left Sujan cold.

We ended the evening back at my house. One moment we were hanging out and chilling, the next the chairs had been pushed back and Sujan and Pradeep had leaped onto each other and were rolling on the floor grunting and growling in a fight. I was shocked. It had just happened – like two dogs. What on Earth I had got myself into?

'Why did you do that?' I asked.

'There are no rules.' Sujan replied.

I was a stranger in this strange land.

A few weeks later I received a letter from the ashram in Pune with a new name, a mala and a message from Bhagwan telling me that when I am filled with gratitude for the whole of existence as it is, then slowly, slowly the fragrance of sannyas will arise. I would be struggling for some time then.

My new name, Ma Prem Vismaya, meant 'wonder of love', but I was filled with neither wonder nor love. My relationship with Nigel was hitting trouble. I was wandering off into the bush as far as he was concerned and he wanted to warn me of the poisonous snakes and insects that could bite me there. I was so intent on travelling that way I found his warnings interfered with the spontaneity I was practising so assiduously.

When I met friends now, I could see them recoil at my orange and beads. I walked into the feminist bookshop where a phalanx of women confronted me and told me to get out, I was no longer welcome now I wore a man round my neck. When I heard myself trying to explain that you enter the unknown when you follow your energy not your mind, I realised I had drifted further from the shore of my previous life than planned.

Someone once asked Bhagwan why we had to wear orange. He explained it was the traditional colour for sannyas, the colour of sunrise signalling the dawning of a new age. But I think it was to mark us out, to force us into each other's arms, as who else would willingly walk down the street next to someone swathed in such a deadly colour. Though it was not long before our robes evolved into reds, pinks and purples – and not only because the Leeds Woolworth's ran out of orange dye.

Each morning I dropped Tim off at the university nursery and drove to Bradford Royal Infirmary Psychiatric Unit with Barbara, now Mahimo, where we worked as Clinical Psychologists, both in our orange clothes and beads. We had managed to persuade them to let us experiment with group therapy and planned to introduce techniques from the Human Potential Movement to the anxious and depressed women of Bradford. Our plan was to raise their consciousness of the Patriarchal context of their distress and help them connect with universal love.

Twenty women in varying stages of depression and anxiety sat in a circle on plastic stackable chairs. We could have done with a few sofas. We began with each saying our names and what we needed from the group.

'Mary. I'm OK thanks.'

'Josephine Brown. Can you shut that window, it's cold.'

'I'm Carole with an 'e', Sinclair. When do we get our tea did you say?'

'Sara Marshall. I can't sleep or eat. My kids are with their gran. I can't cope. Know what I mean?'

'My name's Sophie Smith. Yeah I've got ten kids, but only three live wi' me, the rest are in care. And what do I want? More money I guess. Yeah. And a new flat from the council.'

'I'm Sharon. That's it for now.'

Round we go, several sitting with heads down, say nothing at all.

Our plans to help these women connect with their rage at the Patriarchal Capitalist System, so their anger would release them from their helpless depression, fly straight out the window. We end up with four women having a conversation about which bus to get from town to the hospital, at least three of them are, the fourth seems to be under the impression they are talking about the plot of last night's Coronation Street. One woman accuses another of having stolen her wedding ring. Another begins to weep and says she used to live in a manor house with servants. Several appear to be asleep. Another is interested only in a mark on the chair, while her neighbour mutters and picks fluff off her threadbare cardigan. The tea however is drunk, the biscuits eaten and somehow we get through the hour.

As they left we told them they did not have to come again unless they wanted to. These women have enough on without having to trek across Bradford in the rain to sit on uncomfortable stackable chairs for a few desultory conversations about bus timetables, a cup of tea and a digestive biscuit. We did not expect to see any of them again.

The next week we were surprised, most of them had returned. And they kept on returning. Not every week, not on time, and with no apparent change in their condition or their situation, but they kept coming.

On our last day Mahimo and I asked them what they thought they had gained from the six months we had been meeting. I was dreading this but had to know if anything at all had been of the slightest help to them.

'Well you always remembered I liked four spoons of sugar in me tea. I liked that, it were nice' said Rosemary.

'Whenever I got stuck with my coat and you came and helped me. That was very polite' offered Carole

And from Josephine, 'Once I saw that you were sweating but you didn't ask for the window to be open, and I knew that you knew that for me it were best shut.'

Several asked why we wore orange, but we kept it simple. It was our religion we told them, having long ago abandoned our original goals.

To our surprise, when the time came to say good-bye, we all found we were rather sad. Sitting in a circle doing very little and a love seemed to have grown by itself. Was our group a success or failure? Who can say? Something had happened but neither Mahimo nor I knew what that was. Perhaps we had simply met each other as fellow human beings, and as Gandhi had said – the magic had been in the situation, not us.

The Psychiatric Unit at St James's in Leeds however was not impressed by the magic whatever its source. I had suggested to a group they stand in a circle and massage the shoulders of the one in front of them. I was called before the management. Did I not know that patients must never touch or be touched by each other or us?

It was too late. They had already touched me, and I could not commit to folding my arms across my professional heart if I felt that putting my arms around them was what they needed. I could not betray our common humanity, the true essence, anyway, of all healing. I stood before the management committee and found as I have many times before and since, there was nothing I could say.

Twenty-five years later I heard from a friend who had met the current Professor of Clinical Psychology at Leeds University. He had been one of my lecturers at the time. He asked her if she knew what had become of me.

'She was one of the most gifted Clinical Psychologists I have ever come across', he said, 'it was a tragedy when she left for that ashram in India.'

Why had no one told me I was a gifted psychologist? Perhaps they did. Perhaps I couldn't hear them. Perhaps they did not. Anyway it was not a tragedy.

Apart from trying to raise the consciousness of the planet, we sannyasins meditated daily, though dynamic meditations, where instead of imposing a stillness, which repressed our energy, we jumped up and down, screamed, raged, danced, and cathartically released our madness before lying down. A natural stillness was then supposed to rise organically. Though it could have been exhaustion.

We also went in for raw, anarchic encounter groups. These happened at my house, as I was the only one with enough cushions and mugs. Every

Sunday morning I checked the teabags, milk, biscuits, tissues and turned up the heating before Mahimo, Pradeep, Mahavir, Dwara, Raso, Jayo, Madhur and any other sanyassin wandering through Leeds, arrived. We began with the conversations people have everywhere, the weather, who is making love and war with whom, whether this season's hair is short or long, what is the new black – though we knew that one already. Then we took off our clothes (hence the heating), sat in a circle, naked before the truth and each other, determined to strip pretence bare, encounter ourselves through our encounters with others, while holding in our stomachs the whole time.

Encounter groups are scary. And not just because they're full of fighting talk. You had to be real. The trouble was you never knew whether you were real or phoney until after you had been it and people either went for you or let you be. The idea was to speak the truths you would normally censor as inappropriate, rude, crazy, insensitive and so on, in order break free from society's ideas of how you should behave. Which, as we all knew, was a con designed by the systems of society to keep us down. And back then, those systems had a lot more controlling power over our energy than they do now.

Most people still doffed their caps to their 'superiors' and thought living in sin was, well, living in sin. It was another world. Pink Floyd hadn't yet told us we were just another brick in the wall, Talking Heads were still in the dark and Joy Division were far away. Margaret Thatcher was an ordinary MP and the Shah was in power in a secular Iran. However, the Sex Pistols had recently told us to 'Never Mind the Bollocks', so not only in our encounter groups were we trying to break free.

Inevitably in our groups there were awkward, painful silences as we sat around not knowing what to say or do, especially as the whole point was to jump out of the security of the known into the insecurity of the unknown. None of us had any maps. Share our secrets and we might be revealed as a complete jerk. Tell someone we fancied them and we might be publicly scorned:

Madhur to Raso:	'I fancy you.'
Raso to Madhur:	'Well, I don't fancy you so move over. You are blocking my view of Pradeep and I do fancy him.'
Pradeep to Madhur:	'Yeah. Get out of the way you arsehole.'
Pradeep to Raso	'I fancy you too.'

Mahimo to Raso:	'Lay off Pradeep he's mine.'
Raso to Mahimo:	'Why should I? He doesn't belong to you or anyone.'
Madhur to Pradeep:	'Who are you calling an arsehole, you arsehole.'
Pradeep to Madhur:	'Fuck off, you're jealous that Raso fancies me more than you.'

And this is just the warm-up. There are six more hours of this relentless self-revelation still to go, broken only by tea and pee breaks.

I already knew from my five years of Monday consciousness-raising, that to sit in a circle unpeeling layers of our personalities in order to discover the deeper truths of ourselves is a potent process. So I stuck at it even when I was likened to Miss Jean Brodie and I knew I was much more like Janis Joplin or Joni Mitchell.

Our friends thought Sujan and I should get together; there was 'energy' between us they said. Obvious to them but not to us. But when I had finally told Nigel our relationship was over about the same time Sujan said good bye to his last love, we did find ourselves together under the stars one Easter in Snowdonia. Several days later Sujan moved in with me bringing two boxes, one of LP's, the other with clothes and a few screwdrivers. His family were wealthy and, after he had read Charles Reich's *Greening of America*, he had given everything away and wandered the USA for several years with just his backpack and sleeping bag, before he ended up dancing in the streets.

With my car, my house, my kitchen paraphernalia, cushions and books I was impressed by Sujan's lack of materialism, though wary of the reckless abandon involved. Voices in my head told me I was foolish and impulsive, that it would end in tears, you marry in haste and repent at leisure, we should look before we leap, better to be safe than sorry... But perhaps Sujan and I had taken full measure of what really mattered. Nearly thirty years later, I know we had.

Each morning Tim would wake up wander into my bed and in Oedipal fury, kick Sujan until he went downstairs to make us breakfast. Then he discovered that Sujan not only read stories, he acted them out, and Sujan was allowed to stay.

When Tim was with John, breakfast was delayed as Sujan and I wrestled with our tangled sheets, gazed into the stars in each other's eyes and whispered the secrets of intimacy. I confessed I was a fragmented being who did not know who she really was. Sujan told me he had had bulimia until it had gone, never to return, after the first night we had made love.

I said I felt I had at last met someone running as completely and as blindly into life as I was. He said he felt he had come home.

More people came to our meditations. We took the lease on a warehouse and spent the summer sanding floors and painting. All the great and cool of Leeds, except for the hard-core ideologically correct left, came to the opening party for Sangeet Rajneesh Meditation Centre. We were, after all, with-it hip spiritual guys who knew all the latest sexy dance moves, not weedy pathetic unworldly types who couldn't dance.

Mondays, Sujan ran a dance and movement class, though unlike any other in Leeds at that time. Tuesdays, I ran an encounter group. It was far more fun to lead a group than it was to be in one. For a start you could keep it together and remain wise and serene while all around you messed up their hair and fell apart. Though I kept nothing together when Rajen, one of the spiritual therapists from the ashram, came to run a weekend at Sangeet.

Twenty of us sat naked in a circle. For an hour an oppressive nothing happened. The silence lay on us, a leaden blanket that grew heavier. Even open warfare would have been better than this stuck suffocation. We shifted positions with nervous coughs, all of us stuck semi-frozen on a high diving board, a million things going through our heads, knowing we have to jump eventually but delaying it as long as we could. Eventually the discomfort of standing there was worse than the fear of jumping, and we dived in.

Suddenly we are fighting, shouting and falling into each other and then away back into ourselves. I don't know what's going on. There's none of the empathic understanding and unconditional positive regard of the Rogerian encounter groups that I'm keen on; in here, it's instinctual-anarchic-no-holds-barred-surgery-without-anaesthetic-survival-of-the-fittest. Rajen of the surgeon's knife cuts into our cancerous egos and tells us we are petrified of life, half dead and sit in toilets eating shit. He stares at me with a light-years long challenge. The law of this jungle has decreed he is mightier and I look down first. He invites me into the middle.

'Do everything you are most afraid of', he says as he turns to his beautiful assistant and smiles.

I look at the oh so cool group leader with the ice blue knowledge of hell in his eyes and tell him to fuck off, he's an arrogant arsehole. But that wasn't a real 'fuck you'. I'm only saying it because he told me to. But I do really want to tell him to fuck off. Yet if I really wanted him to fuck off I wouldn't do what he told me and tell him to 'fuck off'. Am I a sycophantic creep or keeping it real? I am way out of my depth here. Rajen ignores me and continues to smile at his gorgeous side kick. I turn and face the group.

What I fear most is if my true ugliness and terrible inadequacies are seen, people will turn away from me in disgust. I decide to go for it. Already naked, I now strip myself completely.

I rub my eyes, mess up my hair, and contort my face to look as ugly as sin. I tell them the truth that lies between the lies is that I live a lie; I fake it so real I am beyond fake. I scream that I hate them all. I stand in front of Sujan and spit at him. I return to my place and sit silently with my eyes closed in the unbearable is-ness of being what I have never shown anyone, not even myself.

There is silence. The life of the group moves on and I breathe. I am still here. I can't remember what it is I have forgotten to remember to forget, but something has changed. I have become one of the demons I had been running from. I looked around the group. When you have done your worst and it has not killed you, you are free of it. I had been in fear, now the fear was in me. That means now I am greater than the fear. The operation had been a success.

It did not escape me, however, that the most powerful women in the group came in for the heaviest treatment. Patriarchy still rules even in the enlightenment business. Bhagwan himself placed women in the positions of power in the ashram, except his of course, the guru is always a man even though we thought him a god. He said men had had their chance and blown it – look at the world – now was the time of the women. Women organised the ashram, ran all the departments, handled the administration, liaised with Bhagwan, and told people where to go, what to do and how to do it. The only positions of power left to the men were as second hand gurus in the groups. Naturally this is where they took their revenge.

It was an interesting reversal to have women with power in the material world and men with power in the inner psychic realms. By 'interesting' I mean both wonderful and terrible. Curious differences emerged, but even deadlier similarities. I now know women and men, all of us, are as bad as each other.

Many people could not understand why intelligent, educated and talented women and men, from all walks of life, who apparently had so much going for them, would want to rush off to India, live in bamboo huts, wear that awful orange and fall at the feet of a guru. It did not help that in our rebellion against the colonisation of experience by the mind, we were reluctant to explain anything. I often tried, but routinely failed. I wrote to my parents, trying to find the common ground.

'Dear Mum and Dad, This man is like Jesus. He is a manifestation of the divine in human form. Just as Jesus was judged and rejected for challenging established religion, so is Bhagwan. But he is teaching us how to love and revealing the truth of the spirit. With lots of love, Vismaya who was Anne'

They increased their prayers to St Jude, the patron saint of hopeless cases.

Not many were convinced, neither parents nor journalists. Bernard Levin, however, was. He visited Pune and wrote glowingly about his experience in the Times. He was pursued for years afterwards. By us, trying to squeeze more good publicity out of him, by others, pouring intellectual scorn on him. And that was one of my difficulties. I could no longer explain in intellectual language what was going on. I could see what had been hidden to me before, that the intellectual mind colonises experience and trades it for knowledge. It asks 'why?' not 'what?' and thinks that to analyse life is more important than to experience it. And along with many other psychotherapists and psychologists, I found more happened in one weekend of these encounter groups than had happened in decades of traditional therapies.

I had walked round my demons for years in consciousness raising groups, co-counselling, and a variety of humanistic therapies. I had thought about them, talked about them, spoken with them, lain in my bed with them, fed them black milk and muesli, yet I had never embraced them. I was too afraid of their raw reality and all my attempts to deal with them were rooted in the very fear that fed them. The only way to deal with demons is to stare into their eyes and know them for what they really are. I had been too afraid of them for this. Yet if your search has at its heart a fear of what you seek, you are not engaged in genuine enquiry, you are on a hunt to kill. And then there's the risk that what you want to kill may kill you first. The more we fear our demons the more power they have.

I do not know another way to acquire the wisdom that knows the difference between the things we need to courageously change and the things we must serenely accept, other than first to try to change it all. God doesn't grant wisdom, the experiences of life do.

I had at last, turned around and looked into the face of my demons. I had invited them to expose me, inhabit me, and become me. My demons had come home too. Our experiment with Bhagwan, was to find out what happened when you made friends with your demons and did not banish them far away for someone else to suffer. We had plans to liberate the demons incarcerated in the deepest darkest dungeons of them all. We were going to find out what happened when you freed the demons of hell itself.

In a group in the ashram I saw the tall blonde German woman stride about the room naked and proud and spit on a cowering Jewish man who quivered in ancestral fear – before they fell into heartbroken sobs and embraced in a deeper meeting than either had ever imagined would be possible. A small step for these two maybe, but a giant step for humankind. In another I saw a man hold down a struggling woman threatening to kill her, before he became aware of the fear beneath his hatred, and wept in sorrow. When later this man told the woman he loved her, she said she did not feel the repressed hatred so many women feel when men say they love us. Another bridge across another great divide. I saw people walk away from despairs that had nearly killed them and with tears of joy running down their faces that they were at last free. I saw old women reach out to younger women to tell them they were beautiful, to give them the love their mothers had kept for themselves. I saw the genuine love that breaks your own heart because its roots are in the real mud of our human struggle with hate. I saw the fierce honesty of a compassion that emerges from passionate anger, rather than the sugar on shit of piety. I saw people in tears as the same ice melted in their hearts as had in mine. I saw innocence lost and paradise regained. I saw myself in all people and all people in myself. Just as I too was seen.

We saw all this and more as angels fell to hell, demons flew to heaven and we all met in a garden in a wilderness, around the feet of what we considered the greatest Master the world has ever seen.

'This very body the Buddha, this very Earth the Lotus Paradise.'

That it all has to happen is part of the mystery.

Chapter 10
The Crazy Wisdom Guru

Bhagwan, or Osho as he came to be known, was a Tantric guru. Tantra is an ancient tradition, older than the oldest known scriptures of the Rig Veda and its roots are in the magic and fertility cults of pre Aryan India. Tantra's all embracing vision of life came directly from our pre-historic worship of nature and mother Earth where the female energies are as powerful and essential as the male. Elements of its teaching can be found in the ancient Palaeolithic cave paintings in Europe and have been woven into the most alive aspects of many religions – Hinduism, Buddhism, Jainism, the Christian Gnostics, the Islamic Sufis, the Tibetan Buddhists, Zen, Taoism. Bhagwan spoke about all these traditions, but the Left-Handed Sinister Tantra was the most secret of them all. Scholars are still searching for the scriptures of this form of Tantra; but there were none written, because the truths you encounter in this Tantra cannot be expressed in words.

Chogyam Trungpa the Tibetan Rinpoche, who first took Tibetan Buddhist teachings to the West, said in his book *The Lion's Roar*, 'Tantra is one of the most secret and sacred things ever heard on this Earth. It is dangerous and very powerful.' Even high-level Bodhisattvas were supposed to have fainted on first hearing of Tantra. The deeper Tantric teachings of Bhagwan, however, were not in what he said; they were in the energy field of the Sangha, the living commune around him. Only those initiated into sannyas entered into these. And there were many levels even within sannyas.

There are said to be three paths to wisdom, nirvana, moksha, and enlightenment – whatever name you give to the ultimate liberation of the human spirit. The first is the 'narrow path' of discipline, simplicity and obedience, the *hinayana* path where you need rules and a spiritual teacher to tell you what to do. The second is the 'open highway' of compassionate action of service and healing, the *mahayana* (greater) path for which you need a spiritual guide to help you learn compassion and humility. The third has no path. You leave all roads marked on maps to wander into the wilderness where you 'dance in the fields'. For this, as Chogyam Trungpa wrote in *The Myth of Freedom*, you need a 'crazy wisdom' guru.

What most people think of as Tantra is really sexual yoga, but Tantra is far more than special breathing techniques and postures to increase pleasure in sex. It involves journeys to heaven where you realise you are God, and journeys to hell, where you realise you are Satan. You don't worship deities and demons, you become them. You experience directly your sexuality, your powers of creation and destruction, and all the pleasures and pains of the body; out of this living experience, awareness and wisdom arise naturally and organically. It is therefore very different from the paths that use self-reflection, detached observation or analytical insight. You incarnate in the very cells of your body the most transcendental truths of the spirit. And to paraphrase Mae West: 'Being good has nothing to do with it'.

Many might be drawn to a spiritual path that includes sex, power and the freedom to follow your energy, but there have always been dire warnings. Tibetan Llamas, gurus and Rinpoches through the ages have issued ominous injunctions about the dangers of Tantra. 'Entering Tantra is hellish.' 'Only Tantra can produce enlightenment in one lifetime. It will either destroy you or enlighten you.' Tantra is like 'walking along a razors edge surrounded by the fires of hell. One slip and you are burned to a crisp.' Better not to begin at all because if you fall, you fall into the 'vajra' hell. The vajra hell, which means the diamond or indestructible hell, is forever. Even remorse for what has happened imprisons you further. Tantra is said to be the teaching for the time of disease, despair and war, which, according to the ancient Vedic scriptures, is our modern age, the Kali Yuga, the Dark Age. As the Tibetan Buddhists say, 'The Tantric guru is in league with death.'

Whatever the rituals and trappings, the central requirement to enter the Tantric path is to fall in love. There are no other qualifications. You fall in love with a 'crazy' guru. The Dalai Llama is reported to have said that Bhagwan was the re-incarnation of the most powerful Tantric master of the Tibetan Buddhist tradition, and that Bhagwan had also been a 'crazy wisdom' guru in other incarnations in other traditions. He said that Bhagwan's incarnation in the C20th was his last, his greatest and most potent of them all.

A 'crazy wisdom' guru is 'crazy' because like life he follows no rules; he is spontaneously himself moment to moment. He follows his energy in an instinctual anarchy that is not checked or interfered with by the conscious mind. If he wants to sit in silence in his room all day, that is what he does. If he wants ninety-three Rolls Royces, that what he goes for. If he wants to kill you, he will. If he wants to kill himself, he will.

The 'crazy' guru's disciples are just as dangerous. In the Left-Handed Tantra you either make love to the guru or kill him.

Some of us did both.

I had fallen in love with the guru of the golden voice without being aware of the many dimensions and depths involved in becoming his disciple; I had simply heard him and fallen. No one can explain why or how we fall in love, and neither can I. Falling is not something we do; it is surrender to gravity. And gravity does not take you the scenic route; you go the steepest way down.

Yet though at first we fall into love, later, the love falls into us.

A few days after Tim's fourth birthday in July, I left him with John and Sujan and flew to Bombay. Sujan was to follow six weeks later. I explained to Tim I would miss him but this was something I had to do, and I would be back for Christmas.

Let her who has never fallen throw the first stony judgment.

I arrived in Bombay a few weeks before the monsoon. The heat slammed into me on the walk across the shimmering tarmac from the plane. Such heat must be blast from the plane's engines and I breathed again on entering the air conditioning of the airport. I then walked out into the sweltering sauna of Mumbai and hit a wall of the same intense heat. I could hardly breathe. Perspiration poured down my face, down my back between my shoulder blades, and my damp dress stuck to my sweaty body. My head thumped in air thick with the clammy heat and sweat of the millions who had breathed and lived in this same air before me. A man on a skateboard waved four stumps at me as I passed. A skinny mother in rags held up a child with distorted limbs, her head lolling, flies crawling in her eyes. An old man with a lunghi filthy with the red dribble of pan, pleaded vaguely around him with blank milky eyes. By the side of road families lived in huge drainpipes, their entire lives wrapped in cloth bundles while they squatted, slept and cooked, rolled together in these tubes. I had never seen such blatant human misery or poverty. Never even imagined it.

The faint wind was not cooling but brought more heat loaded with the thick smell of kerosene, stale bidis, turmeric, incense, jasmine and sweat.

Traffic flowed like the Ganges. A truck loaded with bananas, bright deities and demons painted along its side, leaned threateningly sideways. A taxi missed by inches a bike that veered recklessly between rickshaws, a thin man pedalling, two children on the cross bar, his round wife and her pans dangling off the back. Horns blared as a bus bore down on a flock of bony boys crouched over a game in the dust.

I blinked at the bright peeling colours and the desperate poverty as salty sweat ran into my eyes. All thoughts of staying in Mumbai in this sweaty heat and noise vanished. I turned and went back into the cool air conditioning of the airport to catch the next plane to Pune. India had lifted the curtain only a fraction and I had run in the other direction. Like so many unprepared westerners, I was overwhelmed.

The seats in the plane to Pune were torn and stained, the windows streaked with dirt. In the air the plane juddered and shook as if buffeted by storm winds but the real turbulence was in me. What have I done coming here? I know no one in this whole continent. I am here because I fell in love with the voice of a man I have never seen. Because his voice held the promise he would heal the wounds in my soul. Because he would be my gateway to 'moksha', an enlightenment that is the ultimate liberation from fear and misery. Because he and his disciples would create a new way of being to show the world it was possible to live with love, life and laughter. Yet I have no friend or acquaintance here at all. Just a guru I have never met.

I looked out through the smeared window and could see the wing creak and bend as if about to fall off. A week later this same plane crashed into the side of a mountain on its return journey and everyone aboard was killed.

We landed and I walked out of the airport into the overpowering pre-monsoon heat. Pune was one of the hill stations the British retired to each summer to escape the more humid heat of Bombay, but the air here was still hotter and heavier than any air I had walked through before. Hotter than blood heat. I made my way through porters and men pushing handcarts shouting and spitting red betel nut juice to where a gang of rickshaws gathered. 'Rajneesh lady, this way, I take you.' 'Cheap price to ashram.' 'Look here – clean seats for orange clothes!' I climb into a rickshaw.

The Sikh driver starts the noisy engine and shouts to his friends and at beggars who weave in and out of the traffic, their ragged shirts flapping as they tap on the windows of the rich leaving the airport. Gangs of children run alongside me chanting 'Rajneesh! Rajneesh! Paisa! Pleeeease!' I rock from side to side in the back of this rickshaw as it weaves through bicycles bent with the weight of people and tiffins hanging off handlebars and cross bars, between handcarts loaded with bananas, tins of ghee, cloth bundles, through pale cows and black water buffalo serenely wandering at will. I see buses with people hanging off the roofs, leaning out the windows, crouching on the back bumpers as they bear down, horns blaring, on squatting families by the side of the road. The ubiquitous black Ambassador cars with yellow roofs miss children, cows, carts, beggars and rickshaws by inches.

We weave our way erratically down the main Mahatma Gandhi Road, passing shops selling spices, crockery, incense sticks, saris, astrologers with offers of auspicious dates for intrigues and weddings, typing booths where letters and job applications can be written to look 'unmistakeably official', tyre re-treaders with bike parts hanging all around them to recycle the cycles in this country where nothing is wasted, and even your life is recycled thousands of times.

We drive past turquoise temples with Hanuman the Monkey-King, enshrined in peeling bright golds and blues next to red statues of Ganesh the Elephant God. Unsure of which herbs to pick to heal Rama's brother, Hanuman uprooted a whole mountain and carried it to him returning it the same night. He is now the symbol of devotion to the Master and patron saint of wrestlers. Ganesh had his head knocked off by a blow from Shiva, the elephant's head the first replacement that came to hand. Wrestling with my devotion to my Master, about to go beyond my mind, perhaps I should have stopped and done puja.

The traffic thins as we reach the suburbs and drive through boulevards with larger bungalows surrounded by walls. We turn left into a leafy road in Koregaon Park where orange clad people in flowing robes are walking singly and in groups, towards a large set of gates.

This road, unlike its neighbours, has a row of hawkers flogging lottery tickets, tin monkeys on sticks, bidis, pan, fresh orange juice, incense, newspaper cones of chickee. A boy had laid in front of him rags and rows of gleaming teeth offering to clean your teeth or sell you new ones. Crouching next to him was another boy offering head massage, and a handcart with a battered tin urn serving chai. Beggars stretched out withered arms or misshapen stumps. Other children, with no legs, scoot about on skateboards. A blind beggar holds out an old battered ghee can for passing paisa. The ashram would periodically clean up the road but these destitutes would return, just as did the starving dogs that hung around them, feral and afraid. So many rich westerners mean rich pickings.

We arrived outside the ashram. I paid the rickshaw driver, unloaded my suitcase and stood in front of the large wooden gates. 'Thou Art That' arched in large letters over the top. I looked up at this ancient Sanskrit wisdom and tried to feel the wonder in my name, that I had come to my spiritual home to sit at the feet of the Awakened One – *Buddham Sharanam Gaachami* – the first Buddhist vow. I felt nothing. I was tired, dusty, sweaty, overwhelmed and my clothes smelt of stale beedis and kerosene. I was longing less for enlightenment than for a cool shower and an ice cold drink.

I walked through the gates into a Reception area where a serene sanyassin directed me to the nearest hotel 'until you arrive'. I thought I already had, but clearly my dishevelled state persuaded her I needed to rest before I registered my arrival and bought the lecture pass that would permit me into discourse, where every morning Bhagwan spoke spontaneously and eloquently on various spiritual traditions, interpreting and explaining sutras, scriptures, sacred texts as well as answering submitted questions and telling gloriously irreverent jokes. I booked into the Blue Diamond Hotel where I showered, changed, drank a fresh lime soda, ate mango pulp and buffalo cream. I briefly joined the tanned sannyasins relaxing around the pool, before returning to the ashram.

The ashram was a world away from the India outside its gates. An oasis of green and marble, with offices, workshops, kitchens, canteens, a boutique, group rooms, Buddha Hall where discourse and the meditations were held, and Lao Tzu House where Bhagwan himself lived with the sannyasins who took care of him. Pathways wound through flowers and trees tended by a team of gardeners, people sat with their bidis in 'smoking temples', children played their games on lawns, sannyasins embraced, gossiped, read or meditatively watched the activity of the Buddhafield unfold from benches set in shady groves. First stop for me, the boutique. I had to have an outfit in the crimson I could see was the latest colour. I wanted to look my best to meet Bhagwan. But as he was unlikely to mind what was my exact shade of orange-going-on lilac, maroon, crimson, magenta, purple ... it was really to meet the tanned and beautiful sannyasins from all over the world; who, from their serene smiles and wafty hair I could tell were far more spiritually evolved than I was.

I wandered around, feeling my way into the tribe I had joined.

The next morning I went to Buddha Hall for the discourse that began at 8 a.m. The earlier you arrived the closer to the front you got to sit, so sannyasins would drift in from 7 a.m. onwards. The first eight rows were reserved for the 'close' disciples and allocated to various ashram residents in rotation. We were in place by 7.45 a.m. neither moving nor talking, sitting on the cushions we had brought. Hundreds of us sat every day in a silence I have never encountered again. Even during meditations on Zen retreats, in Tibetan Buddhist monasteries, I have always heard shuffles, coughs, sniffs, and sudden movements. There were never any in Buddha Hall. I have missed this silence ever since. Though there was more than the silence.

When two or more are gathered together for common purpose, something is created greater than the sum of its parts – an energy field, which itself becomes a powerful force shaping what happens. Modern biology explains the patterns of nature as manifestations of morphic resonant energy fields that shape living reality, and Einstein concluded reality itself was a field of energy. When thousands of people have surrendered themselves to the wisdom of a Buddha, an enlightened Master, exactly such a powerful energy field is created – a Buddhafield. A Tantric Buddhafield is the most powerful of them all because it includes the energies of sexuality and the body. By living in this force field, like iron filings aligning around a magnet, we hoped to align ourselves with the enlightened wisdom of the Master and become enlightened ourselves. We would become not only a light unto ourselves, but also a light in the darkness of the world.

That was the idea anyway. Well, it was one of them. We hadn't yet become aware that it is one thing to be an iron filing, quite another to be the magnet. Neither had we realised that all our hearts are of darkness and if they come to light we die.

I sat crossed legged on the cool floor and could hear the same parrots and distant train I had heard on that first tape. I looked around and saw a row of older people with creased faces sitting on chairs rather than the hard floor, but mostly I saw young, healthy, tall, tanned people, the beautiful people who, not at all meek, inherit the Earth. There were stars from Hollywood next to Kulu Valley hippies, a vicar from Christ's College Cambridge behind a Black musician from New York, a Japanese designer smiling at an Australian surfer. Each of us here because the same man who had called me across the world, had called them too. We have each travelled lifetimes to reach here.

Bhagwan arrived in a white Rolls Royce and emerged onto the podium in a pristine white robe. He brought his hands together in namaste, the eastern greeting to the divine everyone, and turned slowly round the hall smiling at us, his disciples. He sat down, placed one leg over the other and began to talk. He used his hands in fluid expressive gestures to emphasise and explain the teachings hidden in the sutras he was interpreting for us that day. He spoke with eloquence and mastery, yet in a simple language that did not mystify the esoteric, but explained it. And, with his charismatic eyes flashing with mischief, he told magnificent, irreverent jokes. Apart from the voice of our beloved Master, laughter was the only sound ever heard in that vast Buddha Hall. Two hours later, he concluded with 'Enough for today', namastéd us once more, and was driven in his Rolls the hundred yards back to his house, Lao Tzu.

Some moved towards the canteens to eat breakfast, a slice of bread and a banana, others drifted over to the offices, others lay back relaxing on the cool floor, perhaps reaching out to embrace a friend or lover. We picked up the shoes and minds a sign outside Buddha Hall had told us to leave there, and gradually the day began. I wandered out into my first day in the Buddhafield.

That morning I strolled about, gossiped with my new comrades, smoked a few bidis in the smoking temple, did a couple of meditations, sang a few devotional songs – 'dancing lightly on the edge of the tide, disappearing into you', hung out round the pool at the Blue Diamond, ate more mango pulp and fresh cream, and began to learn my way around the ashram. In the afternoon I saw some sannyasins arrive at the great gates looking dishevelled and disoriented. Dressed in the crimson that was the new black, I smiled a serene welcome.

At six o'clock that evening, about forty of us gathered for evening darshan, a more intimate meeting with Bhagwan on a covered patio outside his room in Lao Tzu House. Everyone arriving and leaving would have such a darshan, the workers on rotation. We sat whispering to each other, rustling like the night creatures around us emerging in the dusk, including the mosquitoes. For darshan you could wear neither perfume nor insect repellent as Bhagwan was allergic to all perfumes other than neroli oil; but who has a mind for mosquitoes when you are about to meet the Master. We filed in and sat in hushed rows on the floor. One by one we went up to meet him. My name was called and I walked over and sat crossed legged in front of him.

'Hello Vismaya' he smiled 'How are you.'

'I'm fine.' I wish I could think of something more compelling to say but there is nothing, just a smile into his eyes as he smiles at me.

'Very good Vismaya. Come closer'

I shuffle towards him and he leans forward and places his thumb over my third eye. There are no visions or energy rushes, just my heart beating.

He leans back and smiles again. 'Very good, Vismaya.'

Years later, on Safari in Kenya, a large giraffe, with intelligent curiosity and the dignity of her freedom, bent down and peered into our jeep. I sensed a profound and powerful presence as she looked at me and I looked at her, yet in her brown eyes there was no one there. As we gazed at each other for what seemed like an age, I became aware of a vast emptiness. Looking into the eyes of an unafraid wild animal, we see directly into the Soul of the Earth. In the eyes of Bhagwan, I gazed into that same Soul. I saw into a wide open sky where there is no more longing, no more hope, no more despair, nothing but a vast freedom which gazed back at me and smiled.

I went back to my place. After greeting others and saying goodbye to those leaving, Bhagwan turned and went back into Lao Tzu House. I looked up into the night sky. It was a clear night with myriads of stars, but for the first time I saw, not the stars, but the dark emptiness that lies between them.

The Blue Diamond was expensive, so I found a veranda to rent. I got together a mattress and mosquito net, a few cushions and pans and it became home. I hired a bike and before long was weaving through the traffic as if I have always swum in this holy river. Of course, I had come home.

The ashram's main attraction, apart from Bhagwan himself, was the programme of therapy groups, meditation course and trainings. In fifteen acres and slowly spreading into the surrounding villas of Koregaon Park, were concentrated some of the most innovative and creative therapies in the world. These combined eastern techniques of meditation with western humanistic psychology. Vipassana, Zazen, esoteric and psychic work, bioenergetics, primal, hypnotherapy, sexuality and energy work, re-birthing and raw encounter were combined creating intensely powerful processes.

I had been sent a programme of groups while still in Leeds, a list I had been told Bhagwan wanted me to do, but more likely those with places during the time I was there. Though in the synchronicities and magic of Buddhafields, these are anyway the same.

The groups of this dangerous and anarchic Tantric community made it radically different from ashrams where only disciplines of silent meditations were used. We thought an imposed stillness repressed the life force of sexuality, power, need, passion, and desires. Our idea was that when energy flows freely through the body, this direct experience of life would naturally lead to the awareness and wisdom. It is the repression of life that leads to fear, depression and cruelty, not its freedom. And we certainly looked different from the spiritual seekers who meditated in other ashrams. We danced more for a start. We were also sexier.

Bhagwan did warn us that once we had swum in this sea, we would never again be at home anywhere, and I certainly have never come across a tribe like this again. Most people who were there would say the same. But of course, everything changes, if only trying to remain the same, and the whole point was to find the truth of ourselves, to find our home in life, not to remain attached to this particular energy field. Though perhaps when you fall in love with a Master, you naturally then fall in love with the Sangha, the community around the Master – I go to the feet of the commune of the Awakened One, *Sangham Sharanam Gaachami*, the second Buddhist vow. And wherever there is life, there is everything – power in service and the abuse of power, sexual love and sexual abuse, the light of awareness and the darkness of ignorance. That's life. All life. *Dhammam Sharanam Gaachami* – I go to the feet of Life, the ultimate truth of the Awakened One, the third Buddhist vow.

At this point however, I was swimming in a warm ocean in union with both the Buddha and the Sangha, blissfully unaware of the darker, colder, currents below. I had a few wonderful nights of one-ness with several swamis, danced through several groups, meditated into a deeper stillness, and when Sujan arrived six weeks later, I was well in the flow of the Buddhafield. He had been here the previous year and travelled throughout India, so for him, this was familiar territory.

We sannyasins looked continually to find the meaning of phenomena, the hidden significance of which would have been dismissed elsewhere as random events. In potent energy fields, the normal laws of cause and effect cannot explain what happens. For example how a flock of birds and a school of fish move as one creature, how termites build the intricate architecture of their nests, how a single fertilised cell in a womb multiplies itself into identical duplicates yet shapes itself into a body. An energy field acts synchronously on parts separated in space and therefore time, and in the ashram's Tantric energy field, synchronicities, psychic phenomena and apparent magic were everyday occurrences.

We took it for granted that you dream of a friend and the next day they unexpectedly arrive. You get the urge to go to the back gate, where someone there has an important message for you. On a deeper level everything Bhagwan said to us had levels and depths beyond what we could interpret at the time, so we continually invited the unknown mystery to speak with us through dreams, phenomena, flashes of instinct and inexplicable synchronicities.

The morning after Sujan had arrived we cycled into discourse early. Our first time sitting together at the feet of the Master and we wanted to be as close as possible. In answer to the first question Bhagwan spoke at length about the two most important qualities on the spiritual path – wisdom and wonder.

'Only those with both wonder and wisdom have both innocence and experience and can walk with God.'

Sujan means 'wisdom', Vismaya means 'wonder'. We took this as a sign – the Master had blessed our love.

Apart from enabling me to suspend my more critical logical mind, my Catholic training in self-denial came in useful in other ways – whatever happened was my own fault. This always goes down well with any political elite whether Revolutionary China, the U.S. army or the Rajneesh Ashram in Pune. Even when you doubt your own experience, which for us Tantrikas was supposed to be the ultimate authority, 'they' liked it. Though when you have abandoned the authority of your own experience, the only option left is to become one of 'them'. But that is a much later story; here I was still in blissful pre-fall innocence.

I checked in for Zazen, a seven day group where you sit without moving and gaze at a blank wall while being randomly hit on the head with a Zen stick, eating and sleeping in this same spot. Though keen to start with, after eight hours of wall staring, I became obsessed with the squashed mosquito in the upper right section of my bit of wall that was preventing my mind becoming as blank as everyone else's with their unblemished sections. I became impatient for the Vipassana walk where slowly, very slowly; you walk in a circle, gazing at the ground 10 inches in front of you. Our food, not much, was laid out on a long table during the walk. When the food gong sounded, those nearest the table meditatively moved slowly towards it, meditatively took a plate back to their place and meditatively chewed the cud. The others continued to walk slowly in the circle until they too reached the table. I was not the only one who, before the gong was actually rung, became more meditative while passing that plate with the extra large banana. Traffic jammed up near the table in a kind of spiritual musical chairs, before we sped off, relatively speaking, hoping for better luck next time round.

After five days of this I feel a kind of peace descend. When the only distraction is a squashed mosquito, the relative size of bananas and the sounds of your neighbour snoring at night, the only option is to let it go and relax. I clearly have deeper levels of resistance however; I get an awful headache. I feel terrible. I sweat with fever. My vision blurs. Perhaps my Kundalini was rising, though more likely my demons are about to have another go at me. I stagger around in the Vipassana walk well beyond caring about which banana was my lot. The group leader saw me swaying as I gazed at a wall, now far from blank and full of delirious visions, and called me for an interview. I was sent to the medical centre where I was diagnosed with Dengue fever.

Sujan's turn for Zazen came round. I had no doubt he'd enjoy it. He had set up a dance company in London called 'Still Moving', pretty Zen already, and they'd been filmed crossing Waterloo Bridge in slow motion, taking five hours while rushed commuters dodged impatiently round them. I could relax and have fun myself. In Zazen there was no chance of Sujan finding himself in prolonged energy exchanges with the beautiful tanned women with long wafty hair.

Within a day I was in bed with vomiting and diarrhoea. I was so ill I could not move, not even to get to the bathroom, though bathroom is perhaps an exaggerated term for the hole in the ground with a tap and bucket next to it that we used. I could not eat and my frequent shits, when I dangled over a tin by the side of the bed, were just blood and mucus. Before being felled completely I had staggered with agonising cramps to the local market for a few bottles of water, which I rationed as I became too ill to move. I could not even summon help and lay there deliriously hallucinating. Demons were involved, and furniture removal, but the rest is a blur. The sweat ran into the sheets, the days ran into each other and my thoughts ran everywhere. For a while I thought I was three years old. Rats ran under the mosquito net and bit me.

A friend came to find me, as she hadn't seen me for a while. She took one look at the tin can, the soaked sheets and my wild eyes and took me to the medical centre where they diagnosed bacterial and amoebic dysentery. I took a massive dose of Flagyl and recovered. Though I was wonderfully thin for a few weeks and to this day have amoebic cysts in my gut, a war wound that plays up every now and then, when the wind blows in from the East.

Sujan emerged from Zazen and arrived back at the veranda. I tell him of my nightmare week, my near death experience, primal hallucinations and terrible agony.

'Ah is that so', he says with a beatific smile.

I am expecting concerned sympathy and don't like at all this cold hearted disregard, however enlightened he imagines he is.

'You don't understand! I was so sick I nearly died!'

'Ah is that so' he smiles again with serene detachment.

I am outraged at his callous indifference. He hasn't even noticed how thin I am! I am determined to wipe that stupid grin off his face. I am going to make him angry. That will show him where his peace and light is really at. And I know exactly how to do it because I know his vulnerabilities. The secrets we have shared in our intimacy now become my ammunition. I become the witch bitch from hell spitting with fury, pouring scorn and derision on him and all men.

'You self-obsessed, arrogant, egocentric bastard! I nearly died and you are only interested in your fucking pathetic enlightenment. I don't give a shit what insights you've had, you're a complete failure as a human being if all you care about is your detached awareness when I nearly fucking died while you were wanking off on cosmic consciousness!'

He is the cold, rejecting patriarch with the dismissive judgment that condemns such rage to hell.

'You've no idea what this is about, you crazy hysterical bitch, because you are too attached to your own ego. You just want what you want and will do anything to get it. You've no fucking awareness whatsoever about anything, least of all yourself!'

We gaze at each other from opposite ends of the universe and into a fathomless void that has suddenly cracked into existence and split us light years apart. Two hatreds stare at each other with just their antagonism to connect them. Six months of surrender and delight, with the odd skirmish, nothing serious, and now war.

Yet most inventions have had their origins in the necessities of war and many of my deepest understandings have been born in the bitter battle-fields of war with those I have loved. We can't avoid the conflicts anyway, especially as my lovers have resolutely insisted on being themselves and not what I have wanted them to be. Sujan and I managed to reach across the great divide, this time anyway, but now we knew this love of ours was a dangerous business. But even Adam and Eve before they ate that apple, were subject to the law of the jungle – eat or be eaten.

It is a bitter fruit from an even older tree than the tree of knowledge that reveals everything is both good and evil, and even love is a jungle as well as a garden.

In this Tantric energy field, however, there were more than enough psychic phenomena and sudden satoris to keep us distracted. You might be drinking your chai or just strolling about, and out of the blue get zapped by cosmic consciousness. You never knew when a mind blowing insight might suddenly lay you low. Maybe that's why we spent so much time hugging each other in long embraces, we were holding each other upright.

I went into the awareness group. Twenty of us sat naked on wall-to-wall mattresses. Somendra, the group leader, was silent. He put on music, placed us in mandalas and energy configurations and soon people began to shake and fall over, catharting in a wonderful variety of ways, before they collapsed in states of bliss. But nothing happened to me.

We danced. We sat in silence. We gazed at candles and meditated on the sensations in our hands. We let go the boundaries between self and other and merged with the universe. Periodically we sat around him and asked questions. I was wondering what the hell was going on but it wasn't done to ask such a 'head' question, so I watched everyone having spiritual experiences, seeing auras, connecting with past lives and felt inadequate and inferior. Finally something happened to me.

Each night we took a sheet, curled up on the mattresses and, after whatever else twenty Tantrikas might do when following their energy, slept in the group room. The third morning I woke filled with a nameless dread that sat inside me and would not leave. Even the Dynamic Meditation at 6am, where you throw yourself about, scream out your madness and jump up and down, did not move it.

During Bhagwan's discourse it intensifies into a terror that grabs me by the throat. I nearly choke. I look at Bhagwan and suddenly see he is pure evil, a satanic anti-Christ who had brainwashed us into zombie like devotion for his own malevolent ends. I can hardly breathe in this atmosphere full of malice and danger. A terrible and terrifying blackness tightens around my throat. I have never been so frightened in my whole life. This ashram is evil. I will die if I don't escape.

I try to feel the fear and stay here anyway, to stare down my demons not just to run. My mouth is dry. I shake. In the group, all about me, people are laughing, playing and dancing; I am pale, sick with dread and terror. Somendra turns to the sound system and the music of Vangelis fills the room. Suddenly my heart bursts open and I can breathe again. A rush of joy forces me to my feet. My arms rise. I am full of a new wonder and lightness of being.

Somendra comes over to where I am standing enraptured and lightly touches the top of my head. My head explodes into light. I move in ecstatic abandon. I am released. A crippling terror has gone, one, so interwoven with my sense of self, I had not known it was there until it left me. I laugh and dance. Another level of the fear implanted in me as a child has disappeared, another ghost from the past, exorcised. I will never be as terrified again.

The music of Vangelis moves through me and I dance. This new freedom to breathe and move and love is inexpressibly sweet. I am deeply grateful to Somendra and Bhagwan and I love this commune more than ever. For the rest of the group, the others continue with their psychic experiences, memories of past lives, dramatic catharses, involuntary shakings and so on, while I just lounge around and enjoy myself.

On the last day of the group Somendra lined each of us up against a wall while he 'examined our energy'. He told each of us, one by one, where it was blocked and what we needed to do next. When my turn came, he told me he had never seen anyone travel so far in one lifetime. I wasn't sure if this was an acknowledgment of how far I had travelled along the path of self-knowledge, or an expression of shock at how seriously lost I must once have been. He then told me I had the light of awareness and as a result, would get enlightened this lifetime, whatever I did. From being at the bottom of the class suddenly I shot to the top.

In the break everyone crowded round me and wanted to know what was it like to have the light of awareness. Unfortunately I hadn't a clue. I was compelled to put it down to some innate spirituality in my make up. You come across people like that occasionally – naturally spiritual people, with unsuspected depth and the light of awareness. I supposed I must be one of those. Too humble of course to mention this theory I smile modestly.

'I can't tell you. I don't know' I say with an ordinariness that proves how unaffected I am. For a week I bask in the warm glory of a guaranteed enlightenment this lifetime.

Like in all hothouse communities such as prisons, boarding schools, convents, Hollywood, the local WI's and ashrams, we were obsessed with who is doing what to whom, especially who was Bhagwan's psycho-spiritual-sexual flavour of the month. Minor details of the celebrity culture of enlightenment therefore assumed enormous significance. For example what seat we were given when it was our turn to be up front during discourse. Were we placed on the front row or to the side and near the back? When we had darshan did Bhagwan tell us our energy was flowing or that we were full of fear. Was our question in discourse answered with an affectionate joke, or a hard-hitting Zen stick, or was it answered at all. Were we sent to clean the group toilets or given a job in Lao Tzu Library. There may have been a few enlightened souls for whom this hierarchy was insignificant, but I never met any. And so for a while with my light of awareness I was hanging out with the A list. But I hadn't figured for the on-going challenge of having a relationship in a Tantric ashram. It wasn't long before the light of awareness went out and the darkness moved back in.

There was a request after discourse for anyone with video camera experience to report to the main office. Sujan had and went along. Soon he was filming Bhagwan during discourse and darshan. The video department was in Lao Tzu House, the Holy of Holies where Bhagwan lived, you needed a special pass just to get through the gates. Sujan was now hanging out with the spiritual elite, which included the women of the long straight hair, serene receptivity and rarefied energy from living so close to the Master. Then Vivek invited him for tea.

Vivek, Bhagwan's lover and partner, was the extremely beautiful icon of enlightened femininity. It was as if a spiritual Marilyn Monroe had asked Sujan to dinner before slipping into something more comfortable. Though Vivek would already be in something comfortable. I told Sujan I was insecure and afraid, he would probably fall in love with her, or one of the others with long wafty hair, and forget me. He turned to me.

'I wish you'd shut up, you make dramas out of nothing!'

I was shocked. I had thought I was simply 'sharing the truth of myself', like we were supposed to. I knew it! My fear was already manifesting; he was moving away from me into the arms of those more spiritually evolved who do not indulge in such dramas. There was nothing I could do. Clearly it was time to engage my insecurities directly, not just escape them in our intimacy. I hugged him one last time as he went, and sadly tuned away. That's how it goes, as everybody knows, in a Tantric community.

To my surprise he returned and seemed still to want to be with me. This time, however, I did not argue. I smiled and opened my arms.

The sky sulked before the release of the monsoon rain. We bought plastic sandals and umbrellas in readiness for the approaching deluge. The heavy humidity made our embraces sweaty and sticky but there were less of these anyway. In discourse Bhagwan tells us we are born alone, we die alone and in between we live alone. He looks at us with stern frowns, gone are the jokes, while he tells us we are incapable of love unless we first go totally into our aloneness. We leave discourse sober and separate now. The Buddhafield too is full of heavy foreboding clouds.

Finally the monsoon breaks and huge raindrops thunder suddenly down. Even the kids, who loved to splash in puddles, scatter and run for cover. The rain is bouncing off tin roofs and tarmac, turning paths into rivers of ankle deep mud. Umbrellas protect you from the downpour one way but you are completely soaked by the splash back. The deluge is so intense the raindrops become a wall of water crashing down in a deafening roar. It drowns insects, flattens plants, creates swirling rapids in the gutters that dislodge handcarts and send families scrabbling for their bundles of possessions before rushing for shelter. The rain stops as suddenly as it had begun. Steam rises off the asphalt. The children emerge first, laughing as they jump into the ponds in the roads. Gradually life on the street returns, and, like a dog after swimming shakes off water, people flap around sheets and tarpaulins then settle back into their daily squatting by the roadside, by the Ganges of urban life.

Sujan and I too shake off our old life in the West and settle into daily life in the Buddhafield. We plan to stay and make our home here. I go to the office and tell Laxmi I want to return to England to fetch my son to come and live here with me.

'You are welcome', she tells me, 'but wait until the new commune where there will be room for all the children with a school and playgrounds, and space for them to have all they need.'

This mythical new commune is an unknown future, not now. I am about to argue but she has not finished.

'We need you to go back to run Sangeet. Bhagwan needs such centres in the West and you are perfect for this.'

'But I want to be here', I wail, 'not Leeds!'

'Your time will come.' She moves onto other business with Sheela her second in command.

I have promised Tim I will be back for Christmas and get ready to leave. I have a darshan a few nights before I depart. Bhagwan tells me to go and help his people in the West and to come back soon. 'I will' I say. He gives me a box and tells me whenever I need to connect with him, hold it and he will be with me. He smiles and I fall again into the empty sky in his eyes. Lights flash. Music rises to a crescendo. Bhagwan has his thumb fiercely burning into my third eye. The darkness crackles. I free-fall into an emptiness with just silence and darkness.

'Very good Vismaya' he says and smiles again.

I hope this serenity survives my return to a wintry Leeds.

It doesn't survive even the next day.

Sujan decides to stay. The monsoon rains have gone but my heart is as heavy as any pre-monsoon humid heat. I am leaving my spiritual home, leaving Bhagwan, my beloved Master, and I am leaving Sujan alone in a Tantric community. And how that goes, everybody knows.

I climb into the taxi for Bombay. Goodbye Bhagwan with the soul of the Earth in your eyes, who has called me home from my thousand-year exile. Goodbye energy darshans, meditation gongs, Zen sticks, Sufi dancing, Music Group, tea on verandas, bidi temples. Goodbye comrades and fellow Tantrikas. Goodbye Sujan with whom I have fallen even deeper into the darkness of forever and the love beyond even that. The taxi drives off.

In Mumbai I have an overnight stay before my flight in the morning. I wander by Chowpatty beach where a dead man rolls heavily on the edge of the tide, bloated among the seaweed.

I sit in the clean leather seats of the Kuwait Airlines flight to Heathrow via Dubai. The plane takes off. Frangipani blossom, fenugreek, coconut oil, kerosene stoves, tinny radios, packets of bidis, red dust, Ganesh festivals, mango pulp, monkeys, rickshaw horns, beggars, sadhus, buffalo wandering in dirt roads, all fall away beneath me.

I arrive at Heathrow to find my luggage is lost. My presents for Tim, my jewellery, clothes, books, carvings ... all gone. I have arrived back with nothing. The emptiness has come with me after all.

Chapter 11

Cry Baby, Cry

After the chaotic anarchy of India, the first thing that struck me as I wandered through the airport terminal to catch my train to Leeds, was not the cleanliness, the non-peeling paint, the absence of beggars with deformed limbs or temples to monkey and elephant Gods, it was the signs. And I don't mean signs of the synchronous phenomenological magic of energy fields. Signs ordering me – 'Keep to the right', 'Do not drop litter', 'Get passports ready,' 'Please read this sign', 'Entry into designated areas is prohibited to unauthorised personnel'. Mostly the signs were in reds, blues and greens, but there was one orange one – 'Danger, toxic substance. Do not handle without protective clothing'.

You could at least look away from this bombardment, it was harder to avoid the orders over the P.A. 'Extinguish all cigarettes, this terminal is a non-smoking area.' 'Do not leave baggage unattended.' 'Check your hand luggage for dangerous items.' Did that include the box Bhagwan had given me?

Tim and John meet me at Leeds train station. I bend down and pull Tim up and into my arms. I breathe him in as I squeeze him to me. I have been away for six months. I have been away forever.

'Why are you crying Mummy?' he asks, bending his head so he can see me. He is smiling.

'Because I'm happy to see you and because I've lost all my luggage' I reply. Though the suitcases are the least of it. 'I don't even have a toy for you now.'

'Oh that's OK, there's a space Lego rocket you can get me. I know where we can buy one. It's really great. You can fly it into my space station and it clicks into a special place next to the space cruiser, or you can change it and add it to another rocket and make a star traveller if you like...'

He explains to me the arcane lore of space Lego while we sit on a bench in Leeds Railway Station and I hold his little body close to mine. It seems we've both been travelling through the vast freedoms of space.

Tim had started Primary School in September.

'I can write now you know. Did you get my letters?'

They had been in the suitcase, spidery drawings of space men and rockets. The loopy wiggles around the edges were, I think, the writing.

We arrived back at Lumley Mount, the garden bare of flowers in the cold December frost. The gate creaked its familiar welcome as I opened it and climbed up the steps to the front door. I reached into my hand luggage for the keys I had kept safe, a talisman to remind me through six months in the seductive embraces of India and the ashram, that I had also this other home.

I unlocked the front door that opened directly into the living room. Immediately in front of me on the left wall was a Victorian desk with enough drawers for all those papers and numbers that tell me who I am and what I have to pay for it. There was a table under the window to the right that, in a fit of rebellion against the orange, I had painted bright blue. The essential sofa was along the far wall and, though shabby, was well able to do its sofa's job of holding us through cuddles, arguments, story-telling and playing in its time, the many parts it was inveigled into in the super hero dramas.

The living room furniture stares at me, unforgiving that I have neglected it for so long. Tim, on the other hand, jumps on and off the Empire State Building and tells me his favourite dinner is now beef burgers, chips and beans, probably I would like it every day too. And did I know we breathe in millions of germs all the time, even when we're asleep.

A chattering Tim comes with me to Safeway and when the plastic shopping bags are unpacked, the fridge full, another re-entry ritual is complete.

I settle into a different routine. Each morning I take Tim to school on the back of my bike and then pedal onto Sangeet Rajneesh Meditation Centre. Pradeep has been running things while Sujan and I were gone but is about to go to India to join Mahimo, who had flown out not long before I left.

I wrote to Sujan about Tim's new school, about the cat's tapeworm, that I was sorting through the files at Sangeet and how freezing cold it was. He wrote to me of darshans, warm days, how wonderful life is, and that he has married Chetna, one of the long-haired beauties close to Bhagwan.

In those days the British could get into India without a visa and one way to make money to stay in Pune was to marry an American. Sujan however did it for no money, simply because of an odd quirk that makes it hard for him to refuse requests from stunningly beautiful women. I didn't dwell too much on what else he might be giving away freely as I knew full well. You cannot leave your lover alone in a Tantric community and expect fidelity, especially as you'd be doing it too if you weren't in a freezing Yorkshire, thousands of miles away, where 'following your energy' meant you tried to sit as close as possible to the fire without getting chilblains. Pune and Leeds may have been suburbs of the same global village but it didn't feel like it.

I did my best in letters on thin blue airmail paper, to make the details of my daily life fascinating, but there's only so much you can do with shopping at Safeway's, gas bills, bike punctures, tapeworm tablets and bed time stories. Though I did notice that whenever I wrote 'I', instead of the old flourish, with great lines drawn across the top and the bottom, a kind of Corinthian column to hold up the crumbling ruins of myself, there was now just a single vertical line. I hoped this was a sign that the gradual erosion of my ego was going ahead as planned.

Christmas was a week away. Tim helped me put up his home made decorations, chains of paper cut out and stuck together, more surreal than Christmassy, as they were joined in space Lego patterns rather than in an ordered line. He had jumped up and down on a sofa planet Zorg, seeing the presents around the tree.

'On Zorg they open presents *before* Christmas. You didn't know that did you Mummy.'

No I didn't but I got a present before Christmas anyway. Sujan called. He was coming back and would be home for Christmas. At least I think he said 'home'. It's a bit confusing when your heart is one place and your longing is to be somewhere else – which is home?

On the drive to Heathrow I play Roberta Flack, Fleetwood Mac, Stevie Wonder, Marvin Gaye, all those love songs killing me softly, over and over. I am early and sit with a coffee and read about US missiles arriving in Europe casting their long dark shadows. All I can focus on, however, is the arrival of the plane from Bombay. I stare at the arrivals board waiting for the words 'Landed' to appear. Then, for the even closer 'Baggage in Hall'. I lean on the barrier and look for signs of India as I stare at those arriving.

At last a few saris arrive. I see a ticket with BMB on it. My heart pounds. There he is! Tanned, long hair and beard, orange clothes and smiling. I am in his arms and laughing.

On Christmas day we ate nut roast in the shape of a turkey. We pulled crackers, swapped jokes, played hide and seek with new furry toys, wobbled on a shiny bike in the park, cuddled on the sofa watching Snow White, wiped chocolate off sticky hands before a bedtime story to a yawning little boy convinced he wasn't tired yet. I gave Sujan a bright red cashmere sweater. He gave me a beautiful silver belt.

After the groups I've seen, I am walking on the wild side of psychiatry and too far gone to return to working in a psychiatric unit as a clinical psychologist. Anyway I've been given my orders, to run Sangeet. So running Sangeet it is.

Sujan sets up a gardening business and runs meditations and dance workshops. I clean people's houses and run encounter groups. Tim plays on, carelessly enjoying school, super-heroing in outer space with Georgie, feeding carrots to his hamster, oblivious of his future in an ashram in India where there are no TV cartoons, pets or space Lego.

Bhagwan had said that being a mother was the most difficult meditations of them all. Every minute of every day your life was not your own. In fact so difficult was it that it would be better not to have children, and then your whole energy could be available for the spiritual journey. There were, anyway, more than enough people on the planet already. As a consequence sterilisation had become a common occurrence, either in the medical centre in the ashram or back in the West. I blithely booked into Roundhay Hospital, had the snip, but afterwards was ill with a kidney infection. I went to see Shyam Singha, a Naturopath and Ayurvedic practitioner in London who had once been Bhagwan's doctor. When I told him I had been sterilised, he threw his arms up in horror. He drew a diagram.

'Here is the heavens.' He drew a semi circle at the top of the page.

'Here is the Earth.' He drew a line at the bottom.

'And is here is the Tantric connection between the two which is the responsibility of humans to maintain for health of the planet.' He drew a vertical line.

'By cutting your fallopian tubes, you have severed that Tantric connection!' His remorseless pen slashed the vertical line in two.

He gave me a regime of meditations, diets, yoga postures and exercises, followed by a list of pills, vitamins, lotions and potions to take daily. This would be a full-time occupation. Yet, if I had completely blown it this time round, what was the point? He looked at me with eyes flecked with gold. We smiled at each other. He knew I would not follow his prescriptions and instead offered to show me round his clinic. On the walls were photos of him hanging out with Bhagwan in earlier days, both of them on directors' chairs, full heads of black hair, grinning wickedly at the camera.

Shyam pointed to Bhagwan and told me, 'That man is an old rogue. I should know, he's a friend of mine.'

I returned to Leeds to find Linda, now Geeta, had arrived at Sangeet. I was delighted to see her again having no idea she had swapped her orange boxes for orange robes. She had trained as a Naturopath and immediately took me under her wing. I was to do a three-day fast on watermelons followed by a month of no wheat, no sugar, no dairy and three baked onions every day. I began the diet. I began to cry.

I sobbed into tissues, handkerchiefs, toilet rolls, food napkins, and kitchen roll. Even twenty-five years later I can tell you what is the absorption potential of a piece of tissue just by looking at it. Though a true professional in the art of crying will also know you must dab at your tears and not let them run down your cheeks in an unseemly display of unchecked grief. Not only does the salt in tears cause wrinkles, you want to be offered a shoulder to cry on, not to be told – 'pull yourself together!'

I however was too far gone for such subtleties and my mysterious grief erupted without warning all over the place. As I cried I felt my life fall into a bottomless pit of unfulfilled longing. Every now and then I would surface, look around me, drink some tea, and then notice the lonely dog from next door, or read about the famine in Africa and have to reach for the tissues again. I wrote a song.

'All day long I pine for the moon,
All night I dream of the sun.
I hope the truth will dawn on me soon
And this longing and I become one.'
But I was too sad to sing it.

In one of our encounter groups, Sujan suddenly leaped in front of me. The group watched as he held my hand and sobbed. He told me he would have loved to have had a child with me but that was now impossible.

Suddenly, I realise why I have been crying. There is this, the first loss; then there is another. I have cut the possibility of healing my own child-

145

hood wounds through the creation of a happy family of my own. I can never become the good mother of my dreams, the mother I missed, and the mother I had so much wanted to be for myself as well as Tim. As a consequence I am left looking helplessly at the broken-ness in my first family, with no hope of repairing it through my own. At least I can now see this is a natural grief for an unnatural loss, not an unnatural grief for a natural loss. I stop struggling with my sadness and surrender to it. From then on when I cried, I felt ghosts evaporate from my chest, grey shadows that had lived there all my life, leaving me.

With less resistance to its passing, the great mourning finished and the sadness left my lungs. I have never again suffered the colds and coughs that had plagued me every winter up to then, nor the bronchitis that turned into the pneumonia and pleurisy that had killed so many of my ancestors. Neither does Tim have the asthma that affects each one of his eight cousins. Even ancestral grief can be wept out it seems, with the help of several hundred onions.

Tim decided he wanted to become a sanyassin and wrote to Bhagwan.

'Dear Bhagwan, I am Tim. I want a mala. I am 4. Here is a picture of a spaceman. Love Tim.'

We were anyway half way there as the washing machine was slowly turning all things to shades of orange and red.

He got a letter back saying simply 'I give you sannyas because I love you', then the elaborate Sanskrit signature. Bhagwan joined the ranks of super-heroes that travelled through space, saving planets and hamsters.

Meanwhile Sujan and I decided we would prefer to be in Pune rather than saving people in Leeds. In a couple of months the lease came up for renewal at the converted warehouse that was Sangeet. If no one came along willing to take on the responsibilities of running it by that date, we would not renew the lease and let it go. John, Tim's father, was now a sanyassin too and my latest plan was that we could come together as a family in the larger family around Bhagwan.

Late one evening, several months later, a few days before the lease was about to expire, Sujan and I were sitting in the office of Sangeet. There was a ring on the bell. Sujan went down and came back up with Geeta and Clive. They had been driving to Devon when they heard a voice saying 'Turn round and go to Leeds. You are needed at Sangeet.'

'So here we are wondering what the hell is going on!' they laughed.

We all agreed that obviously the Buddhafield had arranged they take over Sangeet. The lease was renewed. Sujan and I pass over the administration and plan our return to India. But we hadn't reckoned on the workings of the Buddhafield in other ways.

A few weeks later Somendra of the energy phenomena, who had noticed my light of awareness in the Pune group, came to the UK. A gathering of the clan was planned in Kalptaru, the Rajneesh Centre in London and the Leeds orange crew piled into two cars and drove down.

The large meditation room was packed with hundreds of sannyasins eager for an energy blast, a spiritual rock concert, and a collective high that would explode us into another level of consciousness. Somendra arrived with his team of mediums, beautiful women whose energy flowed liked their hair. He and Bhagwan would channel energy through such mediums into us more blocked types with self-doubt and not such good energy flow. Somendra stood in front of us, charismatic, dark eyes flashing around the room, about to unleash the phenomena of his energy. He saw me at the back and beckoned me to the front.

'Vismaya, I want you as a medium.'

Imagine croaking in some dive in Tufnell Park and a man from Sony comes over to you waving a contract. Or playing a part in a local radio soap and suddenly landing a major role in a Hollywood movie. Or, if your preferred fame of choice lies in another arena, hanging out on the Mall as the Queen drives by and winds down the window to ask 'do you need a lift? Hop in.' That's what it was like.

As you may remember I have always had a sneaking suspicion I was special. This theory was completely my own, with no other adherents, but then being misunderstood goes with the territory. There was more corroborating evidence for my other theory – that I was a failure. Here, however, was proof to the contrary. I may not be as fucked up as I imagined.

I climb over hundreds of people sitting down. They look at me probably thinking I am one of the serene, nearly enlightened ones, with flowing energy if not hair. Perhaps they are even a bit in awe of me. Ah. I like it.

I like it even more when Somendra puts on Jean Michel Jarre full volume and we four mediums wander around the room touching people who fall over, collapsing in ecstatic abandon. I'm pretty ecstatic myself. These glittering lights seem to suit me.

Hundreds of young people dancing to powerful electronic music completely out of it on ecstasy – the spiritual kind – becoming at one with each other and the universe. We were there first.

After that evening, Somendra, or rather one of his assistants, would call me up and invite me to come to where he was working in Europe and I would go off for four or five days, returning with even more star dust in my eyes. At the end of October I went to Amsterdam to work with him while Tim and Sujan stayed at home. Amsterdam was very cold and very wet, but I didn't see much of it, I was too busy seeing the stars in my own eyes, so that wasn't a problem. What was more difficult was where to find an outfit in the magenta purple that was now the new orange. As an official medium you could not be seen in last season's shade – how would people know you were a special medium and not just one of the punters?

While in Amsterdam Somendra told me that Poonam, one of the therapists from the ashram, had just arrived back in England. She and her husband Teertha had set up one of the first growth centres in the UK, Quaesitor. They had become disciples of Bhagwan and she had been a key figure bringing his ideas back to the UK while Teertha was Bhagwan's main man in Pune, always seated directly in front of him in discourse. I had seen her once at a Humanistic Psychology conference where I gave a talk on feminist therapy. She led some Sufi dancing. As she had the men singing 'be alert' while the women replied 'let it happen', I wasn't impressed at the time. I should have been. She turned out to be one of the most powerful women I've ever met. She had been sent by Bhagwan back to England to expand Kalptaru into a much bigger organisation.

'You should meet her', Somendra told me 'I think you are just the person she needs.'

I arrived back in London for another group with Somendra and introduced myself to Poonam. We arranged to meet the next morning for breakfast at the house in Oak Village where she lived.

We chatted as we nibbled toast and drank coffee. She asked me what my plans were. John, Tim's father has recently taken a job in the States and the arrangement had become that Tim would visit John in the summer holidays and for whatever holidays John wanted. I told her I planned to go and live in the ashram with Sujan and my son Tim and until then was doing various jobs and running workshops. She was interested in the groups so I told her about my background in Clinical Psychology and various humanistic therapies. She leaned forward and stared into my eyes.

'I have been sent by Bhagwan to create an extension of the commune in England. This is now part of the Buddhafield and you are exactly the person it needs. Come next week and live here.'

I looked at her in complete panic. I was being asked to leave everything behind and there was no time to consider it, just her eyes boring into mine.

'Yes', I heard myself say.

To this day I do not know whether that 'yes' came spontaneously from a deep response in my soul or I had jumped so far out of myself I just gave my whole life away in some blind terror. Perhaps in terms of our karmic destiny these are the same, either way the deed was done.

We agreed I would come first, get settled and six weeks later Sujan and Tim would arrive. I hoped they would see it as I did, a step closer to our dream of returning to live in the ashram. I wasn't sure though. I lit a cigarette. It was my first for over a year.

I arrived back in Leeds the afternoon of November 5th. Sujan and Tim had called to say they were building a bonfire in the middle of our cobbled cul-de-sac. As I approached Lumley Mount I could see the Guy Fawkes waving triumphantly from the top of what he did not know was his funeral pyre. I felt sick. Even the news that Jimmy Carter had been beaten by a Hollywood Cowboy was little more than a dull thud from far away.

Tim and Sujan were pleased to have me home and Tim proudly explained the complex construction of the bonfire.

'You couldn't have done it Mummy. Only me and Sujan.'

They have Catherine Wheels, Ice Storms. Roman Candles, Traffic Lights, Arctic Flames, rockets, bangers, and sparklers. I have just one big bomb, without even a four-minute warning.

'I'm moving to London next week to join the commune.'

Sujan is aghast. He cannot speak.

We have many times re-lived that moment and wondered what would have happened if we had taken a different path. If I had paused with Poonam and said 'I need to think about it.' If Sujan had said, 'Don't do it.' Yet maybe we just delude ourselves when we imagine it could have been different, if only… Perhaps this disintegration of my home and family was an event simply waiting to happen, written in the default of my psyche, and a cultural-genetic-ancestral inevitability. Perhaps we just kid ourselves we are masters of our own fate to avoid our vulnerability to the greater forces of life. Perhaps I can blame it all on a sudden rush of blood to the head. Who knows, but Sujan, Tim and I were particularly tender with each other that last week.

During the last night in our own home, I had clung to Sujan.

'What am I doing?' I cried, looking for any sign in his eyes that would make sense of our blind running into this unknown life.

'I don't know. I don't know. I don't know', he replied with the incomprehension that is our first response to catastrophe. His arms held me as tightly as I held him. 'We will find out eventually. One day.' He stroked my hair.

I was once more breaking up a home I loved on a search to find what I did not know and could not describe.

Yet the Rajneesh neo-sannyas commune was my dream, an international community where everyone, whatever their cultural, racial, intellectual caste or class, had equality and respect. Where women and men were equally powerful. Where everyone was committed to this experiment to find a new way of being in which the struggles of sexual intimacy and caring for children were as much a part of the journey as transcendental truths of the spirit. Where music, dance and the life of the body was as important as awareness and consciousness. I could not let a chance like this go by. I had to go. Besides, even if I was walking into oblivion and not the paradise of my dreams, there is a certain call which, if you refuse, a piece of you dies.

The real test is not how much we lost or what we suffered on a path we have chosen, it is whether, knowing this, we would walk that same path again.

Chapter 12

Momma Loves Yah

Before we discovered photos steal a part of our soul, people showed their true faces to the camera. They stared with blank honesty into the flash, not knowing they may be seen by a future they would never see themselves. Now we have learned to lie. We bare our teeth, say 'cheese'. Perhaps with this show of insouciance in the face of the unknown, we hope to defend ourselves from the judgmental gaze of those we may never meet. Was it a desire to protect Tim or ourselves, that made Sujan, John and me smile, when I leaned out of the train for London and waved goodbye, as if this moment would be fixed in a family album to be peered at by a future that might judge us?

Tim's smile was an unfeigned innocence. The worst misadventure he could imagine was to fall out the lilac tree in our garden. He was excited about a move to London and had told his friend George we would be meeting the Queen, who was a superhero, like Catwoman, but with a crown. George had wanted to come with us. I had tried to explain things would not be quite as he imagined, but Tim was urgently called into action as the Incredible Hulk to save the world in a different way from his mother, and ran off roaring as he turned green, the opposite of orange, and broke out of all his clothes.

I arrived into a cold wet London, at the end of November 1980. At Kings Cross I climbed into a cab for Oak Village and through windows streaming with condensation and rain, neon streetlights and flashing car headlights, saw flickering glimpses of the wet city. People huddled against the cold, leaned into the rain with dripping plastic bags. Harried mothers pulled children away from puddles, between the rush to reach a shelter from this rain. People in cars, frowned through windscreen wipers, as they listened to the evening news. On buses in their damp heavy coats, they dropped bags onto the wet floor, scarves unravelled, their umbrellas dripping in the aisles. This sodden rush hour London was now my home.

The cab turned into Oak Village, two streets of white stucco houses, a pocket of wealth caught between the council blocks of Camden and the North London Rail Link that runs along the south end of Hampstead Heath. I paid the cab and hauled my suitcase up to the door of 10 Oak Village, now the hub of the British Buddhafield. Huddling in the porch out the rain, I rang the bell. A smiling sanyassin let me into my new home.

In the two weeks since I had been here, Poonam had gathered around her a team. The garage was stuffed with furniture that had been moved out to accommodate the ten of us now living in this three bed roomed house, with more on their way. Each day we worked in Kalptaru Rajneesh Meditation Centre near Chalk Farm. Each evening, around the kitchen table, we plotted the British Buddhafield.

Poonam had been briefed by Bhagwan to gather about her suitable people to form the new commune in the UK. She was the star around which our planets orbited at a respectful distance. Like all stars that do not pander to their public, she was both loved and feared. Even animals and children would look up when she walked into a room. Yet from the very beginning I had seen behind those dramatic eyes and menacing intelligence and into the same frailty I knew in myself. One morning I woke her. She sat upright, blasted with sleep, her eyes, darted about the room, seeking the parts of her that had fled in the night. In a moment she had coalesced into a person and graciously smiled a thank you for the coffee I had brought.

I met Poonam in the same hidden place I had met my mother; and in an echo of that first love, the one like the umbilical chord, we have to cut to become ourselves, became the keeper of secrets maybe she kept even from herself. As a result I loved her and she loved me, but with one of those dark and dangerous loves, where if the hidden blood pact is broken, the love freezes instantly into a witch's hatred.

The first week of that December the rain continued to fall. In our comings and goings we stumbled over a jumbled hill of wet shoes, squeezing through a widening pile of damp coats that hung sodden in our narrow hallway. In the cold damp and even colder freezing sleet, there happened another event that marks the territory of our time – John Lennon was shot.

We were stunned, hit in our generational solar plexus. We spoke about little else all day, and in the evening, around the kitchen table, we smoked cigarettes, beedis and weed, toasted John with brandy, and imagined a world where there'd be no religion, just the enlightened spirituality of the Buddhafield.

Tim and Sujan arrived just before Christmas. Sujan was told there was no room for him at Oak Village, and was sent to a flat in far off Cricklewood – the first shock. Neither of us had imagined we would be separated. Yet when you are a disciple of a Master, you surrender your personal desires, first to the Buddha, and then to the Sangha, the commune around the Buddha. I told myself that this is the price you pay for a living spirituality, not the anaemic pieties of dead religions that put you to sleep with opium.

Tim joins Poonam's two children, Rani and Soma, in the other half of the living room. They live sleep, play and watch TV in this half room. When someone efficient cleans, mouldering bowls of cornflakes, half eaten toast, primeval Ribena and sweet wrappers are found under their beds. The second shock – the children too must surrender to the regime necessary to build a Buddhafield.

A rota is created to collect the children from school, play with them, feed them, take them swimming, to the movies, read them bedtime stories and put them to bed. Only volunteers are involved, as a result the children have fun, but hardly see their mothers. When I ask for more time on the rota I am told my skills are needed at Kalptaru.

I had rejected a hierarchical chain of command and the obedience required by armies, religions and the Girl Guides, and turned to the consensual collectivism of feminist communities instead. I never imagined I would find myself back here again. I consoled myself – the enlightened wisdom of Bhagwan permeates throughout. Besides, I had only to look at the long list of my failures to see my ignorance would determine my choices unless I was guided by a different wisdom than my own impulses.

In our evenings around the dining table, we play parts in a different theatre – the aikido of psychosexual combat. Deconstructing your ego is what happens when you lose, if you win, you smile the sweet taste of power. This is a Tantric community, not a Cistercian or Buddhist monastery. It all has to happen.

Poonam is the Mistress here. She is a genuine player, who loves the playing, not only the winning. And loves to death a worthy opponent, on the rare occasions she finds one. With her red hair and freckles, she turns to me, her twin sister, her brown eyes gazing a smile into my blue ones. We could be sharing a tender secret.

She serves.

'Sujan's looking rather sexy tonight.' (*Smiles at Sujan then at me.*)

Clearly we are to play for high stakes this evening.

'Yes. He is gorgeous.' (*Forehand return. Smiles at Sujan before smiling back at Poonam.*)

'There are, as I'm sure you have noticed, many women who fancy him.' (*Approaches the net. Smiles at Sujan.*)

'I am not be surprised. Are you one of them?' (Backhand with top spin.)

'I'm more interested in how *you* feel that so many want to sleep with him.' (*Drop volley.*)

'Thank you for caring. Yes, a sexually desirable man for a lover is (*sighs*) so hard. I hope you never have to suffer so.' (*Smash onto the baseline.*)

Poonam is over the moon. She thinks she has found a player like herself. But when a Queen and a courtier compete, they are not playing the same game.

She serves into a different court.

'Vismaya is very beautiful, are you threatened by the number of men attracted to her?' (*Serves. Smiles at Sujan.*)

'Yes. Often. I wish I wasn't but I am.' (*No smiles. Picks up ball and looks at it.*)

'Would you like to explore this insecurity?' (*Second serve.*)

'Yes. I'd like to get through my jealousy. I love Vismaya, but I'm too attached.' (*Walks up to the net and gives her his racket.*)

What kind of game is he playing?

No game. Except maybe no-game is a gambit in the play for enlightenment. Sujan is so sincere and open hearted; he has offered himself to the court. I am afraid for us both.

Poonam is keen to help him through his jealousy. Anugito is asked if he fancies me. He does. We all know that. He is invited to woo me the next evening at our communal dinner, in front of Sujan, before retiring to make love to me, provided he has seduced me enough to want him of course. Anugito is on the line too.

I decide this tennis is more like skiing off-piste down a run as black as midnight, under a sky with no stars. There is nothing to do but go with it. And pray. Though god knows to which gods.

The next night a shy Anugito brings me flowers and chocolates. Sujan, angry and exposed, scowls from the other side of the table. The dinner continues. The women on his side of the table take care of him. I am relieved but also uncomfortable. I know how Rajneesh disciples take care. I retire with Anugito, Sujan is taken home by Hamido.

Sujan and I meet the next day with sheepish grins. He is a player after all, just with different strategies to most.

Meanwhile the Buddhafield was taking shape. We planned a huge party in March with a team of therapists from the ashram to run groups and meditations. We looked for a place big enough to accommodate several thousand and booked every ballroom at the Café Royal, with its appropriate red and gold décor.

Sujan and I walked to the top of Parliament Hill and looked over London. We wondered what this city would be like with a Buddhafield hanging over it, a natural mystic flowing through the air. We knew our vision of people holding hands and feeling truly free at last was more than just a vision in our minds, and though we were dreamers we were not the only ones, all we had to do now was persuade the world to dream with us.

Poonam had been told by Bhagwan to find the right person to run the British Buddhafield and then she could return to the ashram. She wrote to Bhagwan she had found me; I was exactly what the job requires. She told me however, I had the charisma and presence but not the style – the hippy bo-ho thing would have to go.

Bhagwan replies that I am indeed the right person and must come to the ashram for six weeks training. I am flattered, but not happy. This will delay the departure for Pune as a family, which I continue to insist will happen one day. I fly from Heathrow, this time taking Tim with me. In a private fantasy I imagine our trip will be a holiday for the two of us, as well as giving Tim a chance to be near Bhagwan.

Tim and I enjoy the flight. I had wisely brought a bag of games and books, and Tim's favourite soft toy, his Snoopy. We have not had such uninterrupted time together since we left Leeds.

It is January. The heat that greets us this time is a welcoming warmth. We walk out blinking into the bright sun and not willing to risk another flight, take a taxi from the airport to Pune. The turbanned Sikh driver sees our red and orange clothes and smiles.

'No need to tell me where you are going. I can take you there very well. No problem. *Challo.*'

I had been braced for the sights and smells of the Bombay I remembered, but since my last visit a motorway had been built. The wide modern motorway could have been taking us from any airport in the world. Or at least one with palm trees. The large concrete pipes that had been home to many families, no doubt now lay underneath us. I vaguely wondered where these nomads of poverty lived now. A few kilometres on, the motorway narrowed into a single lane. Suddenly the trees vanished and India hit me. I had thought I was prepared this time for the assault on my western conscience, but the slums of poverty, so close to the ordered luxury of international air travel shattered my complacency all over again.

Home made shelters of bamboo sticks and reeds, tied together with string and patched with paper, rags, torn plastic and old sacks, stretched in an enormous sprawl to the horizon. The starving dogs and ragged children, that mark poverty in slums and shantytowns all over the world, wandered between these tenuous constructions that leaned into each other for support. Though maybe I had been inoculated a little, as this time I could see through the crushing dirt and poverty, the appalling destitution, the miserable rags that are the only possessions of the wretched, and was able to see the humanity and spirit of survival that also lived here.

A woman washed a small child in a round bowl, and playfully splashed at her older children running around her squealing with delight. An old man bent down and held out a bowl of rice for four dogs that wagged their tails as they wolfed it down. A team of men ordered each other about, all talking at once, while they mended a roof. A boy led four goats to a muddy stream. A woman peered at her reflection in a cracked mirror to smudge her kohl. A group of children played games in the dust. Everywhere men, women and children, laughed and smiled as they carried water in buckets, bowls, jars, battered tins and chipped mugs.

On the motorway Tim had peered through the window looking for tigers and elephants, now he was distracted by the wandering water buffaloes, the bright turquoise BMW saloon next to a loaded cart that creaked on wooden wheels and was pulled by bullocks.

'Look Mum!' He had seen a monkey jump up and down to reach a banana a man held above his head. A crowd was forming around them and the battered hand written poster that told them this monkey could diagnose illness. Men squat by the side of the road and spit bright red lines of pan, barefoot boys yell for paisa as they run after rickshaws, weaving between buses with people half hanging out the windows. Wherever we look we see bright posters for Bollywood movies, kohl eyed men stare from billboards into the eyes of elaborately made up beauties in saris.

Round the corner, we can see the glass towers of modern office buildings where smooth unruffled men in suits, women in pressed silk saris and Dior dresses, Prada handbags and high heeled shoes, climbed elegantly out of Mercedes. All the centuries meet in Mumbai.

We swung round the city and began the long climb east, up into the Ghats. Our route twisted and turned through dark forests interrupted at regular intervals with the roadside cafes, with their neon lights and Coca Cola signs. The plastic chairs and Formica tables were scattered under tarpaulins and fairy lights. We stopped for a break. I had warned Tim about the toilets, but the reality of a hole in the ground, where to his amazement you could see a great pile of shit if you peered down, was beyond my powers of description. 'You'd better not drop me in!' he told me. We giggled helplessly as I dangled him over the stinking hole. He wanted baked beans, beef burgers and chips. I persuaded him to try a mild vegetable curry, but he spat it out, so I bought curd and chickee, a mixture of nuts and honey, instead.

We drove on, overtaking bright battered trucks that leaned dangerously sideways, but with painted and dangling effigies of gods to protect them on their slow crawling journey up the mountains. Less protected trucks lay on the edge of the road, great beasts that on their final trek had fallen onto their side and died. The taxi driver saw me wince as we overtook one of these lumbering monsters on a bend.

'No need to be worrying, I know this road like the sole of my foot. I have taken many orange ladies to see the guru. Not once a single problem.'

In the abrupt dusk of the tropics, suddenly it was dark. Tim fell asleep. We arrived in Pune late that evening and I walked into the ashram, a suitcase in one hand, and a tired Tim holding the other. At reception I was told they were expecting me and I was to report next day to the main office. Where would we be sleeping? She looked at me blankly. Perhaps a friend could maybe … erm … or someone somewhere… I walked around the ashram until I found a friend and arranged to share their room for the night.

The next morning, showered and refreshed Tim and I return to the ashram for breakfast. Tim wanted marmite on toast but reluctantly settled for curd and honey on bread. Friends came over and welcomed me, filled me in on who was doing what with whom. Tim was teased and invited to visit the carpenters shop. He held out Snoopy to show him the sights, as we walked up to the main office.

Children were not actively discouraged from coming to the ashram, but mothers would be told to wait until the new commune if they wanted to live here. Some women, faced with the painful choice of whether to stay with their children or their Master, left the children with their fathers. An anguish I could only imagine, though I understood the conflict. It was already becoming apparent that these six weeks would be difficult. I would have to find out how other mothers managed to care for their kids and still get to morning lecture.

I am greeted with smiles by Laxmi, Vidya and Arup, the three women who run the ashram. The fourth, Sheela, was away on a trip to the States.

'It is very good that you are going to run the British Buddhafield, I can see you are already a channel for Bhagwan.' How does she know, and what does it mean anyway? But it doesn't do to ask such things. Laxmi smiles. 'What have you planned for her?' she asks Vidya.

The ashram is these days one of the largest 'tourist attractions' in the sub-continent, even in the early eighties it was the largest ashram in India. I am to work in the entrails of the engine that drives the international machine of the ashram. Two weeks each in the records department, books and tapes and the main office. And I was to learn to be like them.

But I knew I could never be like these women, or like Deeksha, Susheela, Puja and the other 'mommas' who ran the various departments. These are the women who hold together the world. The women who in all communities are the gravitational force that maintains the tribal integrity, that stops its many factions splitting off into outer space, who manage the multitude of detail and demand, from babies' nappies to strategies of war. These women were the powerhouse that made the whole project to create a thousand Buddhas viable. Without this terrible and wonderful matriarchy, a few mystics would have jumped up and down in a field somewhere and had a few satoris.

I don't know what on Heaven or Earth gave them the idea I, with my insecurities and self doubt, could be like them, able to sit in such splendid certainties and trust their gut instincts, even with a whole world ranged against them. Which, one day, it was.

Tim, Snoopy and I were taken to the ashram school where a dozen or so children played. Bhagwan had insisted sannyasin children were not to be taught any belief system, not even about him or the Buddhafield. They were to discover the world for themselves. He told us, 'The best gift you can give your child is not to interfere. It is difficult. Great fear will grip you. But let your child walk alone into the unknown. They will grow strong and become themselves, which may not be anything like what you, the parent, has mapped out for them.' I felt this to be so profoundly true;

I was willing to give my child over to the commune for him to have that freedom. Sharna, who ran the school, came over and crouched down in front of Tim. He smiled.

'Which one of you is staying, Snoopy or Tim. We haven't room for both.'

Tim gasps and clutches Snoopy. They have to stay together.

'Ah I see you both must stay. Mmm. O.K. as a special favour to you two. But don't let Snoopy frighten the monkeys!' Some monkeys have swung through the trees and jumped on the roof, screeching. Tim is delighted and waves Snoopy at them. I pass Tim's hand over into Sharna's, a symbolic passing over of responsibility, which Sharna acknowledges with a friendly smile at me too. Bhagwan had said the most important thing was never to be violent to the spirit of a child and had personally chosen Sharna to run the school. It must be all right then.

Bhagwan had told us 'Children are helpless and they are so dependent on their parents, naturally this makes them afraid of you as well as loving you. In the commune, they will have many places to go, many people to care for them – they will not be so helpless. They will not be in your hands as much. They will have more independence and you will not be able to coerce them so easily. They will be a new generation who grow up able to love without fear.'

I watched Tim join the other children. To give Tim a life free from my self-serving interference appeared to me a blessing. To put my energy and effort into the commune where love would be freely available to all the children seemed the best I could do for Tim, as well as for myself and everyone else. This was a necessary sacrifice for the greater good. Must be. I turned to go to work for the commune. I expertly wiped away a lone tear that had dared to creep down my cheek, and went to work.

Work is meditation. You watch your personal trips come and go, while all the time you focus on the immediate demands of the task in front of you. In this way your personal ego dissolves as naturally as a dewdrop in the morning sun. Or did it disappears like a cloud or withdraw 'dancing lightly on the tide', I can't quite remember? Or perhaps it just faded away in the brightness of so much light.

My first two weeks were in the Records Department. I wandered along rows between banks of filing cabinets, full of cards listing every sanyassin and their psycho-spiritual history. Each card had on it a photo, usual details, date of birth and address, and lists of key 'events' such as a précis of a letter to Bhagwan, the groups they'd done, useful skills such as accountancy or plumbing.

In the second week I was let into the secrets of a code written discreetly in pencil on the top right hand corner. 'P.C.' meant 'potential cuckoo' and therefore not to do any of the heavy encounter groups. 'M.B.' meant 'mega bucks' though I couldn't see the point of that. Neither could I see the point of listing people's degrees and qualifications. Weren't we getting away from all that?

Sent to file a box of cards, naturally I went straight to the Va-Vo drawer and pulled out my own. Like typing yourself into Google and finding you've written a book about ballet, gave a paper at a conference on metallurgy and have Irish ancestry from Galway, I found I had written a letter to Bhagwan last year which was précised – 'flowery blurb.' What! My deep gratitude to Bhagwan, revealing how close my ego was to dissolving after the 'Insight Through Expression' group, and the expression of my insights are dismissed as 'flowery blurb'! I move onto the Se-Su drawer – Sujan.

Several days later, I also précised letters to Bhagwan from both his Indian and western disciples. Another fault line running through the rock upon which we built our commune:

'Dear Bhagwan, Please give me a name for the new shop I am opening which will sell pots and pans. Hopefully with your blessing I will sell many. Namaste Dhiraj, the second hut on the left in the alley between the barber and the shoe-mender on Satyaji Rd., Calcutta.'

'Dear Bhagwan, I am overflowing with joy and filled with the bliss of being in your presence. I desire only to be with you and to fall into the endless sky of your eyes. In eternal gratitude, Niranjhana, 2365, SW23rd Ave, LA 91639, USA.'

On one card I copied the name for the shop Laxmi had written, the other I took it upon myself to write 'flowery blurb'.

I was shown the ropes in the Books & Tapes Department by a woman I knew from Kalptaru in London. Sujan had once told me he fancied her, and several people remarked we were alike, but I don't think so. I could tell from the sensitive and caring way she told me how to press the Play button on the tape recorder that she felt superior to me. I thought it strange she should be so competitive with me when it was clear I was immeasurably more attractive and aware than her. Perhaps she imagined to worship in a small office in the ashram was better than having been chosen to run the British Buddhafield.

I fall into a routine. On days when Tim is with friends, I am up early for discourse, a banana breakfast and work. Otherwise it's a later start with

Tim before I take him to school. Tim has made friends and enjoys being there. I know they are not to be taught any religion or history, but I can't make out what they do there, other than have fun. We meet up in the evening for dinner and join others for music group in Buddha Hall. A thousand or more of us sing devotional songs while the kids run around, playing games as incomprehensible to us as is our singing to them.

Black out takes place every evening during energy darshan, when the lights go out for half an hour. When they are switched back on, the mothers try to find their children, who must have night vision, as they can find places to hide even in the pitch dark. Tim and I then go back to the room I have rented and share with two others.

Increasingly Tim stays over with other friends, as they form gangs and want to sleep together. This suits me as I have fallen in love with Nutan and his translucent other worldliness, a legacy from the typhoid that laid him low for months.

My last two weeks are to be spent in the main office with the big 'mommas' where I am to learn the arts of the matriarchy.

I sit by one of the mommas as she deals with a stream of workers, and their various requests, complaints, concerns, fears and confusions. These mommas pour out the love that is the fuel of this communal machine. Often 'tough love'.

A ma wants to change her room, it's too close to the carpentry workshop and the noise disturbs her meditations.

'You wanna be a mystic? Go to California. They hum and dangle a lot of crystals there, you'll like it.' The ma smiles despite herself.

Another ma is called in; she made a mistake in the group bookings.

'But I had an energy darshan the night before and was so blissed out I was gone.'

'Get yourself a sugar daddy, honey, then you can sigh in ecstasy all you want during those moments when you're earning your keep. Here, if you want us to keep you, you keep focused.'

And the most frequent problem of them all – Asha weeps that her lover Vikram has gone off with Madhura. The momma cuts through the crap.

'If you truly loved him, you would be happy he is happy. It was probably your misery that drove him away in the first place!' Ouch! I wince in the seat to the side. Nothing escapes her. 'If you want tea and sympathy hook up with Vismaya here and start a bleeding hearts club. Whaddya expect – this is a Tantric ashram not a convalescent home!'

Sometimes it's compassionate love. A swami has recently returned from his father's funeral and was seen weeping on guard duty at the main gate. He expects a Zen stick, and looks faintly alarmed when Vidya holds his hand.

'Your father will be happy you cry. You must have loved him. Bhagwan has sent you this to wipe away your tears.' She hands over one of Bhagwan's personal linen handkerchiefs. 'And while these tears are happening, we'll move you from the front gate into Vrindivan, the canteen, where you can chop onions, wash pots and cry all you want.'

Sometimes it's 'crazy wisdom love', especially when Laxmi's involved.

A ma arrives with a long face.

'I keep getting it wrong in books and tapes. I'm dyslexic. I'd be much better at cleaning, Laxmi, honestly I would.'

Laxmi promotes her to co-ordinate the books section of the department.

'Bhagwan's wisdom is not in the words; it's in the silences between the words. Who better than a someone with dyslexia to co-ordinate the book department!'

These mommas worked day and night to keep it real, keep us real. If you were genuine, they loved you even as they hit you, there was nothing to fear. Try to manipulate or trick them however, and you were a goner. Their gut instincts were more infallible than any pope's pronouncement ex-cathedra. These commune mommas, the power source of the worldly aspects of the commune, were never off duty, never spaced out and had their feet firmly planted in the pragmatic realities of life on Earth. They had to have what they had to have, or else the whole show would fall down. No open rickshaws, bamboo huts and M.G. Road saris for them – air conditioned Mercedes, luxurious rooms with bathrooms and designer clothes. And if you were a man and one of them fancied you, you'd better be up for it, literally. Everybody knows that's how it has to go, and not just in a Tantric ashram.

When faced with forces greater than you it's wise to take the line of least resistance, and if what they wanted was what you thought was your man, then get it very quickly, he is no longer yours. Else you'd be cleaning the group toilets.

The group bathroom was a large tiled space with showers and a line of eight toilets – with no doors, no privacy, and no clothes, to help us strip ourselves of our false social personas, naked before each other and life. On entering these communal toilets on my last visit I had disguised my shock, sat and gossiped as if I had always done as in ancient Rome or a Buñuel film. I had a conversation with an older woman who told me 'Worse things happened in the war you know' before introducing herself as Lady... She was visiting her son and doing a few meditations. 'And why not my dear?' Why not indeed?

Last time in the ashram, I met my terror of the Buddha and went through it to another level of love and surrender to Bhagwan. This time I encounter my fear of the commune, the Sangha. I sit and listen to the mommas cajole, nurture, bribe, seduce, confront and challenge a stream of sannyasins. A fear creeps into me. Is it reality or my fear that tells me this ashram is really a gigantic hive, where worker bees slave away just so the queen bees and their cohorts can have honey. Suddenly what I thought was love looks like psychological bullying and emotional manipulation. My mouth goes dry. This is jungle warfare not a garden paradise at all. I given myself, in a manic missionary zeal, (for, as Auden said, we become what we hate), only to discover everyone else is on some other trip, caring about one person more than any other, and guess who that person is? Excuse me what planet is this? I may have taken a wrong turn somewhere and incarnated on the wrong one.

This fear settles on my heart, silently creeping into the scars left from old fears of demons and hell. My heart beats faster. I am sweating. There are anacondas in the lotus blossoms. They will soon realise I am an enemy that must be annihilated. How can I escape from the hive that has now revealed itself a spider's web, before it suddenly turns into a lion's den and I'm swimming out my depth in shark infested waters. Laxmi turns to me.

'Vismaya, you don't look so well. Take a break. Go out for the afternoon with your son and lover.'

What! In all the time I have been there, not once have I seen time out being given to anyone. She must care about me, not just the work. How did she know to say the one thing that would stop me in my tracks? That amazing gut instinct of the matriarchy. I walk unsteadily out into the sunlight. Not an animal predator in sight.

Tim, Nutan and I wander down Mahatma Gandhi Road. We buy painted metal parrots and monkeys that do acrobatics on sticks. We bargain for silk clothes and jewellery. We design jackets, and tailors promise them tomorrow, though we know it will be a week. We rest in a bright green juice bar and drink fresh lime sodas, no ice, and mango pulp with fresh cream. Tim piles pistachio kulfi on top of his mango pulp and wonders if he can take some back for John and Sujan.

We watch the Tao flow through centuries. Handcarts wait at traffic lights next to sports cars; a sacred cow with its battered garland of hibiscus nudges a Harley Davidson, its rider in leathers and aviator shades. The scents of spices and perfumes mingle with kerosene and petrol fumes. A cacophony of sound is this river too. The horns of rickshaws, the shouts of drivers, the noisy games of children, the barking of dogs. The cries of people at work calling for customers, calling to each other. The banging and grinding of bicycle repairs, knife sharpeners, stone masons, manufacturers of any car part you need to keep your twenty year old battered Ambassador car going a little longer. To Tim's delight we end our trip at the splendid Victorian Pune Train Station, where in the café they serve fried egg and chips.

We return to the ashram that evening. It all looks beautiful, just perfect. This very body the Buddha; this very Earth, the Lotus Paradise. I am now ready to devote my life to this experiment in communal living that has as its soul, a living Master, the greatest Tantric teacher the world has ever known, and right in its heart, the boundless love and magnificence of a matriarchy devoted to the same vision. I do not want to live anywhere else. This is my home. I belong here. I know I do.

For the second time I go to the main office and tell them Tim and I want to stay.

Sheela, back from her travels in the USA, Vidya and Arup look at me and sigh. I think they may have raised their eyes to heaven but these mommas don't need to call on the powers of heaven, they *are* the powers that be.

'Get real Vismaya!' they tell me. 'Wake up and smell the kerosene as well as the coffee!' What they all know and I and everyone else do not, is the ashram will soon be dismantled and moved to the USA. Sheela's last trip had been to buy the hundred square mile ranch in Oregon that was to become Rajneeshpuram, the city we were to build in the desert of an old vast cattle ranch. They smile and hug me as I sadly get up to leave. They can see I will do as I'm told now.

Looking back of course that was the training. Not the filing, the office organisation, the notations for recording the tapes, the bibliography of the books, group booking schedules, indemnity forms and so on. Of course not. It was this. To bring me into a surrender to the body of Bhagwan in the world, this commune. Their job was done. I had seen how this experiment to create a community run on principles of love and freedom, equality and soul, life and consciousness, worked. Something was happening here that had never happened before anywhere on the planet ever. Women and men were living, loving and working together utterly free from the oppressive alienations and materialist power games that operated everywhere else. We were all committed, heart, body and soul to finding a way of living that honoured every level of human experience both inner and outer, from child-care, creativity, good food, beautiful architecture, caring for the planet, to self exploration, genuine dialogue, real communication, meditation and spiritual growth. I now loved this communal experiment to find a new way of being so much; I would do almost anything for it. That's why they smiled.

Each worker had an energy darshan once a month. I was given one every week. I wasn't sure whether it was to strengthen my Kundalini for the task ahead or because my energy needed a few kick starts to get it started, or my preferred option, Bhagwan saw my true potential for a great enlightenment and was zapping it to me while he could. The mommas had taught me well. However far out I travelled into the cosmos the night before, I made sure I had both feet on the ground the next morning.

I have one last energy darshan. Bhagwan has music playing, lights flashing, mediums dancing as he presses furiously into my third eye. The force blasts me backwards through the gateless gate, this time not into ecstasy, but an endless falling through the night into darkness and the silence of death. I lie on the floor of Chuang Tzu, my cheek against the cool marble. I had fallen to the feet of the Buddha, *Buddham Sharanam Gaachami*. I have now fallen even further, to the feet of the commune, *Sangam Sharanam Gaachami*.

I say goodbye to friends, though we all imagine I will soon be back. Back here, back home. Tim and I climb into the taxi for the return journey to Bombay airport. Tim has wandered through Pune with his friends, jumped in and out of rickshaws, bought chickee and bharfi and god knows what else from roadside stalls. He has had adventures he and his friends giggle about but do not tell to their mothers. He has played in the dirt and streams around Koregaon Park where dysentery, Dengue Fever and unimaginable bacteria lie in wait for us westerners. I had drilled into him time and time again the litany of all those who travel east. No water, no ice, no salad, no fruit unless you peel it yourself – only bottled or boiled water. It seems to have worked. Not once has he been ill with diarrhoea or sickness of any kind. As we walk onto the plane he is doubled up with cramps. Perhaps he too does not want to return to a cold London and an Oak Village, where he has fun, but not really a home. Not the home he wants, with a mum always there to tuck him into bed and read him a story.

Sujan meets us at Heathrow. Tim is full of tales of his adventures and the wondrous sights he has seen. Perhaps Sujan does not notice I am quiet. We stop at the service station on the M4 near the airport. I tell him I love him but I am no longer in love with him. I have fallen in love with another. I can see the red Formica table and I can see Sujan's face. It is white with shock.

Chapter 13
Roots and Wings

Oak Village and Kalptaru were a whirlwind of activity with just two weeks to The March Event, our planned party in a palatial suite of ballrooms over two floors of the Café Royal, though no ordinary party, a psycho-spiritual rave to raise the collective Kundalini of first London, later the world. There were press releases to write, ads to place, programmes to design, food to organise, transport timetables, bookings, airport pick-ups, accommodation to find for the 'spiritual therapists' from Pune, traffic flow diagrams for the thousands of people we were expecting. If you've ever organised a war or a party for thousands, then you will know what was involved. Sujan and I had no time together until late that night.

There's nothing like the material reality of a body to bring you back to your senses. In bed, in the dark, I realise I am in love with Sujan after all. Not for the last time when apart from him, I have fallen in love with the one I was with, rather than remain true to the one I loved. Though there are now three in this bed, even if one is a disembodied entity, here only in spirit.

I am to lead a meditation on the Sunday morning and must therefore be kitted out in a suitable outfit. With the eyes of the British Buddhafield on me, and hopefully all the press we've invited, I cannot wear my usual feminist-hippy-careless, yet in my opinion stylish, ensembles. I am sent to Oxford Street to buy something the Oak Village crew think is chic. But because of their previous lives they still wear nail varnish, make up and blow dry their hair and throw up their hands in horror at the cool hip clothes I bring back. I am sent out again with Adheera. I return and parade in front of a panel of critics in a pleated skirt, blouse, high-heeled shoes and nylons. I look like a secretary dressed for a job interview with a vicar.

I am sent out again with Mangala this time. Mangala has not the slightest trace of hippy boho-chic and her blood red fingernails *never* break. If she can't sort me out no one can.

We enter shops, the windows of which I have never dared to even glance into before. I return, walk the walk and twirl, this time looking like a secretary dressed for a job interview with a Bishop. I look ridiculous, even in their eyes, though they cannot explain why. I can. These straight clothes just do not suit me. They give up. I wear a silk shalwar kameez, flat shoes, elegant. At least I think so.

The weekend is a success. Several thousand of us move between ballrooms, sing Sufi songs, primal scream, meditate, gaze into each others eyes, communicate uncensored truths, accumulate insights, let it all go and dance wildly to a thumping disco beat, a tribe spiralling ecstatically into life, love and laughter. These elaborate ceilings and glittering chandeliers have never seen anything like it, not even in the days of Oscar Wilde. The Press, responding to our invitations, wander freely through this magnificent love-fest. If only we'd known...

We stared at the front pages of all the Monday papers. 'Sex Romp at Café Royal.' 'Drug Crazed Sex Orgy.' 'Sex Guru Followers Make Love in Hotel Lobby.' 'Free Love Orange People Lick Carpets in Frenzy.' Had these journalists been at the same event? Discussion programmes on TV and radio analysed the attractions of these dangerous cults with their harmful 'pseudo-therapies'. There was a question in Parliament about whether such things 'should be allowed'. Fortes, the owners of the Café Royal, banned all sannyasins from entering any of their premises for life. No more TV appearances, invitations to Downing Street or tea breaks on the motorway then. Only good old Bernard Levin argued that something profound and significant was going on. But then he had visited the ashram, listened to Bhagwan and actually talked with us. He knew there was more happening than met the jaundiced media eye.

Clearly our project to turn on the world would take longer than planned.

Meanwhile our vision shifted from East to West as news arrived that the new commune would be created in America on the several hundred square miles of an over-grazed cattle ranch in Oregon. Young Tim also looks west. John now lives in California and Tim wants to go and spend some time with him. John and I agree he goes for six months. On his last day I take him to all his favourite places in London, the games arcades on

Oxford Street, the Oasis outdoor swimming pool, Trafalgar Square to feed the pigeons, Burger King for a non-veggie beef burger, Hamleys for a present for John. 'Probably he'd like some Lego', thinks Tim. The next day Sujan and I drive him to Heathrow.

I try not to cry but gulp back sobs every time I hug him. I attempt to distract myself in details of his packing, has he got his gloves threaded through his coat, does he have enough books and crayons for the flight, will he remember where I have written all John's details down, is his passport safely zipped into his bag... But really nothing can distract me. My little boy is going to the other side of the Atlantic and then the other side of another continent; to his father. Where he will be safe. Where he will be loved. Where he will have a comfortable home and go to a good school. And where he will be further from me than he has ever been. Not just for a few weeks. For six months. Maybe more. This is a goodbye I never imagined I would ever say to the little boy now laughing with Sujan as they skid on the trolley through Terminal 3.

Do children, who live in the moment more than we do, feel less fear because they are protected from the painful futures we so easily envisage, or are they more afraid, because they do not know and have so little power over what lies ahead? For Tim this was an adventure where he would be with his dad again, a dad who earns lots of money and that means new Lego and visits to Disneyland. Perhaps we can only ever be afraid of the return of what has already happened. How else do we know to be afraid? Only a burned child dreads fire, the rest are cautiously curious. Tim has known just a few grazed knees and falls from trees; even the split between John and me was as friendly as could be. Oak Village, though not a traditional home, was much more fun than any boarding school. And he has always been held in the affection and love of all three of us, John, Sujan and me. While my heart breaks through the long farewell, Tim does not weep. He plays with his new Transformer and warns us he will be speaking American when he comes back.

We check in and are introduced to the stewardess who will be taking care of Tim on the flight. He holds her hand, his faithful Snoopy who never leaves him like I do, in the other. They walk through to the Departure Gate. My last view of him is his smiling face, half hidden by his backpack filled with treats and favourite toys, as he turns round for one last shout of good-bye. And is gone.

I am inconsolable and cry all the way back to London, for once grateful for the slow crawl through rush hour traffic. We pass *Evening Standard* placards saying that Bob Marley had died. No woman no cry; but my tears fell and continued to fall – in meetings, in meditations, on the 'phone, on the shoulders of friends on the smokers bench outside Kalptaru. Anywhere and everywhere.

I have always leaned more towards tea and sympathy than tough love, now I am hopeless. I weep when dealing with recalcitrant workers, resistant egos, and resentful disciples. 'Oh how sad!' I cry, 'how painful for you. How can I help?' – not at all what the commune momma's taught me. Some, tougher than me, tell me to stop my self-indulgent whining. Especially one Ma, but she had given her twins away at birth so course she would see it that way. One evening while round at Somendra's for dinner he tells me I have two millstones round my neck – Tim and Sujan. All I have to do is get rid of them and I will fly. But I love my millstones. I don't want to fly.

It didn't help that few relationships survived in this Tantric hothouse, where following your energy was a spiritual discipline on a par with meditation. It didn't help either that Nutan arrived, tall, tanned and sexy from Pune, to be with me. I tried to be with two men but this proved too difficult for me. I have always preferred the personal love of intimacy than the impersonal pleasures of love where you find it. Like making a home and being a hands-on parent, what is a strength in the world is a failing in a Tantric commune. The turbulent struggles this put me through has taught me however, the commitment must be to the love first, not to the person, and with that comes different securities, demands and freedoms.

One thing not possible in a Tantric commune is to dwell for too long on your own misery, if only because more turbulence is always on its way. Poonam has organised a month long counsellor training with thirty participants, mostly women. She has Sujan assist her, which means he takes care of her during the course and does whatever she tells him to. Even when she picks out certain women and tells him to sleep with them, to 'move their energy'.

When he tells me his work for the evening, I narrow my eyes and spit out, it's the Earth that supposed to move. How's he going to manage that? I go to bed alone and privately weep for the loss of Sujan now, as well as Tim. I hate feeling sad, angry and insecure. And besides, a tear-streaked face is so unattractive as well as jealousy so uncool. I can't do much about Tim, but maybe I can break through my attachment to Sujan.

I am to run an encounter group with the counsellor training, which includes the women whose energies have been moved by Sujan. We sit on cushions in a large circle. Rajneesh Spiritual Therapists are supposed to leave their personal selves outside the group room door and become a channel for Bhagwan, a 'hollow bamboo'; tonight I am more a blocked drainpipe. I tell everyone I am angry, hurt and jealous of what has been happening with Sujan. They know this anyway. They've seen my glares in their direction, when they emerge flowing and glowing, after a night with him. I sit in the middle of the group and let it all hang out. The whole she-bang, my inarticulate rage, my fear, my helpless grief. I should have known better than to throw myself onto the mercy of a group of trainee therapists.

One lot let me know what is wrong with me – I am too possessive, full of ego, in my head. Another lot tell me how to fix it – I need to let go, put my ego aside, live in the here and now. The primal therapy crew try to push me into my core pain by yelling 'Get off it – get real!' 'What a pathetic display of shit!' The body workers come to knuckle into my tension. The re-birthers want me to lie down and breathe. The energy workers want me to meditate and open up my higher chakras. My assistant shouts at them' Bloody lousy therapists you lot are!' and puts her arms round me. I sit in the middle in my own private let-go.

A giggle begins somewhere in the region of my stomach. I try to suppress it. I must feel my pain. But suddenly it is apparent we are possibly the most ridiculous event in London at that moment. A few of us catch each other's eye. The absurdity hits us – we are completely and magnificently preposterous. We start to laugh. We cannot stop. We collapse, helpless with laughter. It is infectious. The whole group falls about laughing. Even the re-birthers are gasping for breath between deep sobs of laughter. It is hurting, the tears are falling and still we cannot stop howling. Help! We might die in here! A few curious people poke their heads through the door. We try to explain but it's impossible and we collapse all over again. I don't know how we got out. Possibly our addiction to nicotine saved us when we staggered out for our fags.

I still didn't like Poonam telling Sujan he must 'move the energy' of other women – even less that he followed orders. But she is a double Scorpio, he is a surrendered disciple; *c'est la vie, es la vida, das ist Leben*, in the Rajneesh International Commune. Besides, there are other ways to lay claim to your man.

I bought one of the first Sony Walkmans on sale in Tottenham Court Road with two headphone sockets. People laughed at us as we danced around together, but Sujan and I could no longer hear them. We smiled serenely from within our own world, being blasted by a music no one else could hear. Several years later they were wearing them too. The cooler ones that is – and who cares what the others thought.

No one wore a personal stereo or danced at the meeting where three mommas from the ashram, Sheela, Susheela and Arup, arrived with a message, or rather several messages, about our new corporate image.

Out were eastern or hippie dress, swearing, long embraces in public, slouching, drunkenness, drugs, cigarettes if you have to, but not beedis, fighting talk, dancing in the streets and flowing men's locks. In were – handshakes, polite conversation, designer hair (oh dear), handbags, sobriety, upright posture and civilisation. In the groups there was to be no more nudity, sex or violence. Those working full time would receive full board and accommodation and £5 per week pocket money, and anything we earned would go into the collective pot. Also into the collective pot went our cars. Mine was commandeered anyway by one of the mommas to go shopping on Oxford Street and her driver wrote it off. I never even got a 'Sorry mate!' – just a casual 'It must have been time for you to let it go.'

There was more. Money. On the Oregonian cattle ranch we were to build a city, Rajneeshpuram, and money was needed to finance this project to make a thousand flowers bloom in the desert. Buddhafields throughout the world, especially in Western Europe, were to create businesses to make as much money as possible. We were also to build sacred cities where thousands of sannyasins would live, work, which was now to be called 'worship', and make ... money. Interesting that the work that had been a meditation, such as cleaning every inch of a vast parquet floor with a toothbrush, shifting a pile of manure from here to there, and then from there back to here, became 'worship' now the focus was making money and not Gurdjieffian exercises to energise our souls.

These mommas told us they understood some of us may feel resistant to these changes, so it was important we knew they were coming directly from the main man himself, Bhagwan. We were to be positive whatever our personal feelings. Negativity was to be dealt with firmly because, as Susheela told us, 'One bad apple can spoil the cart.'

We listen in silence.

It's an old dilemma. You hear someone with fresh ideas and insights, as had I when I first heard Bhagwan. Their wisdom makes sense, doors open in your mind. You move closer to listen some more. Old certainties are challenged. You begin to question some of your assumptions. We can learn nothing new if we remain within the confines of our own beliefs, but at what point do we abandon what we think we know? When does an apprentice trust the Master and do as he's told, when does he trust himself and leave? And, when you have loved a Buddha with a devotion that takes you beyond your self, at what point does a disciple kill the Buddha? As even the ancient Masters say this is the only way through the psycho-spiritual Oedipal crisis to become a Buddha yourself.

Most of us at this stage, still loved the dream enough to surrender to the imperfect organisation attempting to embody it. So we breathed deeply, put on our smart clothes, practiced being polite, and even the old socialist-feminists amongst us, got ready to make money as well as love. And while 700 million people watched the fairy tale wedding of Prince Charles and Lady Diana in July, we were busy building our own happy-ever-after.

We sat around the kitchen table with a map of the UK. Where was Medina Rajneesh, our sacred city to be? We dangled a pendulum. It swung over the North Sea. Surely our business could not be in oil? Sujan was put in charge of finding a property and contacted estate agents for large properties within two hours drive of London.

A collection of brochures arrived, one of a mini village in Suffolk that had been an American school. A large mock-Tudor manor house, Herringswell Manor, with thirty bedrooms, numerous cottages, houses and teaching blocks in twelve landscaped acres with no near neighbours. Five of us, dressed in green and blue, malas hidden, drove up to look round it, claiming to be setting up a school, though we neglected to mention this was for Buddhas. We wandered around the gardens and winding paths, through spacious rooms and an array of offices and houses. We had found it. Now we had to find £250,000 to buy it.

Poonam and I tour the UK and Ireland to sell the idea to sannyasins that they buy into the commune – £5,000 and you can stay any time you wish for free. Sell your house and donate enough, and you can live in the Buddhafield, supported completely, forever, however long that is. Though if you were a plumber or an electrician you can come for free – some things remain the same, whatever the community. A two-week tour and we had 25% for the deposit. With no chance of a mortgage we had three months to find the rest.

The next weeks are a blur. We go into overdrive to explain, persuade and sell this possibility to as many sannyasins as we can. Two weeks before the deadline we are £75,000 short. A final push to far-flung sannyasins with savings and, with a few days to spare, we were there.

Sujan and I went to the solicitors to sign the deeds. They had champagne and a celebration planned as in 1981, a quarter of a million was a lot of property. We puzzled them with our complete lack of high or excite-

173

ment. We had to get back for a workers' meeting and for us it was like, OK, what's next.

What came next was I went to Suffolk to co-ordinate the building, decorating, cleaning, buying equipment, organising the kitchen, laundry etc. Thirty of us had three months to get things ready before we planned to move up en masse. Sujan was sent to Devon to help a sanyassin get his farm ready to sell. While Sujan shovelled shit, I played lady of the manor. When he came to visit at weekends I tried to help him see that surrender to the Buddhafield was the thing, not his rages of jealousy. My enlightened wisdom unfortunately failed to illuminate his darkness, so I simply smiled at him with deep compassion, which for some reason enraged him further.

Strangely, there were others, who did not appreciate the gracious way I spread sweetness and light in my position as lady bountiful. One woman took it upon herself to personally supervise the deconstruction of my ego. She told Poonam I had smoked dope, stolen some of her clothes, cut up her precious photos and said bitchy things about Poonam behind her back. Rather confusingly these were not wild spins on real events but complete fabrications. Initially I was angry, and our fights looked like half a dozen of one and six of the other, but someone who lies so completely has weapons that defeat mine and I gave up. Not quite. When she was near I would flirt particularly charmingly, perhaps to remind her I got much more attention than her because I was so much more beautiful, sexy and desirable.

One morning she bursts into my room. Here we go again, I haven't seen her for a while. She tells me she's come up with some great lies for Poonam because she loves to see me angry. I tell her to fuck off and get a life; I don't give a shit. She runs to Poonam and tells her she knocked gently on my door to make friends and I wounded her with my verbal abuse. But this time, we were overheard. I was wise not to fight her directly, when confronted she laughs and says 'Oh well, the game's up.' I'd have been mincemeat in a hand-to-hand fight with this marvel. For two weeks in full view of everyone at breakfast, she is to bow and kiss my feet. She gets the fun and I get the embarrassment – where's the justice in that?

There ain't none. This is a Tantric community, different rules apply.

Bhagwan told us, 'I am against the old family structure because it turns children and adults into possessions. The nonsense of monopolizing love has to be dropped. If your husband is laughing with someone else, it is good. Your husband is laughing – laughter is always good. If your wife is holding someone else's hand ... good. Warmth is flowing and that is good. With whom it is happening is immaterial. And if love is flowing with your partner it will more easily flow with you too.'

Some days it was easy to go with the flow of love, 'the life of the soul'. For example when drinking my daily allowance of one glass of wine or half a pint of beer in our 'Omar Khayyham' bar and I found myself smiling and leaning into a particularly gorgeous fellow Tantrika.

Some days it was much harder. Like when Sujan was doing the smiling and leaning.

It is six months since Tim left. We have spoken often on the phone and John has sent me photos of a tanned blond Californian boy. He flies back for Christmas, to stay. John will send him a ticket every summer for a long visit until/if he decides he wants to return for longer. That is the plan anyway.

I pace around Heathrow once more. The board lights up, his flight has landed. I peer through the crowd looking for a little boy among the business men, families, holiday makers, travellers, as they wheel suitcases, carry back packs, briefcases, handbags, parcels and push their trolleys into England. There he is! A stewardess has brought him through and passes him over to me. Tim and I laugh and hold each other. This is wonderful. We smile and cuddle all the way to the car. He has a new watch on his brown arm and can tell the time to the second. He tells me time is different in America, it is morning for him and early evening for me, which means I will fall asleep before him. It is cold and threatening snow, but this little boy is dressed for California. First stop, some boots and warm clothes, before we drive up the M11 to Medina, our new home.

I explain to Tim all the children sleep in the Kids' House, official name, Ko Hsuan, where during the day there are lessons. There are now six children and about eighty adults living at Medina and more will arrive after December 11th, Bhagwan's birthday, when we officially open. I describe the communal dining room where we eat food cooked in an enormous kitchen, including at least once a week chips, beans and veggie burgers, and the huge oak-panelled hall with a large fireplace, a real fire and eight sofas. I tell him the main house has thirty bedrooms and Sujan and I have a room on the top floor where he can spend the night with us any time he wants to. I explain there is a laundry for our clothes as well as an accounts office, a design studio, a healing centre, carpenters and plumbers workshops, garages, a visitors cottage and in the grounds, an old swimming pool, tennis courts, all sorts of nooks and crannies and hiding places in the woods. Tim is more interested in whether there are boys his age who like Transformers and Lego.

We arrive, deliver the car into the transport office and walk round the corner to the kids' house. Our feet crunch over the frozen gravel as we walk towards the two-storey mock-Tudor building where the school and play rooms are on the ground floor and the kids sleep upstairs. We unpack his bag and I bring out his old toys I have kept safe for his return. The other kids crowd round to examine this new arrival and his toys, then take him with them as they wander through the commune in a pack. Like tribal dogs, they sniff and knock into each other, half in play, half in challenge. I hear one ask Tim if he'll swap his watch for a Star Wars Model. Another asks if he has any comics. The kids are still one cohesive group. They have yet to create the rules and pecking orders that define the territory of their new life. This is all new for them too, and the fault lines that run through all communities to define status and difference, had yet to be drawn by any of us.

I began to organise the Groups Department. We planned a programme of therapy groups and sessions, and created the first healing centre in the UK that incorporated complementary therapies such as naturopathy, acupuncture, homeopathy, massage, with allopathic medicine from two GPs and a gynaecologist, with counselling and body psychotherapy. People came for a week of healing where an individually designed programme of sessions, meditation and diets would be created to meet their unique needs. There was a sauna and a flotation tank too, and in the energy of a Buddhafield, this was a healing of the heart and spirit as well as the body. In the early eighties when power dressing with hefty shoulder pads, not to mention the and hair, were only beginning to threaten us, this was revolutionary. We had many successes when more traditional routes of healing had failed, but like the true source of new fashion, the street, we were never acknowledged for our pioneering work. You only hear about what the fashion scouts have picked up when it walks down the catwalks. Many doctors, healers and therapists came to see how we worked, were impressed, and went away to set up something similar. We would be there still, but there were more important lessons for those of us on a spiritual quest, and for these, something else had to happen.

While I designed and ran courses in psychosexual group dynamics, enlightenment intensives, open encounter, sharing my wisdom like a hollow bamboo, Sujan had his hands in the dirt, digging herbaceous borders and planting a different bamboo. He designed the garden and created a lake. Co-ordinating therapists is very different from co-ordinating gardeners. For a start, what would be their collective nouns – an enlightenment of therapists, a muddy earth of gardeners? And therein lay the difficulty.

I flew high and hung out in the lofty reaches of the hidden hierarchies you find in all communities, especially Marxist, feminist, socialist, spiritual and religious orders, where everyone is supposed to be equal. I was a channel for Bhagwan, dispensing wisdom, blimey I was practically enlightened myself after sharing a particularly deep and meaningful insight. Sujan meanwhile was on his knees digging up weeds, making compost, pruning roses. We swung between these increasingly disparate polarities. Those times when I was on the verge of enlightenment and going with the energy flow of a Tantric community, and all that entailed, Sujan would be storming the grounds in a black rage, until, unable to stand it any longer, would find some fun of his own. My turn to fall into the mud, smoke furiously, swig the brandy, beg Tarot readings from Jaya where I told her to keep the cards turning until one I liked turned up, not those swords in the heart. Jaya was a Tarot mistress, but whatever her Celtic respect for the cards, she had to do what I told her, because I ran the department and that was the way it worked. The chain of command was absolute from Bhagwan downwards. A particularly potent way to break down a stubborn ego if you were very keen, was to have a boss you didn't like and who didn't like you.

As those who live in deserts well know, soil can be worth more than what grows in it; but not many see it that way, and what is rooted in the earth often envies those who fly. And I was rather flying about in those days, especially when regurgitated Bhagwan dropped from my lips and I fondly imagined these pearls of wisdom to be my own. I flew even higher when I began to run groups all over Europe. But while gardeners may be jealous of stars, those with wings need grounding else they fly too close to the sun. At least when you are planting bulbs there's not much room for illusions that you are a guru yourself.

In every group room would be a large full colour picture of Bhagwan with soulful eyes ready to look with compassion and wisdom into anyone opening up their heart. And we were very keen on opening the heart and feeling vulnerable. The group participants that is, not, of course, the therapists. Particularly potent, after exercises with pillows representing parents and forty or more participants were weeping with deep sobs of grief and loss after having screamed out their primal rage, was to breathily speak into a microphone about opening the heart and surrendering to love. I was rather good at this because I also played cool music to back up the message. 'I wanna know what love is, I want you to show me' sang the Foreigners, as I suggested people opened their eyes and looked at the smiling picture of Bhagwan on the wall.

Many years later, full of the bonhomie that can come over you after a good night out, I chatted in the cab home with the Nigerian driver. He was street sharp and disconcertingly perceptive. He told me he thought I would be able to sell anything to anyone. 'You could even' he said shaking his head in disbelief 'sell religion!'

Periodically more instructions would arrive from central office now in Oregon. We were to do Gaachamis every morning and evening. This involved kneeling and bowing your forehead to the floor, chanting the three Buddhist vows to go to the feet of the Awakened One, his Commune and the Ultimate Truth. Like cooking, first you catch your chicken, then you kill it, then you cook and eat it; first you fall in love with the guru, then you fall in love with the commune, then you stagger through to the final fall into the Dhamma, the Law, the Tao, Life. And then people can fall at your feet and the whole thing goes round again. But we didn't read the small print telling us we would have to kill the Buddha first.

The instructions from Rajneeshpuram, referred to now as 'The Ranch', arrive piecemeal. All at once they would have been indigestible. The next one tells us we must be even more positive. Not only must we smile and sing under all difficulties when meeting a suspicious and often hostile public, such as our neighbours now they have found out who we are, we must now flash those shining smiling teeth relentlessly to each other as well. No more negativity, not even between consenting adults in private. With one exception – the plumbers and electricians, a natural aristocracy even in a vegetarian Tantric community. To keep them happy, they could moan as much as they wished over their beef sausages in the transport café down the road before they fixed that leaking tap.

Another difficult pill to swallow. All worshippers were to use allopathic medicine for their ailments, not alternative or complementary therapies. Odd, given our successes at the Healing Centre. But not so odd if you consider, rather than lingering in the slow lane back to health using more subtle techniques, the priority was to get back to work as fast as possible, to sidetrack your ego or make more money, depending on whether you looked through a disciple's eyes or more worldly ones.

During our second year in Medina, another one arrived. We were to point out any undermining negativity in each other by saying 'UDB', shorthand for 'un-divine behaviour'. Not only the plumbers and electricians had fun with that one. I remember 'unusual doggy bag', 'under my dead body' and 'up de bum', but in the worker's meeting when the announcement was read from a fax straight from the source, I was dying for a pee. To leave would reveal my unconscious un-divine resistance, so I held onto it. The longer we were in there, the more focused I became, not on the papal encyclical, but on my bladder.

Had someone really imagined this kind of thing would create a docile obedient workforce? Surely not? But this was just the surface dross of a much deeper process that infiltrated our lives more subtly, like water on the rocks of our rebellious egos that would one day wear them away.

As recovering alcoholics, self employed business men, women who love too much, and children of unhappy parents know all too well, it is possible to love someone or something so much, you suspend your natural self protective instincts and wander into a dark alley where you hope to find whatever you are seeking. But do any of us really know what we're doing, I mean *really*? I have been most blind when I have seen the light, and stride purposefully down that cul-de-sac, fondly imagining I'm walking towards the Promised Land. And in my case, I'm sorry to say, proclaiming the good news to others and telling them to follow me.

Many of us in the commune vaguely sensed another fault line cracking open, but were not aware of its implications. We were headed towards the light and it never occurred to us the light at the end of the tunnel might be the headlights of a train coming towards us. Bhagwan had after all appealed to intelligent rebels, who loved dancing and making love, not losers who couldn't make it in the world. Over half of us had degrees, most of us successful professionals, many with impeccable revolutionary credentials from other arenas. You couldn't be more intellectually right-on than my old lover Nigel, who was so intelligent he could actually explain why the mind is servant of reality not its master, yet even *he* now wore orange and lived at Medina as Bhajan. And we were definitely not anaemic tambourine bashers or bloodless meditators, pale from all that time in the dark. Though we did get up to a lot in the dark, it just wasn't meditation. There were moments during one of our parties, when it was blindingly obvious to us we were in fact the chosen few, an amazing tribe strutting the world's stage, sexier and funnier, as well as with more soul, than any bunch of people gathered together before.

Even next morning in the laundry, when you found your favourite pink cashmere sweater streaked with the purple of someone's sweatshirt, the glitter from the night before still sparkled. Schooling sharks, let alone herding cats, would be easier than training us to follow orders.

Yet there was common ground between even therapists, gardeners and plumbers – we had fallen in love with Bhagwan. He had spoken to our hearts and souls in such a way he had brought us, however reluctantly, to our knees and such a love cannot be argued with. He had a wisdom we had not encountered in western culture with its love affair with rational materialism. Our love affair with Bhagwan, where we played with the real life force and did not just fiddle with ideas about it, took us on adventures more cautious creatures would shy away from, maybe even sneer at. But we knew where it was really at; the instincts and energies of life are in the animal body not the intellectual mind. Plus we had also fallen in love with his commune. The parties helped.

Brilliant musicians as well as mean DJs. lived at Medina. Every Friday was a disco, every Saturday a party. Regularly we would decorate the vast main hall for a summer ball or a winter extravaganza and invite the sannyasins of Britain for a weekend of celebration, meditation, dancing and 'lurve'. There were actors, comedians, singers and dancers who had left their careers in the world and now put on shows for us. Musicals, revues, dance and theatre. Comedians had us in hysterics at their un-divine portrayal of life in our commune. The last dance of Romeo and Juliet, performed by Sujan and Jayananda at one of our Midsummer Balls, was a comedy classic still remembered, with its squashed flowers, streaked make-up, hairy legs in tutus, the competition to be the one the camera lingered on disguised as the romantic love dance of the century. There were days when it seemed we were living in one long continual party where you need never be invited, because we *were* the party. We were the A-list celebrities, so exactly where it was at and so utterly, chillingly cool, even hell held no more threat. And this was long after our instructions to find only spiritual ecstasy meant we had flushed all our weed, dope and coke down the toilets.

And all the while the love grew irresistibly between us.

There is a personal love that grows in face-to-face intimacy, vulnerable bellies exposed as we share secrets and make love. And there is an impersonal love that grows when you stand side by side, shoulder to shoulder, working together for a common goal, personal egos put aside in the service of this united vision. During those glittering nights of celebration and laughter, dangerous liaisons and dancing, sexual intrigues that would have delighted even the gilded mirrors and chandeliers of Versailles; during the times of reflection and meditation, where we would turn inwards and journey into the silence and emptiness between the stars, falling into the other world; during the daily routine of cooking, eating, caring for the children, the laundry, the shopping, the building, the cleaning, an energy field of love was being made. Even now if I meet anyone from that commune, there is still a love. I may not like them, they may even be an enemy, but there is an irrefutable energy field of love between us. And love is more powerful than liking.

Perhaps it's not so surprising in our hyper-connected universe, where sub-atomic particles are forever connected to every other particle they have encountered, even for a nano-second. Old warriors sit around and tell war stories, not to listen to the well-worn tales, but for the love there still exists in that comradeship. Yet we were comrades on the Tantric Path where love is a disembodied sentimentality without its dark twin and soul mate – hatred. An unhappiness too, was slowly depositing itself, layer upon layer, until one day it became a sandbank that would shipwreck us all.

I would like to tell you I was aware of this and spoke eloquently and compellingly of these things; that in the dialectic of our human predicament, caught between compassionate action and detached awareness, we necessarily suffer; that without the suffering we perform a different function, perhaps keep the food flowing into Tesco, organise the trains to run on time, teach children the lessons of history. I would prefer to have been wise then, already mysteriously knowing that an expert is someone who has made all the mistakes; that without the struggle, which in hindsight looks foolish, we cannot create the understanding that will release us from such foolishness. But I can't. Back then I was still getting here, and still had a long way to go.

But how to do we become wise if we are never foolish?

This was never going to be a simple tale where good triumphs over evil, sanity prevails and the light vanquishes the dark. If it were that simple, it would have been told long before, and we would not have to have lived it. It would already have been done.

Chapter 14

Us and the U.S.

Medina Rajneesh, or Herringswell Manor to the locals, thrived. In its second year, over two hundred adults and around twenty children lived there. The number swelled each weekend when hundreds of visitors came for the therapy groups, healing programmes, meditations, or just for a weekend's fun in the Buddhafield. The several thousand who pitched up for our regular psycho-spiritual raves slept in tents or vast dormitories in the ballrooms. Only the meditation room remained silent and empty. The income from successful businesses supported us financially – a building firm, a design studio, a printing press, a programme of residential workshops and trainings, a healing centre, a health and fitness studio in London where, alongside squash tournaments and aerobic classes, we ran meditations and encounter groups. From all this we made enough to send money to the grand project in Oregon too. Especially successful were our groups and trainings in re-birthing, bodywork, counselling, hypnotherapy, neo-Reichian massage, dance and psychodrama, where people were persuaded to become 'vulnerable, open and available' rather than 'defended, resistant and closed'. Beause the hidden agenda of much of Rajneesh Spiritual Therapy was to open your heart to Bhagwan.

Though when a Rajneesh Spiritual Therapist tells you to feel the pain in your heart and look at a picture of Bhagwan smiling down with compassion, then puts on 'Miracle of Love' by the Eurhythmics, it's not hidden, it's blatantly obvious.

This emotional manipulation only worked however, because there was a real healing going on too. The potent combination of western therapeutic techniques and eastern meditations, brought people back to life, opened their hearts, expanded their minds and the energy flowed so much they didn't mind our attempts to persuade them to our way of thinking. People flocked in their thousands to our groups, with or without the hidden added agenda, because they found insights, understandings and a new aliveness.

After releasing our sadness, anger, fear and need, we, the workers, then had to put such personal 'trips' aside. Like logs jammed in a river, these aspects of our ego apparently prevented our going with the flow of the Tao into the oceanic oneness of enlightenment – as well as interfering with the focus to make money for the Oregonian Buddhafield project. So we chained ourselves to a new obedience in order to liberate ourselves still further.

Whatever the commune above ground, quite a different one lives in the unconscious realms below. As well as the one that meets in the pub to tell tales of the other two. Yet the over-ground for us was the underground for most, and vice versa. In a mirror image of the culture and society we were escaping, we allowed rather than repressed, the psychosexual politics of our animal instinctual bodies, though we called it, 'following your energy'. We lived on £5 a week, not much scope for consumer greed there, and, when we weren't following it, we used renewable energy as much as we could and re-cycled our waste. We struggled to bring awareness to our working relationships as well as our intimate sexual ones. Yes, lots of fighting talk, but an awareness arises through such expression that is more usually buried in a quieter desperation. We gave the children a freedom to be themselves, without the intrusive colonising concerns of parents who meet their own emotional needs through the children they think are theirs. The whole community cared for these 'expressions of life's longing for itself', and if any child needed something, any one of us would respond. Even now Tim feels at home in crowds and enjoys working and hanging out in large communal spaces. And, of course, we danced, laughed and made love – above ground.

Underground went so much of what was considered 'normal' elsewhere – monogamy, nuclear families, traditional schooling, accumulation of possessions, insurance policies for the future, building gradually through routine and stability. Our denied, disowned and abandoned aspects, however, put aside in the service of the greater vision, did not just fade away. They went underground, where, unknown to us, they began to plot their guerrilla war against that vision. They were not logs after all, they were crocodiles.

However, in the sacred city of Medina in the early eighties, we were still living in the oblivion of the dream. Also, while the total number of British people out of work at the beginning of 1982 passed three million, we were working twelve to fourteen hours a day, with no days off.

There is a lot of money to be made in the business of spirituality, and I began to travel further afield to run groups in Holland, Italy, Paris, Germany, Sweden, Denmark and Norway. I had sold my house in Leeds, and had passed the cheque straight over to Andrew who ran Rumi, the accounts department. He discreetly put a chunk aside for me to draw on during my travels, as he had noticed my expenses included a maroon leather jacket from Hamburg, sheepskin boots for the Swedish winter, stylish luggage from Paris. 'But I needed them!' I'd exclaim when I brought back the receipts. He knew as well I did, a representative of Bhagwan had to have the gear and look the part. Besides, when Poonam was in London working in our Body Centre there, I ran Medina.

What I really loved were the gigs, I mean the groups. I would fly off to another commune and be met by their sexiest driver in their flashiest car, whizzed to a luxurious room with flowers, champagne and chocolate. And if the driver didn't do it for me, I could gaze around and take my pick of the gorgeous swamis eager to assist this glamorous hollow bamboo, Bhagwan's channel in Chanel. But I was not a temperamental star, more the sensitive type, radiating compassion and love. My particular speciality, ordinary special-ness, had its own cult following. Where else, other than a transcendentally interconnected Buddhafield, could a working class girl from Nottingham, with wiry red hair and freckles, become a goddess without being able to sing or play guitar?

It was that transcendentally interconnected energy field what did it. When two or more are gathered together in the name of a god, in our case Bhagwan, there the god is, a presence more than the sum of its parts. And there is a mystery in this phenomenon that we have yet to fathom. An energy field is geared up for miracles, seven 'impossible' things might happen before breakfast, or would that be more seven types of ambiguity, either way, we began to accept strange synchronicities and 'miraculous' events as normal. Though it helped that a group of people expecting miracles will see amazing phenomena, in a kind of self-fulfilling prophecy, whatever happens.

We were in Paris, forty French and me, in a circle, ready for the encounters between us to unfold. As you may know, the French tend to ignore you if you do not speak to them in their own beautiful language. I speak only vague bits of grammatically incorrect French learned in school a long time ago. I had an interpreter, but that wasn't good enough. A Gallic hostility hangs in the air; probably the same Caesar had to contend with and never quite conquered. There's none of the rapport between performer and audience that allows the energy field to build, so we can take off and fly. I wander out into Paris for lunch. This is going to be one of those dreadful times when the whole show bombs and we sit in the debris of a profound nothing while I die out there, my failure and inadequacy totally exposed. I drink a bottle of Chateau Montlabert with my condemned woman's last lunch, as who has a mind for the bill when you're about to die.

Back in the group room, I look around. Forty pairs of eyes look back at me with the flat steel of million year old sharks circling their next meal. This is it.

Suddenly I am speaking French! To their delight and my surprise, I dispense with the services of the translator, understand them perfectly and speak fluent French the whole weekend. We were off. They even understood my self-deprecating jokes, always useful in situations such as this so nearly turned out to be.

Had my desperation dug into the part of my brain that remembered my school French? Had that bottle of Chateau Montlabert divinely loosened my tongue? Or was this another miracle of the transcendentally interconnected Buddhafield?

Immediately the group ended, so did my French. I was back to stuttering and gestures when, after spending too long in farewells to those lovely *hommes Français*, I nearly missed my flight home. As Gandhi said 'the magic is in the situation, not me.' Like most royalty and people famous for hanging out round people famous for impersonating people famous for hanging out round famous people, however, every now and then I got the idea I was the source of the miracles. We may all lie in the gutter, and some of us look up at the stars, but a few of us fondly imagine we are stars. Having been a working class girl from Nottingham, kept me just enough on the ground not lose it completely as I could never quite get that Nottingham out of the system. My two millstones, Sujan and Tim, also helped keep me dangling somewhere in the region of planet Earth. Though it was a close call.

I was in Sweden. It was winter with a hard crunching snow on the ground, icicles and frozen lakes – hence the sheepskin boots I had to buy; though not, I have to admit, with all the embroidery. The group room was warm, the cushions soft, the carpet deep and welcoming. The lights had a rosy glow, perhaps from a local furniture shop where was gestating the first stirrings of IKEA. Yet despite our sitting so comfortably, very little was stirring in here. They had warmed their homes but not their hearts. I felt a compassion for the hard life of such long cold winters; surely human beings would always choose warm nights on a beach rather than these freezing months of darkness. Perhaps only those driven out of the hot spots end up here, a generational loss that still lived in their DNA. How to warm them so they can feel their frozen hearts?

Suddenly I am able to see pictures of each of them as children. I can see one struggling to bring some laughter into a sad house with an alcoholic father and depressed mother. I can see another running around in an anxious frenzy because his dog is lost and his father will not wait any longer, they must return home and the dog will die in the cold, or be eaten by wolves. I see another was born too soon, so tiny she had to live in a hospital far from home, she hardly saw her parents until she was three months old. I saw how their hearts had been frozen and then broken because water, when it freezes, expands.

There was nothing to do other than tell them my pictures and for them to share their stories, yet that was enough for the ice in their hearts to melt into the tears that released them. And me. I also was a familiar of the frozen wastes they inhabited. Though it takes a lot of love everywhere these days, to keep our hearts from freezing, and perhaps those Swedes can teach us more than interior design. As I write, Sweden is the only country in the western world to have none of the 702 Military Installations of the USA through 132 countries.

Back in Medina, our nearest town was Mildenhall, home to two of the vast American military airbases in the flat lands of East Anglia – Mildenhall and Lakenheath. While we were celebrating Bhagwan's birthday in December 1982 and our second year, over 30,000 women formed a human chain around Greenham Common airbase, the site of the 96 deadly Cruise Missiles housed in the UK. In our own private protest, a group of us old lefties, stuffed malas inside our sweaters and went on the tour offered to the locals by the American Airforce men of the Mildenhall airbase. We knew about the Lockheed SR71-A, the hi-tech American spy plane that flew so high it could not be seen or sensed by any radar yet was able to read newspaper print over anywhere in the world. The Americans denied its existence, but we had seen this giant 'Blackbird', as it flew overhead, taking off and landing with a deep rumbling roar that spoke ominously of the military might of the USA and its attempts to penetrate and police the world's secrets. This 'Blackbird' was as far as is possible from another blackbird, whose songs of love and freedom I had heard in a blue-bell wood, so many years before.

The tall, broad shouldered American airmen, over-shadowing, over-powering, over here, there and everywhere, could not imagine we were other than delighted with their magnanimous offers of gum to the natives. We listened attentively to begin with. Well into the tour we begin our questions. 'What about the Blackbird?' 'Why do you spy on your friends as well as your enemies?' 'How many Cruise Missiles are stored here?' 'What are your real targets?' 'Why does the USA support Israel's murder of innocent Palestinians in refugee camps?' 'Why has the USA supported, and in many cases facilitated, every right wing military dictatorship in the world since WW II, while lying to the world you are for freedom and democracy?' 'Why has the USA destroyed true democracy and freedom in Nicaragua, Brazil, Paraguay, Haiti, El Salvador, the Philippines, and Chile, where thousands have been tortured and killed, brutally oppressed, through the connivance, manipulation, money and military personnel of the US Armed Forces?'

Their smiles became fixed grins, and then fade. We are escorted from the property in silence.

Many years later it emerged, the Cruise Missiles were never at Greenham Common after all, they were down the road from us all the time.

Not long afterwards, so was George Bush. Snr, then the American Vice-president. He arrived in London for a visit to Britain. The Ranch fax us instructions. We are to stand outside the American Embassy with placards to welcome Bush to Britain and requesting the INS to give Bhagwan a religious visa. Chandan and I cannot do this. We first met at the 1970 Women's Liberation Conference in Oxford. We have both demonstrated in the same Grosvenor Square on anti-Vietnam War demos. There is no way we can welcome George Bush. I can't do it. I won't.

I don't. I am given something else to do. Mangala, of the blood-red fingernails, and I, are to find out where Bush is staying, infiltrate his hotel and speak with him about Bhagwan's visa. Why us? Because apparently Sheela thinks we have the panache and savoir-faire to pull it off. The only ones foolish enough to risk being shot by security and deported, more like. I forget this is not a Hollywood movie, I cannot be deported.

'These instructions have come from the highest level. I am not at liberty to say more, but', Sheela pauses for dramatic effect, though whether to threaten us or seduce us I'm not sure, 'the very highest.'

It seems we are all in a movie now.

Mangala and I look at each other. This must come from the main man himself. We'd better do it or kiss goodbye to any enlightenment this life-time. At least we can go in for some heavy-duty clothes shopping, paid for by the commune, before we are incarcerated without trial by the CIA.

We suss out the hotel, borrow a Mercedes, drive to the Churchill Hotel off Oxford Street and sit with cocktails in the bar. We look more like high-class working girls than psycho-spiritual terrorists. We discover Bush and his entourage have booked floors six and seven. We have more drinks, but if we are not going to stagger to complete humiliation, there's only so many cocktails can postpone the reckoning. We go into the lift and press '6'. The doors open. Shit! There are guys with guns at the doors to the lift! We move on up. In what may be our last moments of freedom, we hover between the tenth and eleventh floor wondering what the hell to do. But we are surrendered disciples of a Tantric Guru not jelly-livered conformist individuals afraid to die. We breathe deeply, and press the button for the seventh floor. The lift doors open. There is only one security guard and he's looking the other way! We streak out and round the corner and into a par-allel universe where the corridor is full of people walking the walk of people who know exactly what they are doing and how to do it, speaking into mobile phones before they've been invented.

'Excuse me, may I ask what you are doing here?' A suit is smiling at us. Possibly our lack of purpose and hardware gave us away.

'We're looking for Vice-president Bush', we smile back. The cocktails helped.

'Step this way', he smiles as he ushers us into a side room, his hand held out behind us as if to protect us from harm. The heaviest people in the world are so polite. He speaks rapidly into his phone, then smiles some more at us, 'Take a seat. Someone will be with us shortly.' He stands by the door, arms crossed in front of him, still smiling. It's going to be O.K. These guys are really friendly, not at all as we'd feared.

A tall man, in his early fifties, walks into the room. With the effortless charm of privilege and wearing clothes that cost more than whole towns spend on social security, he smiles. Neither Mangala nor I were prepared for either the whiteness of his teeth or the force and intensity that swept towards us. This smooth operator has cruised in and, before he has said a single word, wiped out every one of our defence mechanisms in one strike. This man is the most charming, sexy, seductive, mesmerising man we have ever met. And all that power is focused on the two of us. No way were we going to survive this encounter.

He introduces himself.

'I'm the vice president's Press Secretary. Now can you two ladies please tell me what you are doing here.' He smiles again. We melt. In any other country a man this powerful would be running the show, here he is helping the guy who helps the guy who runs the show.

'We're here to ask George Bush to grant Bhagwan Shree Rajneesh a visa.'

'And who is he, may I ask?' He smiles again.

'He is an Indian enlightened Master and we are his disciples. He now lives in the USA and needs a visa to remain there.'

'I see' he says. 'I'll look into it.'

We believe him completely.

'Oh and by the way, how did you get in here?'

We tell him. We want to tell him everything. About ourselves, our secrets, anything at all he wants to know. We are too weak to withstand his charm, and only just manage to rein ourselves in, to convince him this was all our own idea.

He escorts us with great courtesy to the lift, and with one more sun drenched smile, leans in and presses the ground floor button for us, his steel hand in such a soft velvet glove.

From that day on I have known the USA would conquer the world and make it their empire.

I was sworn to secrecy about this mission yet when I told Sujan, I discover he is involved in clandestine undercover activities of his own.

The INS in America were investigating the possibility of arranged marriages between Rajneeshies, as we were now called in the press, for visa purposes. An INS officer had arrived in London to meet an ex-sanyassin, Shiva, who had been Bhagwan's personal bodyguard in Pune. In his fury at what he felt was a betrayal of the dream; Shiva had written a book exposing what he saw as the corruption of Bhagwan and the ashram's political machinery. Sujan, and an accomplice, Nanda, were to go undercover, in an unmarked car, apart from the scratches no communally owned vehicle ever escapes, to stake out Shiva's joint, eat pastrami on rye and hope the INS guy made their day. They were to lie low until he came for the low down, from the low brow, low life Shiva, then radio in as soon as they got a visual, spit out their tooth picks, and under no circumstances lose sight of that I.N.S. guy.

They pick up his tail and follow him to his hotel. A while later, he takes a cab. Sujan and Nanda are right behind him all the way from

Knightsbridge to Marble Arch then the black cab swings into Oxford Street where only buses and cabs are allowed. Sujan has a few seconds to decide whether to follow the law or the Dhamma. Sujan chooses the Highway Code rather than the Tao, and loses his quarry as well as his Oscar nomination.

In an agony of remorse, Sujan drives back to Medina. He walks into the main office to confess his failure, both as a spy and a disciple, to find the INS guy drinking tea with Poonam. They were gossiping of gardening and green fingers, marriages and green cards.

We also applied for visas, Visitors Visas. Each year in July, the Buddhafields throughout the world, shut down and we flew to Rajneeshpuram for two weeks holiday and celebration. We arrived in Portland and were driven in fleets of buses up to the Ranch, past signs reading 'Better dead than red!'; and one erected by local Christians, telling us 'Abandon Hope all Ye who Enter Here!' But we weren't bothered. Anyway Bhagwan had already informed us he was going to destroy our hopes in order to deliver us from the tyranny of our dreams.

By the time seven thousand of us arrived for the first World Celebration in the summer of 1982, Rajneeshpuram, an overgrazed cattle ranch with a few rabbits, coyotes, juniper trees and one muddy river, had become a town. Bhagwan had said one of the greatest challenges facing humanity was to maintain ecological harmony and so we created sustainable energy resources, wind and solar power, built a dam and a lake, used new technologies for farming, hydroponics, compost toilets, reed bed systems for grey water. There were sixty acres of organic vegetables, a hundred bee-hives, vineyards, water supplies, sewage and recycling works, three thousand chickens, ducks and geese, and two emus to keep the coyotes at bay naturally. In the early eighties all this was revolutionary, yet more proof to us, we were streets ahead of the rest of the world still caught up in a dangerous frenzy of consumerist greed that could deplete the world's resources and destroy us all.

Roads and pavements wove between the Rajneesh International Meditation University, a complex of therapy rooms, a vast two acre meditation hall, Pythagoras, the medical centre and Jesus Grove, the heart of the machine where the head mommas plotted and planned the whole show. In a shopping Mall were book shops, cafes, juice-bars, stores selling jewellery, Tarot cards, crystals, pendulums and other esoteric equipment for presents to take home; boutiques with clothes in all shades of pink, orange, red, and purple; discos, hair and beauty salons that used only organic vegetable products. We lived in residential blocks, A-frames and mobile homes. There were the massive kitchens of Magdalena, which cooked and prepared the food for the thousands who arrived as well as those who lived there. There were canteens and restaurants, video and tape departments, accounts and legal departments, administration offices, building works, transport offices, a garage to maintain the fleet of cars and buses, including Bhagwan's Rolls Royces, an airport with two planes piloted by sannyasins. And still this city in the desert was growing.

I was proud to be a part of this transformation of a desert into a flourishing city that would show the world it was possible to create a community based on principles of love, freedom, respect for the environment, rather than violence, fear and greed. The children were cared for by the whole community, taught in a school free from repression and control, their intelligence respected not bullied. They were free to create their own relationships with a variety of adults, not just their parents. In the work we had a common goal, the construction of this city, which worked with the environment and did not just exploit it, a living community that was enquiring and genuinely caring for each other. We were exploring radically new ways of living and working together, including our sexuality as well as a spiritual consciousness. We not only had soul, we laughed, made love and danced – a heady mix. It was clear to us that we were, in fact, creating again the paradise from which humanity had been exiled for so long.

There were vague rumblings in the distance, thunder from a different climate, such as the announcement we were to have nothing more to do with Somendra, who had apparently got ideas above his station and was touting his own form of enlightenment. If we saw him we were to literally turn our backs. Odd, but like faint thunder long after the lightening, these storms were so far away I could hardly hear them. Where I lived the sun still shone in a cloudless sky. I loved this dream, and this dream loved me.

During the World Celebrations, we lay around in sunhats, ate Soya bacon sandwiches, swam in Krishnamurthi Lake and gossiped with old friends and new. Bhagwan had, after all, told us only those who gossip can be truly silent. In between shopping in the Mall, drinking in a bar, we danced in one of the discos to Prince and Michael Jackson, thrilled to be cool international lovers. But the soul of it all was Bhagwan.

Each day thousands of us would sit in silence in the vast Rajneesh Mandir Hall until Bhagwan arrived, driven in one of his Rolls Royces. He sat on a podium smiling down at us in his bright robes, a startling flash of turquoise and green, or blue, yellow and silver, or dark black and gold, amongst the thousands shades of orange, going on pink, purple, red, magenta, crimson, damson, puce, cerise... While he smiled, we chanted the three Buddhist vows, bowing down in succession to our Tantric Buddha, our own Sangha, and the Dhamma of all life. The ancient Sanskrit reverberated around the hall and faded into the distance. Then was complete silence. Just the sounds of crickets, birds and the wind rustling in Juniper trees. The only movement in this stark stillness was the rhythmic rise and fall of our breath as we communed with the silence lying under all things. An hour later the note of a flute sounded through the hall and music began, for the celebratory singing, dancing, and all the ecstatic abandonment you could wish for. At least on my first visit. Future visits I had to work.

A team of us gave individual sessions in A-frames dotted about one of the valleys. People booked a session and took pot luck who they would find when they arrived at the designated A-frame. My speciality was relationships. I know of only three other couples, apart from me and Sujan, who entered into the commune together, and, years later, left together – though a lot happened to all of us in between. So while other therapists were giving the party line on intimate sexual relationships, 'the blind leading the blind', 'millstones round your neck', 'co-dependency disguised as love', I knew that what happens with the one you love and who loves you, can teach you more than any therapist could, even a 'spiritual' one, excepting of course the Master himself. As a consequence, I had my own cult following within the cult.

There were compensations for this busman's holiday. I was given a seat up front in one of the darshans. On the first row, which was good, but pretty far to the side, not so good. Did this mean I was getting closer yet only to a B-list enlightenment? Though by now I had worked out the pragmatic matriarchs of Jesus Grove ordered the seating, which meant that other considerations were involved than merely how our consciousness was evolving; like how much money we had. Though how were we now to work out our ratings in the enlightenment charts, who to schmooze and who to turn our backs to? No problem. Bhagwan declared twenty-one people enlightened. Their names were read out before one of the darshans during a July celebration.

One of the elect lived in London. I knew he was nursing a broken heart and had understandably not come over for the celebration. It's not much fun being devastated when all around you are celebrating like fury.

Though I didn't reckon much to the information, even when enlightened you could be depressed and broken hearted. The whole point was when you finally got there, you stepped off the wheel of karma and strolled nonchalantly through life with no more existential anxiety. Wasn't it?

I was sent to inform Deevesh of his promotion to the Premier League carrying with me a signed certificate from the Master himself. I supposed you hung it next to your other diplomas, MBAs, swimming certificates, etc, though, of course, in a golden frame. I called him up and arranged to see him on my way through London.

In the comfort of his beautiful home we had dinner and he pulled out a couple of bottles of wine from the vineyard he owned in France.

'I've been saving these for a special occasion' he told me. 'Breaking free from the wheel of karma is special enough, don't you think?'

I agreed there could be no more splendid occasion to crack open a few choice bottles from his cellar. No resistance from me here.

It was the same wine that had loosened my tongue in Paris, Chateau Montlabert. But a special vintage. He poured the rich red wine into antique crystal glasses, and told me to sniff it, whirl it round, sip it, and notice the taste from the front of my mouth through to the back of my throat. I know very little about wine except that I like it, but this was not fermented grape juice, it was ambrosial nectar. I have never before or since tasted anything quite like it. He told me how much these bottles would have been likely to go for, auctioned on the open market. I won't repeat it as I don't want my laptop to blow its Intel processor. However, I can reveal we had a magnificent celebration and spent the evening amongst the gods on Mount Olympus. I too, for one glorious evening, entered their ranks, and tottered about enlightened, with not a karmic stagger in sight. It's not the taste of those ambrosial wines you pay for; it's where they take you.

Bhagwan had gone into silence when he left India and no longer gave personal darshans or spoke in discourse. He explained he had said all he wanted to and had prepared us through his words to receive his deeper message, which could only be communicated in silence. I was surprised therefore when one July Celebration on the Ranch, I was given a message, I must tell no one but was to be in a certain place at a certain time, freshly bathed and no perfume, because I was to be taken to see Bhagwan.

Six of us climbed into a limousine and were driven across a bridge over a lake with black swans on one side, white on the other, a symbol of Bhagwan's Tantric wisdom beyond the duality of good and evil. We were stopped at two large gates by sannyasin guards with Uzi sub-machine guns, though I don't know what they symbolised – 'don't fuck with me'?

In the time-honoured ritual of suspicious borders between countries everywhere, they leaned in, spoke to the driver and peered into the back of the car. We were waved through and into the grounds of Bhagwan's house. We de-limousined and were ushered, single file, into a cool room with no windows.

We sat in a silent row on the marble floor until Bhagwan arrived, wearing, perhaps it was a bling thing, the largest diamond encrusted Rolex I have ever seen. He namastéd us with a smile, sat down elegantly and gave a rambling talk about the minerals and gold underneath the rock on which the commune was built. I assumed this was a metaphor for inner riches, until he began to talk about the actual drilling. He then gave each of us a hat and a zap on the third eye.

'There is something strange going on here', I tell Sujan later that evening, when I tell him all. 'Those guns are weird.'

The Uzi sub-machine guns began to appear elsewhere around the ranch – at the entrance to the Ranch, in Buddha Hall, in the car that drove behind Bhagwan on his daily drives. Apparently these were to inform 'the enemy' we were not 'chicken shit liberals' but willing to defend ourselves. The Christian Right and local residents were after all increasingly vehement and vitriolic in their attacks on us. And once there was even a bomb in a hotel we owned in Portland.

Another weirdness involved several hundred street people bussed into the Ranch from American cities. No one was coerced, just invited for food and accommodation, but once at the Ranch it seemed they too had to conform to the relentless positivity of no negativity. It seemed to me one thing for us disciples to suffer for the greater cause, but quite another to make others go in for this ego dissolving, psycho-spiritual makeover when they had signed up only for free meals and a warm bed.

I was on a visit to the Ranch at the time, whether to polish up my Rajneesh Therapy skills or because it had been noticed I needed more training in egoless-ness, I don't know, ours not to question, and I was at the meeting where Sheela explained the sudden arrival of several thousand street people. Each of us listening could pick and mix the explanations we could most easily digest. The one I went for was that living in a Buddhafield was a gift to these people, who may be on the streets precisely because they had soul in a soul-less society. To be here was their karmic destiny and unconscious longing for a spiritual home. I remembered my work with psychiatric patients, and my frustration that the deeper meaning of their situation was never addressed. Once again the Buddhafield was doing what I had longed for.

One consideration not mentioned was a local election, where our planning permission might be refused unless we could amass sufficient numbers of resident Americans to vote. Local residents and Wasco County Hall did not quite see this city of the future, where all beings would live in harmony with each other and nature, in the same light we did. What to us was a Buddhafield, to them was 'The Big Muddy Ranch' zoned for agricultural purposes only. The beginning of many long and complex legal battles. Not being one of the high powered sanyassin lawyers brought in to construct intricate legal arguments to do with water regulations, cattle farming, residential zoning and incorporation of Rajneeshpuram as a town, these machinations were distant thunder to me. Storm clouds were massing on a much closer horizon.

At the beginning of 1982 I had gone to Hamburg to run a workshop. A group of us had partied in a gay bar on the waterfront and there I first heard of a mysterious set of symptoms from an unknown disease identified in California. Just a few weeks later it was formally recognised by the US Centre for Disease Control. AIDS had arrived.

There was a snake in our Eden after all.

Chapter 15

Hearts of Darkness

A Tantric community clearly has to find ways to deal with any disease spread by sexual contact. We had three doctors at Medina to prescribe appropriate antibiotics so this had not been a problem. HIV was different. At first we did not realise how deadly it was and simply arranged for everyone living at Medina to be tested. Other communes did the same. Once tested and found negative, for once a 'good thing', you wore a special bead. From then on you could only make love with others of the same bead. If you followed your energy elsewhere, you gave your bead back until, three months of celibacy later, you were tested again. It had to be something extremely strong to tempt you away from that bead.

Then Bhagwan announced, AIDS was so dangerous, it would decimate the world's population. We had to take stringent precautions to ensure no bodily fluids of any kind were exchanged during sexual contact. Kissing and oral sex were out. Sexual intercourse without condoms was forbidden, even between monogamous couples of many years, if any such creatures existed. I didn't know of any. Touching genitals must take place only when wearing surgical rubber gloves. Every visitor to any Rajneesh commune, even if only for a weekend group, must have an AIDS test. Condoms and rubber gloves were to be provided in every dormitory. Anyone found to have a positive result would no longer mix freely with the rest of the commune but live separately in luxurious accommodation, their every need catered for.

Fortunately there were no positive results in Medina. In a few of the communes in Germany and the Ranch, there were those who went to live in isolated splendour. Perhaps to die. AIDS was a death sentence back then.

Though not so desolate or prolonged, I was about to find myself in an isolated splendour of my own.

Sannyasins in Kenya had written to Bhagwan to request he send them a Spiritual Therapist who would run some groups and meditations. I 'got the message' I was to go, packed my bag and said good-bye once more to Sujan, Tim and John. John had recently returned from California and now also lived at Medina. His computer skills had been put to use earning money and each day he went out to work in a nearby city, Bury St Edmunds, with all the office politics that involved, and none of the benefits. His salary went straight into the commune's coffers and he was given back £5 each week. Though the kitchen made him and the other 'out-worshippers' sandwiches for lunch. At least during my African adventure, Tim would have John around. As well as Sujan and his three surrogate parents.

As Medina grew the younger children, particularly, became bewildered at how to flow through this Tao and find what they needed. They had each drawn up a list of three people apart from their parents, who they could call on at any time. Tim had his family within the family to read him stories, tuck him in bed, be with him, and hold him. Though not perhaps the one he wanted most.

I arrived in Nairobi late one afternoon in May. It was hot and dry, bone dry, drought dry. But in African heat, sweat evaporates, which keeps you from knowing how hot it really is. As it turned out, it was fortunate I could keep my cool.

I was met by Hamid, who insisted he carry my bag in one arm, while he held out the other to clear my passage, open all doors and, it seemed, to protect me. When I walked through he bowed each time, not just a nod, a bend from the waist. I thought I heard him also murmur his gratitude. I tried to help with the awkward manoeuvres of holding doors and suitcases while bowing and keeping the way clear, but he was horrified. It seems I must do nothing myself. I decided he was an old fashioned Indian gentleman.

Hamid tells me his family come from Bombay, and that he is now, 'thank Bhagwan', very successful in the import-export business in Kenya. 'My family are all disciples of Rajneesh, and have been since soon after he moved to Bombay. Since 1971, Rajneesh is our family's guru', he told me proudly, as he opened and bowed me through the final set of doors.

We emerged into bright sun. For two seconds its equatorial heat hit me hard between the eyes while Hamid's driver leaped out the limousine parked by the kerb and opened the door for me. I slid gratefully onto the cool cream leather of air-conditioned luxury. Hamid switched from gentleman to boss, giving orders as abruptly as he had been solicitous. The driver was Kenyan, wiry and electric. I could imagine him in the import-export business himself, his lop-sided smile would suit a shifter of dodgy contraband through illegal borders more than it did serving Hamid as a driver in a cap and uniform.

We drove along the road that leads from so many international airports, a motorway lined with swaying palms and boards advertising hotels and car hire. We were soon in the city of Nairobi with its tall office buildings, multi-national logos, white marble steps leading through wide courtyards with fountains, up to glass doors and the uniformed doormen of hotels and headquarters of trans-national corporations all over the world. In their smart livery, I see them open doors of black shiny limousines, to men in suits, who stride into the building, doors opened for them all the way through to whatever air conditioned meeting is their destination. I see too the police who stand in pairs and look around them with a casual indifference, which they can afford because they have guns.

Only on the pavements are there signs I am in Africa, not Europe or America. Everywhere women and men wore startling dramatic patterns in exuberant primary colours. The bright greens, yellows, reds and blues, with unmistakeably African designs of leaves, birds, animals, nature's shapes, woven into patterns, wrapped under and over and round each other, mirroring the manoeuvres of the crowds. Large wrapped bundles of merchandise bob up and down, on the heads of even children, a colourful surf on the sea of humanity that flows through the towering glass and stone buildings. In between the unmoving shrines of international wealth, are market stalls, Coca Cola signs, and mangy skinny ribbed dogs. Children chase each other, playing with sticks and shouting. Women stand, babies on hips, bundles on their heads, flashing bright white teeth in timeless gossip. Men lie asleep in patches of shade, waiting for a dusty bus to arrive, sometime. Everywhere the bright material stamped with shamanic talismans of Africa.

I can see the laughter and gossip in the flashing white teeth and eyes, but in our air conditioned bubble as we swish through down town Nairobi, I can hear and smell nothing of Africa. Hamid is telling me they have a party arranged to celebrate my arrival.

'I hope you are feeling hungry' he says, 'there is a lot of food being made.'

'I am', I reply, graciously assuming the royal role he has arranged for me.

We reach the suburbs. The wide tree-lined streets are empty, apart from an occasional sighting of another black shiny limousine. There are no skinny dogs and market stalls here, proof of the wealth behind these high walls and metal security gates.

We arrive to gates that open automatically, and crunch over the gravel to the front door, opened, before the car stops, by servants dressed in black and white. I repress the impulse to open the car myself, and wait until the driver opens it for me with another bow. Hamid gestures towards the front door.

'Welcome to my house. May your stay here bring us many blessings.' He bows deeply again and smiles. I smile. The servants smile. We all smile. And I realise they are waiting for me to enter the house first. We enter a large hall with a curved staircase, everywhere is marble, glistening brass and crystal. Gathered to greet me under the chandeliers, are about thirty Indian disciples of Bhagwan, in saris and suits of all shades of orange. I bring my hands together and bow slightly, as I namasté them in greeting. They namasté me, not with slight bows, but deep bends from the waist. Some go down on their knees. Some fall onto the floor prostrate. Some emerge from the throng and throw themselves at my feet and kiss my Clarke's sandals. I hope my feet are not too dirty and sweaty from the journey for their sakes. But I suppose a princess does not bother herself with such things. I then discover I am not royalty.

I had thought they were saying 'Bless me!' as they fell at my feet, as in 'Bless me, what is the Master doing sending someone with red hair and freckles to the equator!' But no, they mean. 'Bless me!' as in the guru blessing the disciple. It dawns on me that because Bhagwan has sent me as his representative, I *am* the guru.

My heart sinks. I touch them on the head, the blessings of the Master flow into them. They are happy. A rustle of women show me my room and offer to help me unpack. I ask for a few minutes alone. They completely understand I need to meditate. They namasté, smile and withdraw backwards out of the room. If there is anything I am needing? I must simply please ask. They reverently close the door.

I fall back onto the vast bed, surrounded by more marble, brass and crystal. So far, I have only played at being enlightened, dispensing wisdom with a serene smile, tossing my head as a flowing medium. All my friends know full well, I am insecure, need constant reassurance and am attached like crazy to Sujan and Tim. If enlightened I would be free from all of these, as well as no more gossiping, neurotic Tarot readings or witty remarks that stab at existence rather than gracefully accepting it. Here I must play it for real. I cannot disappoint them.

The next weeks are a blur. I run meditations, an Enlightenment Intensive, Vipassana, Zazen. I give discourses, interpretations of sutras, answer questions, and offer guidance. I give talks, darshans, and individual sessions. All the sannyasins in Kenya come to sit at my feet and absorb my wisdom, bathe in the energy of the Master coming through me. I have everything I could possibly wish for, delicious food, drink, whatever I want cooked for me, a swimming pool, Jacuzzi and sauna, all in the comfort and luxury of this beautiful home. There is always someone offering me a gift, a drink, a massage, to check if I have everything I need. I am never alone.

And I have never been so lonely in my life.

Many years later, when our dreams had become our nightmares and Rajneeshpuram had disintegrated so catastrophically, I could understand the terrible loneliness of Bhagwan, Osho as he was then called. His old friends, such as Laxmi, had gone, manoeuvred out by Sheela, or had left because the dream had shattered and they were in the process of killing the Buddha in order to come home to themselves. The best of his crop of disciples had left him, as planned, and he now had around him only those who hadn't surfed the wave, who had held tight to their boards, perhaps thinking the board was the thing, not the ocean. Every country he tried to visit refused him entry and he had returned to the ashram in Pune. Then his partner, Vivek, committed suicide. She presumably killed herself because she was in unbearable pain, though this is never talked about. Her suicide is seen as a personal aberration, she was manic-depressive, ill. There is no enquiry beyond that, into how our collective dream had made her so unhappy. The commune betrayed her too. Just as it did Osho. Just as it did us. Yet we were the commune. We had betrayed ourselves.

I think by the time she died, Vivek alone was carrying the full burden of Osho's humanity. Everyone around him, in all directions as far as the eye could see, thought him a god. By that time, those of us who had worked out Osho was a man, with all the shadowy dark turbulence that involves, were deep in our own dark turbulence. We were angry at the sense of betrayal all devotees feel when their god reveals himself to have been like them all along, a human being with the same frailties and failings. There was no one left close to him, who knew him as a man, who fought and argued with him, lounged around and watched videos with him, laughed in irreverent disrespect. Except for Vivek. Perhaps this profound isolation is what led her to kill herself. And perhaps the same terrible loneliness led Osho to do the same.

At the time Osho and Vivek died, I was living in north London with not an orange robe or mala in sight. By then, I had abandoned that dream and begun another, so it is hard to know what exactly happened, but reading between the lies that lie between the lines, perhaps Osho asked one of his close disciples to give him a lethal injection. Perhaps the same that had been rumoured as lying around for years ever since Rajneeshpuram, part of a secret agreement with those so surrendered they would do whatever Bhagwan asked, including poisoning him. Which is why, the story goes, one of the mommas was lined up at a festival darshan with a lethal injection to stab anyone who, given the sign, was ready to leap forward with their lethal injection to kill Bhagwan. Not being party to these pharmaceutical plots I do not know if there was another syringe full of more poison waiting to plunge into the momma's arm should she lunge towards the devotee if they lunged towards Bhagwan. Busy blissing out en-masse in a celebratory ecstasy, we, the ordinary disciples, had absolutely no idea there had been this lethal line-up in our midst. Those who loved him as god, and so would do anything he asked, even kill him, against those who loved him as a man and would do anything to save his life, even kill.

There was certainly one celebration when Bhagwan threatened to abandon the project to create a field of Buddha's, and would 'leave his body' during the celebration darshan if he sensed his disciples were not up to scratch. We were all warned during that celebration to be even more relentlessly positive than ever, as Bhagwan's connection with the body was increasingly tenuous. But we surpassed all previous ecstasies and kept the Buddha in his body a while longer. Though this is why he had to have 93 Rolls Royces. They were ballast to keep him on the ground of this Earth, as well being something to challenge the hypocrisy of religions that preach poverty while being the richest institutions on the planet. Also, these gifts from devoted disciples were the manifestation in form of our love being given back to him in return for the inner riches flowing from him to us – and to blow our minds that confuse spirituality with a body-less anaemic piety. As I've mentioned, you could pick 'n' mix whichever explanations you preferred.

However, at the time when I was furiously channelling him in Nairobi, our guru was very much alive. Killing the Buddha was something Zen monks did if they happened to meet him on the road – like cutting off their eyelids to stay awake for meditation, running at people with swords and wearing shoes on their heads – but only as an esoteric teaching and not for real. Furthermore, our Bhagwan was living like a freshwater fish in the salty water of the West.

In the East, a guru is an integral part of the community. He holds an enlightened wisdom not possible for those struggling with survival, bringing up children, the machinations of business, the work of farming, and so on. The guru's enlightenment is not his alone; it belongs to, and is in service of, the community. And anyway, you become a guru because it is your fate, your karma, not because you want it for the psycho-spiritual status or the jewellery. Just as one person's destiny is to become a farmer, another a soldier, so another's karma is to be a guru. And all work together for the whole, which lies in the community, the tribe, the family, not within the individual.

In the West, however, in our time, we play many parts, and it is not society that contains the whole, but the great 'I' with its community of inner selves. And we western disciples were going to get enlightened in the same way we could win friends, influence people and get to the Moon – through our own efforts. We were just going to 'do it'. And with the god of that 'I' on our side, a ruthless naked individualistic ambition in the service of a spiritual materialism, we couldn't fail. There are many gods in the East, but only one in the West – that magnificent 'I'.

So when the wicked will of the West meets the surrendered psyche of the East, there are profound misunderstandings on both sides, to say the least.

The loneliness of a guru in the West is absolute. There is no one who speaks his language. No one to see the common humanity between the guru and his disciples. No one to be a friend and meet his simple human needs and frailties. There is no community to serve, just wilful individuals who want what he has, and will kill him to get it. How lonely is that?

As the rapper C-Murder said 'Fuck the celebrity shit, I like the chill in the hood. I wasn't born in a White House, know what I'm saying?' This guru too was not born in a white house. Bhagwan was born into rural poverty in a basic hut in a small village. Of course there is the dark side of guru-hood too. While the guru carries the light for the community, the community carries the darkness for the guru. The community with its survival struggles, power battles, accumulation of money and possessions, supports the guru; in return the guru provides the silence and peace of serenity and wisdom. Together they make a whole.

A guru adrift from his natural Sangha, as was Bhagwan in America, begins to embody the darkness of the world because there is no one near him to do it for him. We western disciples certainly wouldn't. In pursuit of our enlightenment, we would have nothing to do with all that worldly stuff.

During one celebration, there was a raffle for one of Bhagwan's Rolls Royces. The sanyassin with the winning ticket approached the stage to receive his prize from Sheela, and promptly gave the Rolls Royce back to Bhagwan. We all cheered because we each would have done exactly the same. What did we need a Rolls Royce for? We were headed for the stars, not Wall Street.

Perhaps a profound loneliness is what killed this Buddha. And we did it by simply being the most devoted of disciples.

Meanwhile, surrounded by African splendour, I too was a fish out of water, lost in a role not written for my western psyche, with its different enlightenment – and after weeks in the loneliness of the long-distance guru, I too lost myself. I drifted through the days, serene, wise, and calm. I smile graciously, a source of benediction to all who come into my presence. Many of my everyday confusions and fears have faded. Tim and Sujan are in my heart but as memories from another life. I am a detached awareness. I am a source of unconditional love. There is a fragrance around me of an unworldly light. But I am not me.

A western sanyassin turns up out of the blue, from where he has been living somewhere out in the bush. I nearly fall at his feet, but locked up as the guru I cannot disappoint these caring and kind people who care for me so assiduously. He asks if I would like to go on Safari with him. Like it! I would love it. To run from this enlightenment into the wilderness of the bush. To put on loud music, fling my arms wide and dance dirty. To mess up my hair. To laugh and make fun of each other. To be as neurotic as I wish. To stamp on the muddy Earth, more heavenly than any heaven.

He arrives a few days later to pick me up in his jeep. A smiling band of devotees namaste me off. Maybe they are as relieved as I am. Perhaps as soon as we are round the corner they too will be delighted to fall back into squabbling loudly, screaming insults, arguing over whose turn it is to wash up – thoroughly enjoying all that fighting talk, abdicating responsibility, and blaming each other that is such a relief after consciousness raising of any kind.

As we drive towards the Kenyan Safari Park, we leave the city behind, but not yet civilization. A brand new road cuts through the landscape, its tarmac-ed perfection ending abruptly in the dirt roads that lead off it. A car drives by, flashing lights. This warns us the President is soon to drive by. We must stop, get out the car and turn and face away from the road. This important man must not be looked at by anyone. Cars pull over and people stand, heads bowed, and their backs to the road. Why do I find this more shocking than a curtsey to a highness? Perhaps because to see and be seen is the essential foundation of all community, even a cat can look at a king. Not here.

But then you are never alone in the bush. There is always an eye on you, an animal, bird, reptile or insect, observing you in its own way. The plants too. Leaves of trees, the grasses, the tendrils of plants, the roots of what grows in this blood red earth, all vibrate as they register your presence. And take its measure. There is nothing too small to escape the notice of this vast natural awareness. As I stood on the edge of this wide open plain, which had appeared profoundly empty, I suddenly felt more exposed than I have ever felt in a city surrounded by thousands. The air was dense with a sudden silence. Even the chirruping and clicks of beetles and crickets had stopped as two humans appeared and stared into the distance, their backs to the road. The island of majesty that is the President sweeps by. We climb back into the jeep and drive off just as the creatures of the bush, no doubt, begin to rustle and move again as we disappear.

Where I come from you are someone only when you are seen. Here, not to be seen is what marks you out as a somebody. I wondered to Wajid, which is more lonely – not to be seen because you are someone, or to be seen because you are no one? He just told me he'd rather see than be seen any day and pointed out distant zebra.

The dictates of the city gradually gave way to the disorder of villages. Battered rusty trucks parked at all angles in the shade of four thorn trees around a single old petrol pump. Chickens pecked in and out of houses. A straggling village of huts, mud-baked bricks topped with straw and a few official corrugated tin-roofed buildings of concrete, belonging to the church, the government or the railway, are scattered along the road. Wealth is now measured not in liveried servants, limousines and stock options, but in goats, cattle and sons. Laid out in front of huts, at various stages of being washed and dried, are the only things people in every culture possess, clothes, cooking utensils and blankets. We are in territory where even a ladder is a precious possession owned not by one person, but by the village. A place where you lose everything unless you work hard to keep it.

We leave behind the yards bright with purple bougainvilleas, pawpaws, melons and pumpkins; where cattle gaze over fences, before they amble off to tug at the sparse tufts of hard grass near a muddy creek; where bars with broken plastic chairs sell maize beer under Coca Cola signs; where packs of skinny dogs strike my western heart with their gaunt bony bodies and stark ribs, where sitting in the shade of the lean-to verandas, people enjoy a vacant eternity we seem to have lost.

Wajid and I drive into the Park and into territory where you can walk all day and get nowhere. Acacia trees, their great white thorns sharp against the sky, their small grey leaves, favourite food of giraffes, fringe the wide edges of the plain. Dirt roads. Blood-red earth. Scrub bush. The singing emptiness of the plain, with patches of bare ground so hard and dry nothing grows, until the rains. The blue shimmer of distant hills. Skies where if you look too long into them, you lose your soul. This Africa is bigger than any of us.

We drive off the main dust road onto a narrow track that suddenly broadens out into a clearing. There is a permanent water hole nearby that many animals drink from. Wajid grabs my arm, and gestures me to be silent, not to move. I look to where he indicates with a slight nod of his head, and above the fringes of the grass and brush, see the back of large animal, moving restlessly to and fro. The grass thins at one point and suddenly we could see this back belongs to an enormous lion. The hair on his huge body is shiny with vigour and threat. He is so close we can smell his sharp pungent sweat and raw-breath. He is aware of us, can smell our human-ness. For a timeless moment we three meet in the stillness. Then the king turns between the long blades of elephant and buffalo grass and stalks off into the bush to find another shade to sleep through the heat of the day undisturbed.

We drove on into the sudden rush of green crowding round a water hole. Hoopoes, louries and tiny birds sang from the tops of thorn trees. I saw a hippopotamus yawn and looked into his untamed mouth ready to swallow a world. I saw the smooth glide of an alligator, then her wait, as sudden and still as death. I heard the piping of water birds, the chorus of frogs, the thrilling of crickets, an orchestra, whose swamp music no one hears in its raw purity, because the sounds change in the presence of a human. Further away, on the desert edge, was the faint laughter of hyenas. Wajid told me the Masai and Kalahari tribes predict the future through these sounds of wilderness. Several years before WW2 they had tried to warn everyone, the birdsong had changed and told of a dreadful catastrophe about to engulf the world. Though no one listened.

We drove on. Past dried river beds and shallow hollows fringed by tall, brown, burned out reeds, that only spring to life when the rains come. On the far rim of the plain was a tumult of dunes, covered with bush and thorn trees. The heat lifted the line of bush on the horizon and it became

205

a wavering line suspended in the sky. Wajid told me the horizon was not the few hours away it appeared, it would take two days to walk there. The red earth was scarlet now. A blood-crimson, as red as my sanyassin clothes and then redder. In the distance we saw herds of zebras, antelope, wildebeest. Above us, the greatest hunters in the skies of Africa, vultures with wingspans wider than a house, circle and glide, their huge wings outstretched. We saw a lone rhinoceros swing his bulk slowly round towards the green of another water hole. The most dangerous animal in the park, Wajid told me, they kill more people than any other mammal. But what is dangerous for us is a friend to others; through binoculars I saw small birds riding on its back.

Wajid tells me how to see the animals; you don't look, but gaze vacantly, and let the wildlife find you. This way I spy a rare lone elephant far away, moving on a quest only he knows. Sometimes we stop the jeep and wait. Giraffe arrive. Having never been hunted by humans, at least for several generations, they have no fear of us and come close. One tall elegant sister bends down and looks directly into my eyes. This animal is wild, untamed, belongs only to herself, yet in her eyes there is no one there, just the naked curiosity of her freedom. Our two freedoms look into each other. Life gazed timelessly into life. What she saw I will never know but as I met the gaze of this unafraid wild animal, I saw into the Soul of the Earth.

Bhagwan had often said the day would come when we would find ourselves hanging over the void, with only our connection with him to support us, held over the abyss by the thread of love between the disciple and the master, symbolised by the mala. Then one day we would realise – there is no thread. There is no holding. There is no one there. There never has been. And we fall into the void. *Dhammam Sharanam Gaachami*. We fall into the life we came from and into which we will return. The life we had to lose in order to find it again differently. I saw the same empty presence in the giraffe's eyes that I had seen in the eyes of my Master. I had not realised until that moment that when you fall in love with a Tantric Guru, you fall straight to the feet of life itself.

There is a home that can be found only far from home and in the red-streaked dawn, with the dew of the night on spiders webs hanging from elephant grass and thorn trees, and the soft rustling of the bush all around, every sound is from a world I do not know yet belong to. It is thought the first humans came into life and were born on the dry and dusty plains of Kenya. Adam and Eve were perhaps in this very same landscape when, millions of years ago, our first parents had gazed at a new strangeness in each other. We are all out of this Africa. Yet this Eden too has its snake. Many snakes.

We drove by a sparkling black mamba hanging by its tail from a branch. A saffron-yellow cobra sat upright in the dirt road, its hood erect, then suddenly fell inert, a coil of rope, before it wriggled away into the bush. As our jeep startled them, black cobras with white rings round their throat, spat poison on the run. Emerald tree snakes hung from thorn trees. Adders lay still, coiled bracelets in the yellow grass, waiting as only a snake can – forever. And once we saw a python, the shape of his last meal in its slow-moving, lumpy body.

Wajid and I lost ourselves in the bush for several days. Though I suspect only I was lost, he had maps and knew where we were all the time. And during that time the singing plains of Africa showed me the greatest story ever told is written in our bones and, when we learn how to listen, we can hear it in the singing in our own ears.

I returned to Nairobi with a different darkness in my heart – the darkness of Africa, where nights in the bush are so black, a star can blind you. The darkness of beneath the earth and within the womb, without which, nothing would give birth to nothing. The darkness of the interior of that Dark Continent, our body, which is the source of all we know. Even the light of our reason is born from the sensations that arise in the dark instincts of our animal body. All our hearts are of this darkness. Like so many western white people before me, Africa had changed me forever.

The beauty of that wild darkness was the perfect antidote to the beastliness of my enlightenment, and my last days in Nairobi were full of laughter. We fell naturally into our common humanity and I left Hamid and his family and friends with the hugs and real smiles of human friendship. They had known all the time; I'd just been doing a job.

I watched Kenya fall away below me from the plane, the raw and mystical interconnectedness of life that nourished and sustained our ancestors still throbbing and beating its pulse through the African wilderness. I had only been here a short while yet even I had seen Africa is a country that can break your heart. And keep on breaking it. Yet perhaps any country, tribe or family we love enough to suffer its darkness, will do the same. Just as the darkness in my tribe was about to break mine.

During the celebration that summer of 1983, Poonam was told she would be staying on the Ranch, not ever to return to Medina. She was informed that she had been on a personal power trip, and now one of the mommas on the Ranch would take over personally those reins of power.

This momma was warm, ruthless and never wrong. Her first job was to weed out the old guard. She held meetings where she talked about the dark energy of Medina, how Bhagwan had been banished by the old hierarchy and we must re-educate ourselves away from the oppressive regime of the past. The cultural revolution began. Adheera, Weechee and I, the three remaining members of the gang of four who had once ruled, were marked women. Just after reaching 99 on the snakes and ladders board, I went from guru to taboo in one slide down that snake.

People began to remember the evil done by the old corrupt elite. Public confessions were offered of unwitting collusion in past wrongness. Fresh news of our abuse of power arrived daily. We three sat silently in the back during these meetings, guessing at our fate after this ritual humiliation was complete. I was glad Tim was not here to witness his mother's fall from grace. He was in California with John, who fed up with £5 a week and sandwiches, had returned to more lucrative employment in Silicon Valley.

The frustrations and fear that had lain buried under our less than perfect leadership were now manipulated by new masters and took their revenge. In the jubilant celebrations of release from old tyrannies and devotion to the new leaders was, of course, an old story in a new disguise. 'The queens are dead – long live the queens!' Though I had never imagined I would find myself this side of the barricades, amongst the ruined remnants of a glorious revolution that had lost itself.

I later heard the people in accounts had been ordered to go through the books with a fine tooth comb to find evidence we had been secreting fortunes into private accounts. When no sign of this could be found, because we had never even thought of it, they were told to look again; and to find some. Hard evidence was needed to discredit us further – for the good of the Buddhafield. I think the bewilderment of the accounts department made the new guard back off from this one. If I had known then what I know now of the corruption on the Ranch, I would have been able to draw strength from the innocence of Medina. As it was, although I knew how sincere had been our intent, I could find no righteous indignation, just shame.

Within a few weeks we three remnants of the old guard, were put on planes to Rajneeshpuram, separate planes so that we would not re-infect each other with our wrong thinking. When I arrived, I was sent to assist Rajen in one of his encounter groups. Frozen in shock, dislocated from my friends and family, lost, bewildered and confused, I sat there, a dazed and estranged statue. At one point he told me 'take over running the group'.

So far exiled from myself, alienated from even my shock, I couldn't speak. No one helped me. None of the 'spiritual therapists' reached out to me. Perhaps spiritual therapy was only for those who paid.

I was called to Jesus Grove. I sat in a lonely chair in front of a line up of the heaviest of the heavy mommas. They were all there. Sheela begins.

'You have the negativity of life times to deal with. You are a deceitful, manipulative, cowardly liar who has used Bhagwan's words for your own advantage. You have utterly betrayed your commitment as a disciple. You have an iron will masquerading under a false surrender. You are a solid rock of negativity with no flowers growing in our soul. You...'

I am punch drunk and begin to lose all sense of myself and reality. The women who run this show are no fools, and all six of them nod in agreement and add their own version of how fucked up I am. I stare at them. I must have been insane to have ever imagined that I was even remotely O.K.

Sheela continues. 'You must never work with anyone again as a therapist because you are pure poison. You have a heart of stone that has never held Bhagwan in your heart.'

I crack and begin to cry. But these mommas have not finished.

'These tears are phoney, nothing more than an empty manipulative drama. You are completely unconscious of the true motivations of your vicious and vindictive mind. This is a pathetic trip and must stop immediately.'

They continue. I don't know for how long. I am brutally and completely smashed into tiny pieces beyond where I have been before. Even my worst acid trips were a picnic compared to this.

But being systematically annihilated by the Matriarchy is no picnic. Not a tablecloth or cucumber sandwich in sight. Not a blade of grass left growing. Stripped naked on bare earth, I am left not even my bones.

Chapter 16
The Worm Turns

I stagger out having vaguely understood I am to report for work to the kitchens of Magdalena. I return to the dormitory, wash my face and try to write to Sujan. The pen meanders all over the page. 'Help me', I write. 'Help'. I can think of nothing else to say.

'Help me' I say to Satyarthi who meets me as I wander through the Mall dazed and in shock. He takes me to his mobile home, pours me a large glass of wine and orders me to drink. He tells me to lie on his bed. I am light years lost and do as he says. He holds me in his arms. 'Breathe' he tells me. I breathe. In. Out. I cannot cry. I cannot rage. I cannot feel. He holds me for a long time. I may have left for the far reaches of the universe never to return but for his warmth, calling me back from somewhere very far away.

The next day I climb onto the bus headed for Magdalena. I report for duty and am sent to wash dishes. I scrub the massive pots and pans, scraping away the stubborn burned food. I hope these tears are washing me as clean as the pots. This is a favourite spot for re-education and I am not the first to weep into the dishwater. Those around me are quietly kind, which makes me cry all the more. I feel I do not deserve their kindness.

I spend my days in a lonely world with shame and disgrace my only companions. There are some who kick me when I'm down, but when you're on the ground you've got nowhere to fall anyway. Each day I am called in to see the kitchen mommas so they can check the progress of my re-education. I sit in front of them numb, and can think of nothing to say when they ask me how I am doing.

'I'm deep in it' is all I manage to come up with. I know they want more.

I return to the pots having failed a test in a language I cannot decipher.

I receive a letter from Sujan. We are in different worlds. He is delighted to have been promoted to a spiritual therapist, something he has long wanted. He even asks my advice about a group process, but I can think of nothing to say. When I speak with Tim, he wants to know when I'm coming home. Home. I do not know what that is or where it is. I am lost.

Yogini, the head kitchen momma calls me in for my daily meeting. Today, exhausted by shock and grief and having spoken with Tim, I burst into tears. She holds out her arms. I fall into her. She holds me and strokes my hair as I sob lifetimes of grief and pain into her lap. This is what the mommas have wanted all along, for me to surrender to the Mother, to fall in love with them as deeply and irrevocably as I have fallen in love with Bhagwan.

But we have, all of us, already gone through this with our own mothers. She was our first guru. We were once at one with her. We came to life inside her. Don't they know that the mother's last gift is to let you rid yourself of her so completely, you find your own unique self? No. It seems not.

I work fourteen hours a day, every day. On breaks and briefly, before I fall exhausted to bed, I meet up with friends. Mahimo, my old friend Barbara from Leeds, has been stripped of her privileges too, her re-education happening through the hammering of nails in the construction of hundreds of A-frames. She failed some test of commitment when helping Puja co-ordinate Pythagoras, the Medical Centre. She wasn't sure but she reckoned it was because she preferred to hang out with lovers and friends rather than with the heavy-duty mommas plotting further great leaps forward in the glorious Buddhafield. Later it became clear she had been moved when one of the jobs of the Medical Centre became to research poisons. She could not be trusted to make her patients ill rather than heal them.

When all is stripped away you discover the essential and what is immediate assumes great significance; a tea break is as pleasurable as once was a party, a joke as sweet as a love affair. We 'rebels' hang out together and the healing begins. Though I'm not sure it's in the form the mommas had in mind. Where there had once been simply a 'we', I notice now an 'us' and a 'them'. They have cars, guns, ironed clothes and Motorolas. We don't.

After six weeks of pots I am called to the main office.

'Pack your bags. You will be leaving for Germany tomorrow.'

The woman does not even look at me.

'What about Tim and Sujan?' I ask.

She looks at me.

'Can't you say 'yes' for once!'

Obviously not.

It turns out I am to stop over in England for one day to pick up Tim and a few clothes, then travel onto Köln.

I arrive at a cruel and self-righteous Medina, where I am publicly shunned. Though many seek me out and in private wonder at what is happening. Is there much difference between being bewitched by witches as in the old order, or possessed by mothers, as in this new? I don't think so. And anyway, are they not the same?

Sujan was torn. His ambition to run groups was being fulfilled. He felt free from living in my shadow. Yet he also loved me and was puzzled by my withdrawal into myself. I tried to explain this was my protection, but he wanted me happy and laughing as in the old days. We were no longer travelling together. He was now on the high road and I on the low road. Familiar strangers. He loves me, he loves me not.

The next morning Sujan drove us to Harwich. Tim and I were to take the ferry from there to the Hook of Holland, then a train onto Wioska, the Rajneesh commune in Köln.

Tim and I stood on the deck and looked over the rail down onto the quay far below. We could see the tiny figure of Sujan wave us goodbye as we slowly drifted away. We waved as Sujan became smaller and smaller and smaller. We waved though we could no longer see his waves. We waved until he was a tiny red dot – and then gone. We waved until our arms ached, and then some more. I did not expect to see Sujan again. If we happened to re-meet it would be as old comrades who would smile at our memories and then return to our separate lives.

Tim and I turned our backs on England and went inside to find a seat.

The last time I had visited Germany I had flown and been chauffeured in luxury, this time I travelled by train with no flowers or champagne to greet me. My ordinary arrival however, was the least of my worries.

Wioska was the largest of the huge German Rajneesh communes, the others were in Hamburg, Berlin, Munich and Freiburg, each incorporating centres in almost every major city in West Germany. The Germans it seems had taken to the *Leben, Lieben und Gelächter* of this new way of being in a big way, where the work within the Buddhafield would make you free. The German communes made more money than any other arm of the International Commune, especially in their discos. Every night the young of these cities would come in their thousands to dance to the new heavy bass beat that had begun to make itself heard in the rhythms and sounds of dance music. Wioska owned discos in Köln and Düsseldorf as well as other businesses, offices, restaurants, shops and apartments spread through Köln, Dortmund, Wiesbaden and Düsseldorf. It was also a Siberia for those rebels who had neither cause nor reason for their resistance to the mommas.

I am given a bed in a room across the street from the block that houses the children, the central offices, the kitchen and canteen. Before I go there I take Tim to the second floor where the children live. The successful German businesses require more labour, which is being shipped in from all over the world. The communes in South America, Italy and Spain have been closed and the residents distributed through the German communes. Tim and I walk through the door into the children's area and into chaos. The Brazilians and Spanish arrived a few days previously, with far more children than expected. We find other mothers and children in a bewildered unhappy confusion, far from home, as unhappy to be here as we are. There is nowhere for personal toys, just one jumbled communal shelf, and very few toys and books. There was not even a play area, just beds squeezed together. The children must play, run around, and make friends and fight, all in the gaps between the bunk beds. And there was no school. Tim and I stared at all this and then at each other. One of the most painful periods of our lives was about to begin.

The other children spoke German or Spanish, not English. In Spain and Brazil where family is central, they had lived with their mothers, not like this. They had not evolved the complex codes, however anarchic to our adults' eyes that order such things. And neither did they have the toys and books that Tim had brought. Whenever Tim left his bed and his carefully arranged stash of Lego and soft toys, they were raided. He spent most of his time fighting lonely battles to get them back.

In Medina Tim could wander freely and find me anytime. Here, he could not cross the busy road on his own to visit me and was not permitted to leave the kids' area after 6 pm. I was tied too in way I had not been before. I worked in the kitchen from 8.30 am until 9 pm, with strictly controlled short breaks announced over a public address system. I spent most of my time on my knees cleaning the floors. I should have taken the opportunity to pray for deliverance. The only break was when I chopped vegetables. Then I sat at a table with people who talked German and took no notice of me whatsoever. Not even when I stuttered simple questions in my rudimentary German. Later I discovered this was because they had been told to ignore me as a dangerous rebel. Dangerous! I was so buried in despair; I had not the spirit for rebellion.

213

After the potatoes, carrots and leeks, I'd slide back to the floor for more cleaning of the lino, until the ten-minute break when I would rush up two floors to find Tim playing lonely games or fighting for his toys in tearful angry Spangldeutsch. By the time Tim and I had agreed our next meeting, I would be late for lino-duty and called in for yet another dressing down by the kitchen momma.

I had a kind of dazed rapport with the Spanish and Brazilians, but they had each other. I was on my own. Each night I would fall into bed with aching arms, sore knees and a well of loneliness. Each morning would be the dread of another day on the tiles.

To be oneself or to become oneself, that is the question. It's a big choice to remain the same and change your situation, or to adapt and stay where you are. I took the Darwinian line, it is not the conditions that lead to extinction but failure to adapt, and decided to stay and somehow take the unhappiness out of myself rather than myself out of the unhappiness. I got ready to encounter yet another family of demons I had been running from. But whatever name we label our unhappiness – ego, original sin, existential anxiety, the unconscious tyranny of the id – before you can be free of anything, you must first know you are enslaved. I discovered my slavery on the kitchen floors of Wioska where I fell onto the tiles and into my own nuclear winter.

Through the cracks in my psyche, my old demons poured gleeful reminders of my failure. They told me I had been on a meaningless road to nowhere all my life, my existence was a profoundly flawed mistake and while the sins of others were minor crimes and misdemeanours, mine were mortal treasons. Old terrors and dreads flew in, flapping their wings like vultures. More arrived forming a dark cloud. They fluttered around me until their massed ranks blocked out the sun completely.

Hello darkness my old friend.

In desperation I ask to see Ramateertha, the commune co-ordinator who everyone agrees is a 'good' guy, kind, compassionate, understanding. A few days later I am called for and go up to his office on the first floor. I sit on a large sofa. The soft comfort of it shocks me after hard floors and plastic kitchen chairs. I am awkward and do not know how to begin. He does not help me.

I choke back the tears that are threatening to fall as I tell him, 'I am struggling with a deep unhappiness. Nothing seems to reach or help me. I feel full of grief and shame. I need some help.' Ramateertha, according to instructions, hardens his heart.

'You are clinging to your ego. This is your negativity, the result of your abuse of power and rebellious lack of surrender.' His hard voice beats me further into my shame. This is so unlike him it can only be further proof of my profound unworthiness. I return brokenly back to the kitchen.

A rebel loves her cause even if the cause is just her rebellion, but I had no cause worth fighting for, not even myself. Deprived of any other mirror, I begin to believe the propaganda about myself.

While I was deep in losing my life in order to find it, Tim, unencumbered by shame and unworthiness, was making a life for himself. He was now fluent in the spangleutsch the children spoke. He went every day to a German school, where he was lonely, but fought the bullies who laughed at his red clothes. He made friends with a shoemaker who lived nearby. He took me once to meet him and they gossiped in a German I could hardly understand. Tim was surviving with the resilience of a healthy nine year old, but he was not happy. Yet I was too lost in a deep aching hole to take us back to a better life. Besides, I was so worthless, even this commune was a better parent than me.

Sujan calls. He is coming to Wioska.

I weep when he arrives. I weep when he unpacks his suitcase. I weep when we are together in bed. I weep the next morning. All these tears will put out the fire of love if I am not careful. I am not careful. And anyway how can he love me when I do not love myself?

Sujan told me that one day in Medina after I had gone, his possessions and clothes were messed around, stuffed into a plastic bag, some taken, some shoved into another room. He knew this was because of his connection with the old guard. He had been shocked. I could not get him to understand that was a minor violation compared to how profoundly broken into pieces I had been. He knew I had never really abused my power; I was too insecure in myself, so he could not understand why I was suffering so. Especially as he was delighted to be in Wioska where he was seen as a person in his own right, not just as my appendage.

My loneliness grew even more acute when he turned to women who were more fun than me. And there were many of those.

In Medina we had tried to make it straight to the Lotus Paradise directly, in Germany the core dynamic that would dissolve our egos was making money. Christmas came and went, we hardly noticed. There was no celebration, no decorations, no special food, no treats for the children. I tried to create a little Christmas cheer and invited Tim and Sujan to a late night feast on my bed, where I gave them chocolate, Sujan a scarf and Tim, a small piece of Space Lego.

This was no life for a child. Others must have thought so too as it was decided Medina would become a boarding school for all the commune kids of Europe. Tim is delighted at the thought of returning. He will be with his friends, hiding in the woods, climbing trees, stealing carrots, jumping in the lake, in the Medina school, his toys safe in his own personal locker. I weep, of course, when he leaves on the bus with the other children. At least I am no longer weeping alone, mothers are crying everywhere. Tim comforts me.

'It's a sad day for mothers, but a happy one for children, mum.' We hug.

I wave another long farewell with the other mothers, tears streaming down our faces. The bus turns the corner. None of us know when we will see our children again. That is how much we loved this dream. More than ourselves. More than our families. More than anything else. Because we thought this dream was the best hope for our children as well as the world, we were willing to suffer even the heartbreak of losing them. We turn forlornly back to work, I mean worship.

That night Sujan tells me he has fallen in love with another woman.

I have been so preoccupied with my suffering I have neglected the eternal vigilance required to keep a sexually attractive man by your side in a Tantric community. With Tim gone and now this, the last remnants of fight leave me. I am too bereft even to weep. The next morning during the ritual bowing of the *Gachaami's*, my forehead touches the cruelly familiar floor and I cannot rise. All the exit routes out of my suffering have been blocked. There is nowhere to go, nothing to do, no one to turn to. Hell is not other people. If we can blame someone else it is purgatory, not the seventh level of hell that is no one's fault but our own. I fall into an ontological void full of shame, self-condemnation and self-hatred.

In one of the few acts of kindness I received in Wioska, I was left undisturbed to lie with my wet cheeks against the cool tiles. Perhaps my complete indifference to whether I lived or died communicated itself in a stillness they respected. I must have got up eventually, and no doubt cleaned the floors as conscientiously as always, but an old struggle in me had gone. What is the difference between surrender and being broken? In one you smile, in the other you weep.

The pace of 'ego dissolving' heats up. We are to be allotted a sleeping space and every two weeks randomly moved. We are permitted two black plastic bags of possessions, no more. The commune co-ordinators, three women and Ramateertha, rifle freely through our shelves and take any-thing they feel to. 'Zenning' they call it. I can think of another word.

My non-attachment seems to be coming along nicely. When Sujan tells me he does not want to see me very often, because if he did he would fall back in love with me and he is enjoying not loving me, I hardly blink. When everything you love is lost, you discover yourself differently. If noth-ing else, when you live through your worst fear, it no longer has the power over you it once had.

I become friends with a black Brazilian guy who's never been further than a few hundred miles from the equator. He told me after his first day in Germany,

'No sun, the whole day! How can this be?'

The next day too was cloudy.

'Oh my God!' he exclaimed staring out the window, 'not to see the sun for two days! It's unnatural!'

I do not share with him chilling tales of the German winter. We've each got enough on just getting through the day. The third day.

'Aaah, I am going crazy! It is impossible to be happy without the sun. Grey for three days! I am going to fade away.'

A week of grey skies go by. He is frantic.

'I am going to die. I have no dancing in my body. There is no joy in my mind. No love in my heart without the sun to feed me. No one can live like this. My soul is shrivelling.'

I know how he feels.

He is saved when a friend from Rio sends him a tin of Guarana. He and I swig back tablespoons of the stuff dissolved in water. After six months of relentless despair and loneliness, some of that Brazilian sun re-enters my life.

I continue to have my regular 'battering-of-the-ego' sessions with the commune co-ordinators, spend fourteen hours a day on my knees – new instructions, longer working hours – but an old familiar spirit in me is returning. Only my stubborn refusal to leave until I have got to the end of this lonely tunnel keeps me here. Though when you're a worthless worm, your worm's eye view sees what's hidden underneath the table. And that is far more revealing than what is displayed above. I now laugh on my tea breaks, and not always with a politically correct positivity. I am turning into a bit of a rebel after all.

One day I am queuing for lunch when I spy some friends from the Ranch. I am delighted. I can gossip in English again! As we eat our lentils and mash I find that, like me, once high in the scheme of things, they have been brought low through some fault in their surrender. 'Dangerous rebels' are increasingly sent to the German correction facilities, though some are mysteriously confusing in their reports of why they have been sent here.

More 'rebels' arrive. With the freedom of nothing left to lose we congregate at meal times and thoroughly enjoy ourselves. For one hour at least. There is a 'crunch' going on most of the time now, which means we work sixteen hours a day to make even more money for the Ranch. The Wioska Politburo notice at dinner we laugh more loudly than other tables. A new directive arrives. Those from England and Oregon, are not to sit together at meal times or laugh loudly. I assume because our comradeship of rebellion and cynicism could infect the more politically naive.

Instructions from Oregon come thick and fast. All centres in Europe, South America and Japan are to close and we are to live in the great communes of Köln, Munich, Berlin, Hamburg, Zurich and Amsterdam. All children are to go to Rajneesh School in England. Meals are to be standardised and cooked according to strict recipes so we eat the same rations on the same day in every commune. And last but not least, more money is needed on the Ranch therefore we must work even harder for the Great Leap Forward.

Another message arrives for me. The co-ordinators of Rajneesh School, tell me my regular parcels to Tim of tiny toys and chocolates must cease. They make the other kids jealous. I am also told I must stop my phone calls. After speaking with me Tim is tearful and tells them he misses me. I tell them, I feel like that too, and completely ignore them. Though I am no longer sure if Tim receives his parcels or not.

The worm is turning.

When you fall in love with a person, a family, a tribe or a dream, you give them permission to do their worst to you. At what point does this become a license to kill?

I am suddenly ordered off the kitchen floor and into the disco. I join the team who leave each afternoon for Düsseldorf. We drive up the autobahn to worship in the gleaming temple of Disco, with its white marble, shiny steel and pale wood, and return at 6.30 the next morning. Life is a dance floor, Buddha is a DJ

Three of us work behind the cocktail bar and shake cocktails all evening, every evening. My Brazilian friend and I are together again, this time with different spirits to keep us warm. Before long we are moving to the music, juggling glasses, shaking cocktails, dancing together in elaborate rituals, throwing in just enough extra to make sure we 'test' each drink after we've filled the glass. We were not pathetic wannabe holy types after all, we were cool dancers and party-hard.

Wednesday, Friday and Saturday were the big nights. Thousands came. In the run up to the spectacular finale, we slip the DJ's tequila in exchange for our favourite tunes. They turn up the sounds blasting from the gigantic speakers. The power surges through the crowd. The pulse builds. We emerge from behind the bars, a Tantric shamanic energy team, the base beat in our blood, the rhythms of these urban hymns compelling us to dance. And still the energy builds. Thousands of bodies in frenzy of abandonment become one body dancing towards a vast rapturous communion. The heavy bass thumps through the speakers and into our souls. We are lost, nothing can save us now. Yes! Yes! Yeeeessss!!!

The explosive climax releases us into delirious orgasmic ecstasy. Screams, laughter, sweat and collapse. And breathing as the music turns into a soothing caress. Our sannyasin Tantric speciality – ecstatic orgasmic abandonment. No surprise when several years later, the first large-scale manufacture and distribution of the drug Ecstasy, was organised by sannyasins.

After the disco has emptied, we polish every surface, wipe glasses until they gleam, drink the left over wine, scrub scuff marks from the dance floor, and when several thousand have partied 'like it's 1999' from 9pm to 4am, that requires a heavy duty industrial cleaning machine, and drive down the autobahn as fast as possible to get to our beds for six hours sleep before we begin again.

Too much ecstasy, even for a Tantrika, is dangerous, and two weeks of disco shift alternate with more grounded work in other departments. I am sent to Rajneesh Buddhafield Transport – RBT.

My first time driving a left hand drive, I manage to manoeuvre a small van though the streets of Köln, delivering bread and messages, to the various bars, cafes and restaurants of the Buddhafield. I return to base to be told I must drive one of the buses to Frankfurt Airport, as there is a load of sannyasins arriving from the Ranch. More rebellious individuals needing training in the art of surrender I presume. Three buses set off in a convoy. I am the third. This is my first day driving on the right. My first time driving a bus. I do not know the way. I have been given no maps. It is pissing with rain. And growing darker. I must not lose the bus in front.

We weave through a cold wet Köln, headlights flickering, reflected in rainy puddles, windscreen wipers on full. The lead driver has all the street-wise cunning of those who know their terrain in all weather, and all vehicles. I slip through a red light to keep up – and this is Germany where you do not even cross an empty road if the pedestrian light is red. I hunch over the wheel stiff with tension at the speed we weave through these city streets.

We slip onto a ring road. I am confused by the unknown signs. The traffic flow is strange. I cannot read the road. I need to slow down. I cannot. I must stay behind the leaders. My hands sweat and slip on the wheel. Our convoy swings onto the autobahn. Our speed picks up. There is no speed limit on these roads and I dare not blink in case I lose the bus in front. But I can see no bus, just small red wavering lights. I stare at them through the fierce dark rain that batters the windscreen. Sometimes they appear to waver in the air, sometimes they disappear completely and I fly blind. I cannot look away for a milli-second. Everything is blurred at this speed in this rain. Those taillights merge with the red lights of others racing down the autobahn at speeds I dare not guess. I just know I have never driven so fast in all my life.

I forget where the indicators are. I can hardly breathe. There are sheets of water on the road. I am going to skid. I will slide through the central reservation and crash. This bus will be my twisted metal coffin. I will die. Maybe burned alive. I grip the wheel. My tight muscles ache. I may never relax again.

When the going gets tough, the tough get going. At least on these roads, at these speeds, you stick to one lane. Here, with that right foot right down, the journey is not the goal. The goal is the goal and the scenic route for wimps. If you can't stand the heat, get off the street. Do not swerve. Do not look away. Be total. Do not lose sight of the lights in front. Follow them blindly and you will arrive. I know the tune to this one!

We arrive at Frankfurt. The return journey will be even more of a nightmare with sixteen dazed refugees from the Ranch in the back. I ask the lead guy 'please drive more slowly on the way back'. He looks at me blankly. 'We weren't driving fast. Just stick behind me. No problem.'

It finally happens. Somewhere on the ring road round Köln, I lose them. I drive about randomly, hoping I pick up their trail. I fail. There is nothing for it but to pass this journey over to a higher power. Vague landmarks must have spoken to my unconscious as I eventually pull up outside Wioska. I stagger out exhausted and stare at the lead driver with red eyes. 'Like I told you', he said, 'no problem'.

No. The Rajneesh commune was not a problem to be solved, it was a mystery to be lived. Sujan and I are told we are to drive a van to England to deliver stuff to Rajneesh School. For one glorious week, I will escape the regimented life of Wioska Rajneesh, 33-39 Lutticher Strasse, Köln, Germany. I will have time with Sujan. And, after three months apart, I will see Tim.

Sujan and I hardly see each other these days. He has been 'enjoying his freedom', and in a Tantric community everyone knows what that means. He is pleased to be free of his attachment to me – good for him. But he has not reckoned on what being close to me for days in a van will do to this serene detachment. He is resistant at first. Cool, as in separate, rejecting, superior, and judgmental. Not for long babe. My old ways are returning. By the time we are driving through familiar roads in England, we are laughing, gossiping and confiding in each other as intimately as ever.

We arrive at a Medina we do not recognise. It is a boarding school, not a home. We drive through the gates, past a checkpoint that radios our details into the office before we can proceed. We move slowly up the drive and swing round into the main square. I peer at all the children in their red and maroon, looking for Tim. I cannot see him. We make our way to the office. One of the two who co-ordinate the school is a friend, but it is best we do not speak what is in our hearts. I come straight to the point.

'Where's Tim?' I want them to know I care more about him than any commune business.

'Sit down. Have some tea. You must be tired after your journey.' They smile imagining they are being thoughtful and kind.

In that moment I fell out of love with the Sangha. These people think they know better than me what is right for my son. They think they are loving, while they violate one of the most profound loves on this planet. They think I would prefer to sit with them than see my son who I have not seen for nearly three months. They are completely and complacently wrong. How could my friend do this to me?

Because I was doing it to myself. Because I had done it to others. Because we were all doing unto each other what we were doing unto ourselves. We would sacrifice ourselves and all that we loved, in our dedication to the greater cause of love and freedom for all. As have human beings throughout history.

Without a love that extends beyond our immediate family, we would still be in caves with no justice, no democracy, no hand of friendship across the divides of race and creed; just the law of the jungle and tribes at war. And I had seen what many in our individualist, capitalist, materialist, culture loved enough to die for – money, whatever it costs. Even if it costs the Earth.

Like the Saints of Christianity. Like suicide bombers. Like the soldiers of WW1 going over the top at the Somme. Like Ché Guevara. Like Gandhi. Like Joan of Arc. Like Mao. Like Jesus. Like Stalin. We're all 'gonna have to serve somebody', but how do we know, in advance, if what we serve is good or evil? Jung says it's whether you laugh at yourself. Sartre tells us this is the existential anxiety none of us can escape. Nietzsche might say – who cares? Osho would say in the living of it you find out. Me? It all has to happen, but I don't know why. Though I knew all children suffer their parents' love, and ours did too.

I stand up in the office of Rajneesh School and announce I am going to find Tim then abruptly turn and leave. The co-ordinators do not argue and send someone to find him. They invite me back onto their comfortable sofas for tea, but I do not go back into that room again, the same office where once I had plotted and planned a glorious revolution that had failed. I stood outside and waited for Tim. I see him.

He is taller and thinner, and a little bit of a stranger. I run over to him and we hug. He feels stiff in my arms. What is wrong? He pulls away. I can see it is to protect us both from the tears that threaten to flow.

'I've made you a cake, come and see!' He pulls me towards the kitchen.

We sit in the hall eating the cake, with a wriggly 'for Mum' written in green icing. I love him. He loves me. But we no longer live together and each has a life the other knows nothing about. Is this what made mothers suffer so in the days when tender boys of seven would leave home, cuddles and cushions for the discipline of dormitories, cold showers and hard benches? How can this be right?

It is not. With no words spoken I make a secret vow to heal this split whatever it costs. And I have. But first I had to travel further into the darkness simply because so much of that darkness lay in me. It had travelled down generations and wrapped itself around me, dislocating my being from my self. It had beaten the love out of me and all my love could do now was pour itself into the world and hope enough would find its way back home to me.

To become the mother Tim needed, and the one I so much needed for myself, I would have to travel further into that darkness. I would have to chew it, eat it, swallow it and digest it, so thoroughly, the sins of my ancestors could no longer contaminate the future. My greatest gift to Tim perhaps lay in this invisible work of love.

Perhaps my vow began its homeopathic healing immediately. The school called me a few days after I returned to Köln. Tim wants to leave Medina. They pass the phone over to him.

'I don't like Medina anymore, mum. I want to go and live with John.'

'If that is what you want then I will sort it out for you.'

'Thanks, mum. I don't know why but I just don't like it here anymore.' His voice trails away.

'Don't worry Tim. I'll call John, then call you back and let you know what we've organised.'

I call John. John sends the plane tickets immediately and within a week, Tim is on a flight to Santa Cruz where he would be happy and cared for by John.

I should have been upset that Tim was leaving the safety of the Buddhafield for life in the cruel and dangerous world. I should have tried to explain to him that sometimes we have to suffer in the pursuit of happiness. I should have said a lot of things according to the gospel according to Rajneeshism. But I did not.

I returned to Wioska and continued my journey to discover how far my love for the vision of a new way of being would take me into its opposite, a nightmare of ages old human abuse of power. That is how much I loved this dream.

What I did not know for a long time was how much the dream loved me too. Though not at all as I had once imagined it did.

Chapter 17
The Birth and Death of a Religion

Tim now lived with John in California and attended school there. His regular phone calls, happy gossips about his pets and trips to Disneyland made me feel lighter and out came the old rebel that had been hiding in the fields since this new order's guerrilla war with my ego had begun. I began to see why I had been seen as dangerous. I can make people laugh. I can tell good stories. And when I'm in the mood, can sell even rebellion to disciplined, organised Germans. Especially as behind all the regimented order there was, anyway, an instability inherent in the Zeitgeist.

As part of complex legal manoeuvres going on in Oregon connected with visas and planning permission, we now belonged to a new religion – Rajneeshism. Religious teachers can allegedly get Green Cards more easily. When the fact Bhagwan had not spoken for several years went against his religious leader status, suddenly – a miracle! It was discovered Bhagwan had been adopted by an American couple as a boy and this had been completely forgotten. Here were the papers to prove it. I think the couple were relatives of Sheela – another amazing synchronicity.

In line with now being a religion, we were each given a book outlining the basic tenets of Rajneeshism, a little red book, a Tantric Catechism. There was even a Rajneesh Bible. It seemed we were collectively becoming what we hated.

I could perhaps have spared a compassionate thought or two for the mommas and co-ordinators who had to be on message and uphold all this rubbish with a straight face in meetings. But I didn't. I felt less compassion and more hostility. The worm was really turning now. An oil tanker has apparently a turning circle of eight miles; I can only conclude my inner worm was extremely long too.

It was an ordinary evening shift in Rajneesh Buddhafield Transport with two of us available to ferry supplies or taxi people around. We had eaten the sandwiches, and were half way through our flask of coffee, reading the Rajneesh Buddhafield Newsletter, describing the latest outrage perpetrated against us by the wild citizens of Oregon and tips on how to open the chakras with deep breathing, when a call came through for me to collect Ramateertha and take him to Köln Bahnhof, the railway station.

I wove through the streets of Köln, driving the Mercedes like the well-seasoned Deutsche Autotreiber I had become, and climbed the two flights of stairs to his rooms. I helped carry down the luggage of one of the more surprising 'rebels' who'd arrived from the Ranch, Jayananda, Sheela's husband. I never did discover what he had done to be sent here. Perhaps he was dangerous because of what he knew rather than what he'd done. Or rather not done.

The two of them sat in the back as we drove through the streets of Köln to the railway station. The hairs on my neck stood on end as I heard that Sheela and her crew of head mommas had quit the Ranch. They were on a flight to Switzerland. There was chaos and confusion on the Ranch as they had told no one they were leaving, and had taken an enormous amount of money, jewels and all their designer clothes. And everyone knows, when you pack your Prada and diamonds, you are not coming back.

There was about to be chaos in Europe too. Dipo, who controlled the European finances and had complex dealings with Swiss banks, had also abruptly left the Zurich commune. He had booked a hotel for them all and called to say Sheela wanted Jayananda there too.

Jayananda left on the next train to Zurich. As we drove back to Wioska, Ramateertha and I wondered what was going on. He told me he would speak with the Ranch and call a commune meeting the next day.

'Don't mention this to anyone, Vismaya, you must keep this quiet' he told me, visibly shaken.

'No way! You can't expect me to keep this kind of stuff to myself!'

'I suppose not', he sighed.

I dropped him off and drove round to the disco.

Many of us would drop in for a drink at one of the bars in the disco, where we were allowed one glass of wine or lager a day. I arrived and ordered a double Malt whiskey. The crowd was heaving towards the explosive climax due in about two hours. I had a different bomb to explode.

'Sheela and her crew have left the Ranch. They've taken loads of money and are now holed up in Zurich probably emptying the Swiss Bank accounts.'

It takes a while for people to get I'm not bull-shitting. A crowd gathers. The DJ's see something is happening at the back bar, but there are too many dancing to stop the music. Eventually they realise something too hot to ignore is going on and fade out the tunes. We crowd together while I hold forth and manage to weave a story out of the meagre details I have. The trendy *volk* of Köln cannot follow the theories, rumours and conjecture we share so excitedly, but our fever is a buzz anyway. They hang out with us as we wander into the night and gather in the groups that gather everywhere, when a community is in shock and tries to grapple with the incomprehension and bewilderment, which is its first response. No, the first is denial – 'It's not possible!' 'It cannot be!' – perhaps to give us time to marshal our defences against how naïve and foolish we've been.

Soon we start to remember things that had escaped our attention before, or that we had pushed conveniently away into some dark recess of our minds. We re-tell old stories with a new slant. The fabulously expensive designer gear Sheela wore, was shockingly now revealed, not to be a manifestation of Bhagwan's magnificence but of her greedy materialism. The joke she had told on TV – 'How do you fit a hundred Jews into a car? In the ashtray!' that had once been an irreverent 'fuck-you!' to a hypocritical society, was now suddenly a blasphemy.

There's more chaos and confusion the next day when Ramateertha calls a commune meeting. He tells us Sheela and her gang have embezzled the commune of millions of dollars and were about to be exposed when they ran off with the money.

Faxes from the Ranch are posted daily on walls around the commune. Sheela and her gang had listened to our private conversations, had wire-tapped offices on the ranch, bugged people's bedrooms. They had even bugged Bhagwan's rooms. A group of them had wandered around The Dalles, a town in Oregon, with Salmonella on their hands touching food and over 700 people had required treatment. During one of the festivals they had poisoned a load of salad to make us ill as well. It was these guys, too, who had planted the bomb in our own hotel in Portland. Though quite why they would want to poison and blow us up, had yet to be revealed. Sheela had also ordered one of the pilots to drive over Portland Council Building and drop a bomb on it. Ah so that's why he's here – he refused. That's also why when, surprised to see him, we had no planes in

Köln, I'd asked 'What are you doing here?', he had told me, 'You don't want to know', and continued to chew his tofu.

We have more commune meetings where Sheela and her gang are denounced as capitalist free-loaders, dangerous commies, psycho-spiritual bullies, take your pick which revolution or counter revolution we're living through. They had manipulated us, abused their power, had the negativity of lifetimes and had never had Bhagwan in their hearts.

I've been here before.

Spiritual Therapists are flown over to help us work through our anger at what has happened. In an abrupt change from the relentless positivity, we are invited to voice our criticisms and concerns. There is an awkward silence. I stand up and announce that parents should be with the children, not in different countries. Prasad replies that Bhagwan had known nothing of what had happened to the children of the European Buddhafield, and had been deeply shocked when he'd heard. Sheela had done this so we would be less distracted, work harder and make more money. There is a howl of anguish and rage from the mothers. To have entrusted our children to the enlightenment of a Buddha is one thing, to have Sheela and her gang divide us is another.

Prasad told the mothers to put a cushion in front of them and let out our anger and pain. A hundred mothers are soon bashing cushions and screaming, sobbing out their rage and grief. I am silent. I want to think my own thoughts, not make it alright.

We crowd round the notices posted up daily and I read them as avidly as everyone else, but I cannot point the finger with the same fervour as others at the baddies in the black hats. And when all the Rajneesh Bibles were ceremoniously burned in the yard behind the disco, and I hated them as much as anyone, I could not dance around the flames. I stood with other counter-revolutionary veterans from where we silently looked on from the shadows.

The faxes became increasingly surreal. Sannyasins had been infected with diseases to make them too ill to tell what they knew. Some had been drugged into week-long sleeps. Some had been falsely informed they were HIV positive and sent to live in a cordoned off area of the Ranch. Plans were found to systematically reduce the protein we ate so that we would become more docile and less sexually active. Information obtained through phone-tapping was used to blackmail people into giving all their money.

Then Bhagwan himself stepped onto the stage.

After years of communing with his disciples in silence, he began to speak again. He knew nothing of what 'Sheela and her gang' had been up to. He was shocked to discover they had tried to poison his doctor, his dentist, Laxmi, Jefferson County DA, the Dallas water system and even himself. They had walked off with $10 million of the commune's money. Sheela and her cronies had robbed and set fire to Wasco County Planning Office. Poisons and dead mice in cages had been found in a secret tunnel behind Sheela's house, together with syringes of HIV-infected blood. Stashed there too were classified CIA material on the effects of poisons and how best to kill people without murder being suspected – several former members of Mossad, ex-Vietnam veterans and an ex-CIA agent had been in the 'Peace Force' who had wandered around the Ranch with Uzi sub machine guns and Israeli-made Galil assault rifles. Also hidden in this secret tunnel was $25,000 of ammunition and a lavender hot-tub.

Bhagwan exhorted us to learn from these mistakes and create an even better commune. He described Sheela and her cohorts as 'fascists' and 'Stalinists'.

I've been here before too.

I was told Ramateertha had a personal message for me from Bhagwan. I climbed the stairs and sank once more into the deep soft sofa, the scene of many an ego-bashing, consciousness-raising encounter. Bhagwan wanted me to know he had been shocked to hear how I had been treated. He had not known. To recompense me for my unjust suffering I could do any work I wished, in any commune in the world. I could even do nothing at all if I felt so inclined.

I was then given a message from the group department on the Ranch. They were sorry for how they had treated me; it had all been a dreadful mistake. I could run any groups I wished, whenever and wherever I wanted to.

They were not unkind, these Köln co-ordinators, not really. The proof was they looked sad and uncomfortable speaking to me like friends for the very first time. They apologised. Ramateertha said he was sorry for how he had treated me but he had been told I was a dangerous rebel who must be kept down at all costs. He looked me in the eye, genuinely remorseful. He told me he could now see this was Sheela's way of dealing with anyone who might interfere with her plots. I was welcome to stay in Köln, or he would help me go wherever I wanted to.

'I need to think about it.' I told him.

And I really did need to think about it. We all did.

Meanwhile back on the Ranch, Bhagwan, along with Sheela and six others, was indicted for conspiracy to evade immigration laws. Bhagwan, and his closest disciples, secretly left the Ranch in two chartered Lear Jets that landed at Charlotte where two further jets were waiting to take them to Bermuda. A team of Federal Customs agents boarded the plane and arrested Bhagwan at gunpoint.

At a press conference a Congressman announced with grim, but undisguised, delight,

'We've got the biggest one of all. The Bhagwan himself!'

The prison was inundated with flowers.

Bhagwan appeared in court chained in manacles. I saw the footage and was shocked. I had no idea that prisons in the USA still went in for this barbaric practice. Then too, this was the guru who for me had been a manifestation of the divine, and who I had wanted to shower with gifts – 93 Rolls Royce's, diamond watches, the petals of 50,000 roses. I had fallen to his feet in utter devotion. I had danced in ecstasy for him. I had communed in silence with his soul. I had loved him with the only love a devoted disciple can have for her Master, more than my lover, more than my child, more than my life. And I had continued to love him despite no longer loving his Sangha.

Tears came to my eyes even as an anger that he had betrayed me, that he had lied, began to stir in my belly. I had loved him totally, now I was about to hate him just as totally. Because when you have loved someone more than yourself, the journey takes you right out of the gravitational pull of your own fears and desires, into a spacious liberation free from your desires – that's the theory anyhow. (Though on a Tantric path it's a little tricky as you are also free to follow your desires, should you wish to.) Then, so the story goes, having lost your life, you must make the return journey and find your life again. Like all great journeys however, though the place we return to may be the same, we are not.

I decide to find myself again in the UK and pack my bags.

Sujan is still in love with the glorious revolution and decides to stay.

I wave, with smiles this time, as the train pulls out the station. I am pleased Sujan cries as I leave. I have cried a river over him. I have cried an ocean over this commune. But no more. I set off home dry eyed, even though I am not sure where that home is.

I arrive back in England, older, wiser and fatter. The cocktails that had helped put me back on my feet have also given me a protective padding against a cruel world. I have pain in my knees from all that kneeling. And I never want to clean another tile or piece of lino ever again. But I can drive very fast, mix a mean Margarita and know all the latest dance tunes.

But, as all astronauts who have travelled to the stars well know, the only journey more difficult than leaving the gravitational pull of Earth, is the return journey home.

PART THREE

Falling in all Directions

My third eye opens and
I see The Dark

Chapter 18
A Cross-eyed Daughter of Kali

I make my way across London to Poonam's house. While crawling under the foundations of houses on the Ranch to lay bricks in the freezing cold, it had occurred to Poonam she had better things to do with her life, and she had left. She now lived with her two children in a three-storey terrace in Camden. Adheera had already arrived; Suresh was on his way, Udbodha on a flight from the States. The Oak Village regiment was reforming. Champagne flowed, as did our war stories as we re-enacted the bloody battles of Berlin, Hamburg, Munich and Köln, and proudly displayed our war wounds and decorative scars.

For nearly seven years I had worked every single day for a ration of chocolate or five cigarettes, and a glass of cheap wine. I now sat on soft chairs, lounged in a bath, drank tea out of a china cup, flicked through magazines with no pictures of smiling Buddhas, except in the interior design, Feng Shui section. When I was tired, I sat down. I changed my clothes and no one took them. I lay in bed until I felt to get up. I left and did not tell anyone where I was going. I walked on Hampstead Heath not knowing when I'd be back. I had time to myself, alone.

Later that day I took £100 from the cash-point – real money. A friend had cashed my Child Benefit for me over the years and there was enough to support me until I got my life together. I marvel at the £20 notes, crisp and full of promise. In the commune we'd had cards each month and the date ticked when you picked up your daily allowance. Economic life had been simple; you pulled out your creased pink card and knew exactly the state of your finances. Though we had to keep track of our illegal insider trading deals – five of my cigarettes for your glass of wine, and half tomorrow's chocolate, which can get extremely complex in prisons, boarding schools and Tantric communes. I stuff the notes in my pocket. I do not have a purse, I must get one. And then ... shopping!

I wander into Sainsbury's in Swiss Cottage. And stop dead. In the years I have been away, food has become a packaged, multi-coloured consumer item; we can have anything we want not just what we need. This store is massive. Rows of sauces. Seven kinds of sausages. Ready made Indian, Chinese, Italian, Thai. A fridge full of yoghurts. Frozen deserts to die for. Out of season fruit. Oven chips. Even tofu-veggie burgers! I have been out of mainstream society for so long, like a prisoner emerging into sunlight, my eyes take a while to adjust. Though by the time I had walked past the fruit and veg, I am pushing the trolley through the aisles like an old hand, choosing between balsamic, sherry or cider vinegar where once I just reached for the malt.

I go back to the bank sooner than expected.

Sujan realises he wants to be with me more than his revolutionary comrades. Tim decides he wants to come back to England too. Our family is coming back together!

To begin with, we squeeze into one room in a communal house, but I want a home. I want a kitchen with my own crockery, a bathroom where I don't have to queue for the loo, I want to buy cushions again and design my own bedroom. I want Turkish carpets and fancy lampshades. I want to drink Rose Pouchong out of a china cup. I want my own glorious sofa. I want ... I want, therefore I must shop.

To make money, I set up a counselling practice and run groups. Sujan gives bodywork sessions. Tim goes to a school nearby. Eventually we have enough money to rent a flat in Belsize Park. We will soon have enough for a mortgage. It appears we are landing on our feet.

Bhagwan, meanwhile was having trouble landing anywhere. He had paid a fine and been expelled from America. India refused to renew the visas of those travelling with him so he flew around the world seeking a place to land. But no country would risk offending the USA and he was turned away from Italy, England, Ireland, Germany, Holland, Sweden, Portugal, Switzerland and Jamaica. He came temporarily to rest in Crete until armed police stormed the villa and he had to leave. Canada would not even let the plane land to refuel. Uruguay allowed him in on a three months visa but would not renew it. In the end he returned to Pune, to the ashram that had been tended faithfully by a team of Indian sanyassins.

Like a herd of cattle disperses once it has crossed the dry plain and reaches the fresh pasture, sanyassins spread across the globe and began to look for fresh grass and new ecstasies. Those astute enough to have held onto their wealth bought beautiful houses in Hawaii, Australia, Thailand, California and the South of France. The rest of us congregated in cities. We had now to learn the arts of survival and making money. But when a dream turns into a nightmare do you conclude that you messed it up and try again, or that you have been dreaming the wrong dream and switch track? Only a few began to question the dream, most of us were dazed and aimless, waiting vaguely for the next instalment of the Rajneeshie dream.

Bhagwan began his teaching again. Sannyasins travelled to sit at his feet, again. The new way of being full of 'life, love and laughter' was apparently up and running – again. Many of us re-aligned ourselves behind new blueprints for the 'Lotus Paradise', because it was too painful to face the death of the dream directly. Though I imagine those left with the job of dismantling the Ranch and selling it had a more painful dose of reality than the rest of us.

The demonization of Sheela and her mob continued. Years of self-sacrifice and relentless positivity had created a well of repressed rage and hatred. I suppose all that accumulated negative counter-transference had to go somewhere. Every God must have his Satan – else we might start hating the god. Having been an object of vilification myself however, I could not go along with the pre-Kleinian crudity of 'us good, them bad'. Besides I well knew I had one good breast and the other bad, I just did not know yet, everyone has. I began to unravel the dream.

Before re-cycling was fashionable, the poor did it anyway; they had to. My step-grandmother unravelled old sweaters to knit new cardigans. 'Waste not, want not' she said, as she showed me how to wind wool into balls round my fingers so it would not stretch. 'A penny saved is a penny gained' she told me, when she put tiny pieces of left over soap into a machine that squashed them into a multi-coloured cake until this, too, became a tiny piece in another bar. So when you have woven a cloth of magnificent colours, and for seven years have given everything to the weaving, and the dress does not fit – you are careful when you take out the stitches. There is magic in that cloth you will want to use again in the making of another frock.

There was, however, no shortage of frocks in the shops. I could wear any shape, pattern, design or colour I wished. I no longer had to blank out the greens, blues, yellows and blacks, nor turn away from patterns and swirls. Neither did I have to dress like an undercover spy, a Bishop's secretary or a sexy cocktail shaker – unless the fancy took me. I was free; kind of. You are not really free when driven by rebellion.

For a while I wore only green or turquoise. Then I bought a black silk dress with green and brown flowers. But I wasn't really liberated until, many years later, I bought an orange kimono of my own free will. For a long time, however, I thought I would never again wear any shade of red, orange, pink, maroon or purple, ever, despite the fact that at this point, I was still a bit in love with Bhagwan. Though around this time he re-named himself Osho. I was not at all in love with the commune, however, not even the new, up-graded version. I had anyway always loved the *idea* of the commune more than the living reality.

I threw myself into creating a home with gusto. I enjoyed the whole process, even housework, except for washing pots and cleaning floors. Sujan, however, was still in love with both the Buddha and his Sangha. Just when I thought our new home was taking its shape, he announced he was off to Miasto Rajneesh, the commune in Italy. The house fell down.

Feeling a crumbled ruin once more, I sought out a therapist. I found several, probably wise and compassionate with their other clients, but they judged and condemned me for what they did not understand – my journey with Bhagwan. You cannot heal your wounded inner child if your therapist thinks their job is to teach you how foolish you've been. There are levels and hidden depths to the game of master and disciple, secrets hidden to all but the inner circle; of course an outsider would dismiss these unless they had been on a similar journey. So I found therapists who were Buddhists, Taoists, who had walked these eastern spiritual paths. But they also condemned the Tantra they did not understand. I turned back to Rajneesh therapists, but they still preached the old 'let-go', follow your energy line. With one exception.

Amitabh told me it was more important to be interested in what was happening than trying to change it, heal it or make it better. This is it. Be with it. Be here, now. But he was only here for a week and then he went back to the States.

Perhaps I needed meditation at this point, not more therapy. I began to meditate again, though I must confess, sitting comfortably on the sofa. In the synchronous magic of all deep love affairs, as soon as I turned inwards, Sujan turned back and came home.

We bought a house and began to put down roots. Tim was now at secondary school. He had a cat, two mice and a hamster. He was making friends at school. We were gradually returning to ordinary life. Or so I thought.

Sujan was invited to teach on a bodywork training course in Holland at the Rajneesh Commune there. As the training drew to a close, we planned a romantic long weekend in Amsterdam. I flew over to meet him. When we met I sensed a subtle misalignment, a hairline fracture in our continuum of being, perhaps because he breathed in slightly more than he breathed out. It was hard to tell. Sujan denied anything was wrong so I assumed we just needed time together.

There were three days left of the training. During the day I wandered around Amsterdam and in the evenings hung out with the group. I asked him several times,

'Is there something you're not telling me?'

'Not at all. Why do you ask?'

In the time worn reply of fearful confusion I replied,

'I don't know.'

The training finished and we checked into a hotel. We sat with our drinks in the bar before dinner. Alone at last, it would now be alright. Sujan stroked his chin.

'I had an affair with a woman on the course.'

He now told me all. How he had fallen a bit in love with her. How he had made love to her. How he had felt a depth of connection with her he had previously experienced only with me. I found out that everyone on the course had known and had been complicit in keeping it secret. I had even had a friendly conversation with the other woman and liked her. My first reaction was relief; I was not crazy and paranoid. Though it wasn't long, before the fury came.

This was the first time there had been secrets and lies in our bed. Whatever turbulence had come upon us in our long sojourn in a Tantric Commune, we had always told each other the truth. We had never made love without having spoken what may have lain between us otherwise, an invisible barrier to our nakedness. I felt betrayed, we were not in a Tantric community now, and was enraged at the lie.

Yet I knew we all lie. My lesson of the long blonde wig had been we all have to. It is how, when and to whom we lie that matters. Sujan lies with his words. 'I didn't say that!' he shouts, when we both know he did. But when he is not happy it is written all over him, he frowns, his lips tighten, and his face never lies. I, on the other hand, rarely lie with words, but will disguise myself with a long blond wig, smile while my heart sinks. When lovers learn to read each other lies, there can be no deception, but I self-righteously accused him of lying to me anyway and unleashed the furies.

The first blast from an atomic bomb is not, however, necessarily its deadliest. There is a wind that follows, with a fall-out that cannot be seen or felt, that blows it deadly contamination down generations. So although the betrayal of the lie enrages me, this fury unlocks a far deeper rage in my heart.

I was born in the Chinese year of the Ox, both the year and the time being of the element earth, which makes me a 'Double Earth Ox'. Like an ox, when committed to a person, a cause, a vision, I am solid, dependable and reliable. I lean hard into the wind, follow the line of duty and determinedly see things through to the bitter end. Among more western stars, however, I was born on the first day of spring, on the cusp of Pisces and Aries, where the beginning and the end of the Zodiac meet. A solid earth ox, a fiery impulsive ram and a deep-water fish have very little in common. Perhaps this is why I have managed to be both a rebel and conservative, pulling to the left and other times pulling just as hard to the right. In my case too, rising up to heaven and, as often, falling with gravity down to hell. That sign of the cross was written in my stars.

Many times, after what may have been years of solid strength and reliable building, I spontaneously combust and vehemently turn against everything in a wild rage, roaring against the bitter winds of fortune, shaking everything I have accumulated off me, like a bear who emerges from hibernation to find his coat has become home to an army of parasites. And I leave. I walk away from what I loved so much; I gave too much and lost myself.

The second, more deadly, wind begins when we return to our home in London.

Sujan has always protected himself from the dangers of intimacy, while I have been more threatened by aloneness and nurtured relationship. Suddenly I don't care. I am enraged with Sujan, friends, the commune, my family, his family… I cut up his clothes. I throw his possessions out into the back yard. I smash every single one of an antique china tea service with his family's crest on it. I refuse to listen to reason or threats. I am never going to serve anyone again. No lover, no family, no friend, no guru, no God.

The rage burns its way into my soul. Like underground fires that burn for centuries in ancient peat because they cannot be extinguished, this fire slowly but surely ignites, and a wall of flame rushes towards me.

There is no fury like a woman Tantrika betrayed by her Master. With the red eyes of a true daughter of Kali I see Bhagwan now as a psychopathic liar and a megalomaniac energy vampire. I have dedicated the best years of my life to a vile criminal posing as an enlightened master and given everything to a corrupt and malignant force for evil. He is the Anti-Christ, the Beast of the Apocalypse, Satan in human form.

I ritually burn my mala. The golden bits that won't burn, I hammer furiously to pieces. I stamp on the tapes of his meditations. I rip to pieces his books. I tear up and throw onto the bonfire all the pictures of Bhagwan I can find. I cut my red clothes to shreds, they too then go on the fire. I destroy all the presents he gave me. I cut up his robes and smash to pieces the watch, the pen and the special box. I refuse to make love with Sujan while he wears a mala and calls himself by that Sanskrit name. I am enraged from the moment I wake up, all through the day and until I go to bed.

Asleep, the rage fills my dreams. I am the rage that burns with the heat of hell and the ice-cold hatred that freezes eternity. I am a demon witch scorned by what I had loved more than my life; this fury is the only way I can crawl back to myself. I spit out a hatred as ancient as the Earth, a darkness, so pitch-black, it eclipses all light. I am the Black Latifa. I am the source of black milk, Satan's wet-nurse, who poisons those she loves as well as those she hates.

Poonam and her daughters come for dinner. We open a bottle of Rioja and eat a salad of goat's cheese and walnuts with rocket and a balsamic vinegar dressing. Second course is pasta with a rich tomato sauce and garlic ciabatta. Delicious we all agree. Suddenly Soma pushes back her chair.

'I'm going to be sick she says, and rushes out the room to the toilet in the hall.

'I'm sick too' says Poonam and she runs upstairs, hand over her mouth, to the bathroom.

One by one we run to a sink, a toilet, the bath, and are violently and wretchedly sick.

We return to the table. What have I done? We go over the ingredients. Carrots, tomatoes, mushrooms. I fetch the remaining mushrooms, they are regular supermarket variety not hand-picked deadly poisonous 'Destroying Angels' or 'Death Caps', or at least of the biological kind. What else?

'The onions you mother gave us' I tell Sujan.

'What!' he exclaims. 'Those are daffodil bulbs!'

I poison even my friends.

Maybe with that catharsis, we vomited out other poisons as well. Sujan announces he is no longer Sujan, but Martin, and throws away his mala. I am no longer alone with my fury as he now encounters his sense of betrayal, his anger, his disappointment and loss. His was a quieter, less fiery, turning away. He buried his mala, did not burn it, kept his red clothes and re-cycled them for gardening. But he had not been brought either so high or so low as me. Had not give so much away, such as a child.

Tim is happy to have a room of his own, in a home, with a mother who cooks for him and reads him bedtime stories every night. He has pets to love. Majid, his best friend from Medina, lives down the road. He makes new friends. He learns to skate board and play games on his first Sinclair computer. But like us he goes through withdrawal symptoms from so many years of communal living. Haverstock Hill, a state comprehensive with over two thousand pupils, was a world away from Rajneesh school. He saw fights and knives, drugs and bullying, language and stories that shocked him. His entry into north London urban street life shook him as profoundly as our entry into the world of money and survival was shaking us.

There were times when our boat rocked so much it nearly sank. Then one or other of us would find a way to right it, and we would sail on, hoping to find what we were seeking as we sailed off beyond the sunset. Because I still had not found what I was looking for.

Before I could walk, I had learned my smiles could ease the divisions of war and had continued to hope my smiling efforts would save the world. When my mission to spread peace and love everywhere failed, I did not realize my omnipotent fantasy was a delusion, I concluded I must find new cures to heal the ills of the world. Any poor limping creature who crossed my path, whether it wanted it or not, was the recipient of my experiments and solutions. And in working to save the world, I abandoned my own family. Just as I had abandoned myself. For some of us, home is where the hurt is and why we have to leave.

Sujan took care of Tim, while I went to find what I did not know and could not name, in a Tibetan Buddhist Monastery in Tuscany, on a meditation retreat with Ram Dass, an old friend and ally from years before, a psychologist who had experimented with LSD as a tool of cosmic consciousness and had become disciple of Neem Karoli Baba.

Tuscany in late spring is a slice of paradise. Paths, edged by box, rosemary and lavender, wound their way through the monastery gardens to benches and pergolas where you could meditate and listen to the bees in the sweet peas, the roses and camellias. The air was filled with the scent of borage, thyme, sage, oregano and mint. Butterflies clustered around the buddleia and lilac. In the kitchen garden, the silver of artichokes contrasted with the vivid orange and reds of nasturtiums, cherry tomatoes and strawberries. This was a place of serenity and peace.

From the grounds you could look out over soft rolling hills, olive groves, vineyards, medieval hill towns unchanged since the Renaissance. And then wander into the meditation room where Ram Dass, a Jewish Hindu, taught Zen Vipassana to a lapsed Catholic disciple of Tantra in a Tibetan Buddhist Monastery. All bases covered, can't fail.

Yet failure is an old friend of mine. My learning has been circular not linear. I have had to spiral many times back into what I thought I already knew for even deeper experiences of it. I have had to repeat failures, break my already broken heart and make the same mistakes again and again. Though when you fail, do you learn the lessons of failure and try again, or do you learn this is how it always goes and give up? If you don't know, you've no choice but to try again. Maybe many times; it's never the same river the next time you step into it anyway.

Though it is always a river. Some things do not change. There was a snake in this Eden too. And the snake that tempted me in this garden was an old familiar.

One day the resident monks invited those of us on the retreat to a special meditation. A high-ranking Llama from Dharamsala in north India, was visiting to celebrate the feast day of Tara, the Green Buddha of compassion. She sits in half lotus with one leg outstretched, to leap into action should anyone need her. Still in my revulsion to orange, I wore a bright green dress that day and, not supple enough for a full lotus position, sat with one leg outstretched. The visiting Llama saw me and ordered his monks to bow to me and give me flowers. I was, he announced, an incarnation of the Buddha Tara. I was a goddess again.

And as I bit that apple, I found it sweet.

The Greek Myths warn us time and time again, when a human meets a god, the immortal mortally wounds the mortal. And before destroying us, drives us mad. But I am past the point of no return. Just watch me burn.

In the late summer of 1987, while the country, in a fit of madness, voted in the Tories for a third term, in a different kind of madness, Martin and I took off on another adventure to the stars. Martin was initially reluctant but I persuaded him. I can blame no one but myself, though naturally I have tried.

It worked out perfectly. John, Tim's father, was returning to the UK and would live in our house with Tim. Martin went ahead of me and after John had arrived, I was to join him a month later, in a Villa in Italy, where a group of us planned a six months journey into the far reaches of the human psyche. Martin left with promises he would write and phone, but I received neither letters nor calls. Anxious about this, I called the Villa. A friend answered. I asked to speak to Martin and she hesitated.

'What's going on?' I ask.

'Well, Martin is spending time with another woman here.'

Spending time means more than a night here and there. What is there to say? I put the phone down and promptly go out and buy a packet of cigarettes. I have not smoked since Medina, not even during my time in Wioska. Later Martin called me.

'I am free of my addiction to you' he told me.

I took a drag on my fag, reached for my wine and bit into the chocolate.

'Fuck you!' Not original, but what else to say?

'I need to explore my sexuality with other women. I have repressed myself with you and not been my true self because I was afraid to lose you.'

'I see.' I am not going to cry. I am not going to cry. I am not going to cry because I can tell he is gone from me and my tears will drive him further away, not bring him closer to comfort me.

A close friend is in Berlin to sing the lead in Stravinsky's opera 'The Rake's Progress'. I call Philip for his sympathy. Before I can tell him about Martin's intemperate, dissipated progress as a rake, he tells me he has an infection in his eyes and cannot see. He lies on a sofa in Berlin in the dark, cucumbers and chamomile tea bags on his eyes, afraid he is losing his sight. I lie on my sofa in London chain smoking, afraid I am losing Martin.

Over the next few weeks, we have the kind of long mournful conversations Schopenhauer would have approved – the world is governed by a blind unconsciousness, despair is our only hope. We laugh, hollowly, as we stare into the void, and the void stares remorselessly back. When we realise our sole purpose may be to serve as a warning to others, we laugh again, just as hollowly.

I didn't manage even a hollow laugh when I arrived at the Villa. The first thing Martin told me was that it was over between us. Paul, the guy playing the lead in this show, had helped him see that personal relationships were the primary obstacles on the path towards Self Realisation. They were, therefore, to be removed and destroyed.

I was not ready to face the heartbreak waiting for me in ordinary life, so I ran into the extraordinary, where the heartbreak found me.

Chapter 19
Angels Fall In All Directions

Villa Volpi, an exquisite 17th-century mansion in northern Italy, complete with balconies, towers, stone steps, terraces and courtyards, sweeping stairs and wide halls that led into elegant rooms with marble floors, antique chandeliers, gold mirrors and beautifully faded colours on the walls, overlooked Lago Maggiore and the Alps. There could not have been a more magnificent setting for our Grand Tour of the far reaches of human consciousness. In Renaissance splendour we planned to go beyond the material world and enter the realms Zen monks reach through their Zazen and koans, indigenous peoples through hallucinogenic plants, shamans through trance dances, Hindus by yogic postures and chanting, Taoists through meditation and martial arts, Judeo-Christian-Islamic mystics through fasting and prayer. We were going to sample and re-mix bits of all of those, plus our own Tantric speciality, making love and dancing, to give birth to old understandings in a new form in a great party of the Nagual. That was the plan anyway.

Paul had gathered around him ex-sannyasins and ex-spiritual thera-pists, as well as other 'seekers on the path'. My closest friends from san-nyas were all here and sixty of us gathered to 'explore strange new worlds, to seek out new life, to boldly go where no one has gone before.' Let's hear it one more time for the glorious dream of love, consciousness and free-dom from the pains of this earthly existence.

We gather in one of the long elegant rooms while Paul tells us these six months will liberate us from false beliefs about who and what we are. The material reality we imagined was fixed and solid would dissolve, other dimensions of reality would reveal themselves, we would discover our true magnificence. There was a catch. This process would involve the death of our personal egos and our attachment to any person, even our intimate sexual partner, would have to go. Ah. So this is Martin's excuse for loving another.

I decide to play it cool. I want Martin back. But this is going to be tough. The woman he is currently 'spending time with', is a young, beautiful, extremely wealthy heiress who drives around in an open topped Mercedes with leather seats, a heavy duty sound system while her hair wafts gracefully. How tough can it get? What's more she demands nothing from him. (Give her time, honey, give her time.) My Oscar winning performance is so convincing that in one exercise where we are asked to vote on who is closest to enlightenment, I am voted into the top three. I totter out on my high heels and bathing costume, toss my red curly hair, smile at the cameras and reveal my ambition is to become enlightened and further world peace. But this is a lie. Not only am I gearing up for war, I am completely freaked out of my mind, unfortunately not in the direction beyond our minds Paul is directing us.

I stagger around a while longer in the myth, but on the third day descend into hell. I turn to a friend in tears. She tells me I am needy and demanding and must get beyond all this. What! I have spent hours holding her hand through the grief of her love affairs! Then I notice she smiles when I am publicly exposed as an example of someone who is stuck in the personal. All these years I had thought her a friend with, ultimately, my best interests at heart, and suddenly she is revealed as an enemy. This is more than ordinary envy.

That night I cannot sleep and wander through the vast palatial rooms alone, surrounded by splendour. Through tall windows, the radiant moonlight shines in from the lake. Golden mirrors, held up by cherubs, reflect a thousand points of light from magnificent chandeliers on ceilings which display the brilliance and grandeurs of heaven. I recall an old story of Lucifer, the brightest of all the angels. When God finished making Adam and Eve, he ordered Lucifer, meaning 'bringer of light', to bow down before these frail and mortal human beings. Lucifer refused, saying he would bow down only to God. For this he was expelled from Heaven and entered the Hell he rules as Satan. In this story it was not his pride that led to his exile from paradise, it was his ignorance of the power of vulnerability.

I stand underneath the luminous angels and archangels painted on the ceiling as they flicker in the light of antique candelabra, and wonder. Gods and angels, with their might and glory, are immortal. They are never vulnerable, cannot be mortally wounded, do not die. Their power and glory can shock and awe and make many things happen, but they cannot make love. Only we terribly frail mortals can do that, with our imperfections, insecurities, needs and inadequacies, our awful mistakes, our dreadful existential anxieties about death and annihilation. We wouldn't need love otherwise. You don't need love when you're already perfect. You don't need anything. Though a bit of adoration and worship might not go amiss.

Lucifer had looked down from his great height at these naked human creatures, shivering in awe of the magnificent light that clothed him in glory and had not understood he should bow before this terrible and wonderful vulnerability. And neither did we. I had forgotten my catechism; even God had to become human, able to be wounded and killed, to create the love that would redeem the suffering of this world. We were trying to save it the easy way, without the suffering.

I looked at the serene countenances of the angels and deities above me, at the Olympian gods on fading frescos on walls. We can only paint what we know. The landscape of myth is the landscape of the human spirit and we are, each of us, both Lucifer and Satan, proud and vulnerable, divine and animal. If we want only half the story, then we must either murder our humanity to become divine, or kill our gods to stay as we are.

I had also forgotten, lying in our naked vulnerability, enfolded in the arms of the one we love and who loves us, we know the pleasures of an intimacy that may make even gods and angels jealous. What else would tempt our disembodied souls to swap un-incarnated bliss for the pains of life in a body? Reality TV shows? Take-away Pizza? I don't think so.

I had had many such nights of loving with Martin. Only Aneeta and Peter here have had a similarly long relationship through years of Tantric communal living, where you either move on or go deep. There were those who were jealous of me, with a more corrosive and insidious envy than I had any idea. Such jealous gods and angels are to be feared.

Be warned. Hard hat area. Danger of flying unreconstructed revenge.

Martin will not speak with me. I pass him on the stairs and he looks away. I sit near him at dinner and he completely ignores me. In a bewildered grief I ask him,

'What is going on? Please talk with me. What have I done that you should be so cold? Please, please speak with me.'

I am long past the cool performance of Act 1, and well into the abject misery of Act 2.

He is cold and distant.

'You are the past. The past has gone. It is over.' He moves swiftly away.

I am uncomprehending. So sudden a break, so violent a rupture, with no explanation, no discussion, no tender worlds of 'good-bye, I loved you', nada; the love and intimacy of nine years completely denied. This violent end to our relationship has been so abrupt that I cannot believe it is happening. I will wake up tomorrow.

But the next morning this life-crash is as real as the day before. I live in a hope more terrible than loss and wander around in shock, blown open to the winds of circumstance. Anyone who cares to can see my heart has been wrenched out of me while still beating, flapping around in a shaming daylight that shocks it into pumping blood in all directions.

'Help me!' I beg friends, holding out my broken heart, a wounded bird in panic, fluttering in my hands. 'I'm bleeding to death, look.' But they are tending their own concerns in this crusade to murder our humanity. When striving for immortality there will inevitably be mortal casualties, anyway, for without the human sacrifice, no god will deign to live in the temple.

With nothing to hold or contain me, I spiral even deeper into a void that has lain in wait for me for nearly forty years. A long overdue meeting between me and myself with no distractions, not even a lover, to come between us.

Meanwhile. we worked hard to build our temple to old gods in new disguises. We reach out for what lies beyond our reason. We go with the flow of the energy, rather than our ideas. We gaze into each other's eyes and share insights, stray strange thoughts, flashes of images that come to us when we sit, unmoving, for hours in darkened rooms. Our dreaming becomes as real as our waking. We listen to what we can hear in the spaces between the sounds. Our energy moves us in strange dances. We sit for two-hour meditations. We place ourselves in energy mandalas and special configurations then shake and vibrate as we let go into the energy field created. We spend five days and nights, naked in a room, leaving only for the toilet and a shower. We channel instructions for hi-tech orgone pyramids. We practice telepathy and telekinesis. We astral travel. We leave our bodies and have near death experiences. We encounter the spirits of the shamans and the gods of the Mahabharata. Through all this we dream the dreaming that gradually becomes the reality.

We join together fragments of a psychic jigsaw that piece-by-piece is revealed. Twelve of us, many ex-Rajneesh Spiritual Therapists, are apparently a special team of beings who have incarnated in many forms, in other dimensions, on other planets, from other realms. We have come to Earth to raise the collective vibrations of humanity, to facilitate a leap in consciousness, but somehow we lost our way and have forgotten our true nature. The 'Chosen Few' meet twice daily to break down 'bourgeois individualist conditioning', I mean the 'human conditioning of the personal ego'; though how I got chosen as one of the twelve, wallowing in the mud of so much human misery, was as much a mystery as what was being revealed. In these meetings we were to be utterly transparent to each other, tell the whole truth and nothing but the truth. So help me God.

Though I wasn't the only one at this point praying to a higher power to help me let go of my attachments. The second month of the project, October 1987, Black Monday wiped out chunks of the wealth of some of the people here. I noticed that Paul was concerned too, but apparently attachment to money is less of a problem than attachment to people.

When you cut away all human ties, you float easily into other worlds. People began to remember previous lives. Disembodied entities arrive and communicate with us telepathically. A space ship visits during a meditation. We channel the wisdom of higher beings. The archetypes come alive and take up residence – within us. We discover our true names. We are what this Earth has been waiting for because as our collective vibration rises, this will trigger a raise in the collective vibration of the planet.

It was a far cry from those long ago Mondays when I raised my feminist consciousness on sofas in Leeds; and I'm not just talking Yorkshire MFI versus Italian Baroque, yet the principle remains the same.

The pressure is on for me to change, to get it, to move on, to let go. In the mire of my human unhappiness, I am blocking the whole planet it seems. I try. I meditate. I focus on the here and now. I refuse to think of Martin. But then he sits opposite me and strokes the arm of the woman next to him and cruelly whispers intimacies. Or he follows his energy in the group room into long tender sexual embraces, but with others, never with me.

It took me a while to realise that sometimes Martin flaunted his latest conquest to purposefully disturb me; I had never imagined he could be so cruel. But what threatens even the most carefully constructed ego, more than anything else is love, and such a profound denial of his love for me merely revealed his desperation to escape it. Just as it occurred to me Paul was trying to escape his love for his ex-partner, who now sighed in the arms of another. But then self-doubt assailed me and I did another meditation hoping to see through the glass less darkly.

We are encouraged to announce to the group any psychic experiences we've amassed that day. People have realised past lives, seen visions, encountered spirits, and remembered living on other planets. I came up with a few feeble offerings. One night I astral travelled to a friend's house and saw her asleep in her living room. Later she called me. She had had a vivid dream I had appeared at the end of her bed, which was temporarily in the living room as friends were in her bed. Another time I had a tele-pathic communication that Martin wanted to meet me, but he must have forgotten he'd sent it, because when I arrived he said,

'What are you doing here?'

Once an angel flew over me, though not like the sweet angels of my Catholic childhood, more like the massive space ship in the opening cred-its of Star Wars. But this massive, throbbing force that moved slowly through the universe, was too awesome to speak about, so I kept silent. I was beginning to realise you mess with these powers at your peril.

If a particularly amazing revelation hits us we ring the bell and call the community together for the latest revelation. The bell goes at 2 am. This had better be good. It's Martin. He has become enlightened. Everyone claps, except one – guess who. In another meeting Martin announces he has not only achieved Self Realization, he has also realised he never really loved me. Ah, yes, when you are going beyond your humanity into your godhood, your worst enemy is your vulnerability to love.

Martin bestows a smile onto his latest groupie, who sits receptively and adoringly by his side. I glare at him, eyes narrowed all the better to focus my hate. Everyone is enamoured with him, his energy is beautiful; he is such a wonderful man. But I hate him. I spit out, this is to do with his mother – unresolved Oedipal stuff and cowardly revenge against the power of the Woman. Like every other guru, he is afraid of women and this Tantric teacher posturing is nothing more than his dark revenge. He makes me sick.

No one agrees with me. Women emerge flowing and glowing from their private Tantric meditations with him. Martin is full of light while I am dark with fury. Clearly I am the one that is angry and sick. I am the one with the problem.

Some of these people had been my friends for ten years. Poonam, Adheera, and Weechee were comrades from Oak Village. Our gang of four has been to one hell and back together already. They have been my 'family', I love them. I had thought they had loved me. With such a line up of trusted friends telling me I am the one that's crazy, perhaps I really am. Maybe so mad, I don't know it. I can no longer trust even my own experience.

I flip between terror and rage; one moment a deer in panic, petrified and blinded in the headlights of a hunter, the next a witch spewing vile hatred into a cauldron of spiteful spells. Caught between such extremes, I am lost. And there is no one to help me. I am so completely in pieces, I cannot even help myself.

When I was six years old I went into a huge barrel at Chester Zoo. It rolled continuously and you were supposed to run through at a diagonal and out the other side. I fell over, and could not stand up. I rolled and kept falling. I struggled to find my feet, but each time I nearly made it upright, I'd fall and the great barrel rolled on. All the postcards I'd bought of my favourite animals fell out my pocket and tumbled with me until they were creased and bent beyond repair. My purse fell open and my money fell round with me in a mocking confetti of change. And still the barrel rolled. I was frightened, and began to cry. 'Help me!' I cried. The other kids laughed, my little finger bent back, suddenly I was in a nightmare, with no escape. Public exposure of my knickers, my money, my tears, my shame and complete humiliation. And still the barrel turned. Someone eventually turned off the power, and a stranger handed me my postcards and money. Before I could run away, he pointed out a notice saying only children over 11 years old were allowed in the barrel.

There had been no notices warning me Martin would be so cruel, my friends so hard. Though I can imagine my tears are a drag when you are impatient to get going for the stars. I was judged and condemned for my refusal to let go. Especially as I was apparently letting down the whole planet as well as my friends.

Meanwhile I fell and kept on falling, in all directions, completely unable to find my feet with my heart is blown open, its secrets displayed for anyone to see. This public exposure of my devastation fills me with shame. I cannot eat and feel sick most of the time. In cold turkey from addiction to love you are your own worst enemy. You sink your teeth into your own flesh, chew on your own intestines and rip out your own heart. And howl with the insanity of utter despair. We are encouraged to write in diaries our latest revelations and insights. I write a howl.

'I am visiting every room in hell. Each cell in my body screams with longing, barbed wire wraps around my organs, razors slice into my heart. There is no cure for this craving that crawls through my body and is killing me. I am willing to destroy everything to feed my hunger. To serve Satan forever, for just one night with this man, even if it is only to say good-bye. I am willing to kill even my love, that's how far I have fallen.'

Here I did not just suffer withdrawal from my long relationship with Martin, I saw him with other women nearly all the time. It was driving me insane. I was going mad. We all were. But if it has not been done before, who can judge whether a work is of genius or madness until you dissect it in the aftermath. And even then… But as Mao Tse Tung said when asked what he thought of the French revolution: 'It's too soon to tell.'

I share a room with Aneeta, who used to sing the Sufi songs in music group in Pune with her partner Anubhava, now Peter, one of those very rare couples still together despite years of Tantric temptations. Perhaps this is why I felt them to be an oasis of humanity in this place so hostile to such love. But even their love cannot withstand the winds of karma and strange design that move us. Aneeta begins a love affair with another man. Peter is devastated and there are now two of us staggering under the humanity the rest run from. For a while we are each other's only refuge, and there is a sweetness in our intimacy neither of us knows is the disease or the cure.

The deep waters of this sea of cold impersonality is threatening to drown others as well. We group ourselves into threes and for a week each three eats together, walks together, sleeps together, washes together, and is never asunder. If one wants to pee, all troop to the loo. If one fancies a stroll round the grounds, all wander the shrubbery. I cling to this raft of human warmth and notice others hang onto their lifeboats with similar relief. Though the original idea had been to dissolve the boundaries of the ego identified self, not to find comfort in our common humanity.

We continue our journey to create an energy field that will shift us, en masse, to a higher consciousness in a kind of psycho-spiritual quantum leap. Though more like a psycho-spiritual entropy, some of us drift in the other direction. Back towards each other.

But the experiment is not over. We channel instructions for strange rituals and energy configurations for our meditations. We meditate for hours at a stretch. We have no chocolate, caffeine, alcohol, sugar or cigarettes, and eat only vegetarian organic whole foods. We no longer pop out for coffee, cream-cakes and shopping. We remove all addictions, not only those to 'love'. We do not read the news or watch TV – except for those who sneak in newspapers to monitor the market's recovery – apparently, unlike 'love', money is not potentially addictive. We stare into each other's eyes in prolonged energy exchanges that reveal the secrets of our souls, even those we have no idea were in there.

Apparently, I was once an Empress of China and abused my power by ordering whole villages to be put to death. On the other hand, allegedly, I have three beings of light that hover around me and most people only have one. You win some, you lose some I guess.

Paul is particular good at telling us what we do not know about our-selves. He can apparently see right into, not only our souls of this lifetime, but previous lifetimes as well. He can tell us of our amazing lightness of being or disgusting darkness of ego, depending on whether we are flavour of the moment or not. No prizes for guessing which was my lot. A co-dependent love addict with periodic delusions of grandeur, I hadn't a chance.

Paul snaps his fingers fiercely and glares at me.

'You can drop this right now, if you want to. Right now!' Then with dismissive disdain, 'You are too attached to your darkness.'

He turns away – as do, one by one, each of my old friends.

Aneeta is sent to the States to put in a bid for money at a private gather-ing of a wealthy charity for the spiritual well-being of the planet. She calls Peter. She feels very different, she tells him, out of the energy field of the Villa. Peter is not to repeat this to anyone, but as soon as the plane took off, she realised what was happening at the Villa was a collective insan-ity. Peter is shocked and, swearing me to secrecy, tells me. This is dyna-mite. Aneeta is no lightweight; what she says will have a profound impact.

Aneeta returns and closets Peter in a long whispered meeting. They call me in. They are going to leave. We have collectively fallen into a spell that Aneeta has now realised is a curse. I help them pack their bags and will drive them to Zurich. They go to Paul and explain they are leaving, because what is happening at the Villa is dangerous, and not at all good. He quietly explains they must leave immediately without saying good-bye to anyone, and promptly calls everyone else to a meeting.

We gather in the group room. Paul explains in a soft and gentle voice that a poisonous element has entered our experiment and must not con-taminate us. We are to have nothing to do with Aneeta and Peter, not even to say good-bye. They have life times of negativity, have never had true love in their hearts, and are a source of 'evil'.

Fade in the base beat and slowly let it build. I've heard it all before. I've heard it all before. I've heard it all before.

Presumably I am so fucked up and contaminated with negativity already, there's no point attempting to persuade me not to speak with them and no one tries to prevent my taking them to their train.

I drive Aneeta and Peter through the long dark tunnel drilled into the granite rock of the Alps of the St Gotthard Pass. My best allies are leav-ing, so why do I feel strangely happy? Why, when I stand on the platform and wave them good-bye, do I smile through my tears? And why, as the train pulls out from Zurich Station and the two who have shown me most warmth and friendship leave, do I feel lighter?

Because a part of me has left too. One fragment of my being has stealthily gone, like the two of them, from insanity to safety. Which is just as well, because when I return to the Villa, events there turn even weirder.

Paul reveals himself to be the incarnation of the head honcho of a bunch of ascended Masters, The White Brotherhood, and the guys allegedly in charge of the spiritual progress of the Earth. It was like being the ruler of the universe – God, really. Out-enlightening the Buddha is as good a way to kill him as any, I suppose. Though, to take on the mantle of the Supreme Being takes a certain 'chutzpah' to say the least. It also gives you a mesmerizing power over any ex-Catholic who gets too close because, as those experts in guerrilla marketing the Jesuits said centuries ago, you can take the girl out of the Catholicism, but you cannot take the Catholicism out of the girl. So when the S.B. himself tells a good catholic girl she is bad, mad and sad, she knows it's true – even with the voices of feminism, existentialism, D. W. Winnicott, R. D. Laing, Buddha, John Lennon and the goddess trying to reach her with a different message.

The sensible thing to do at this point would be to leave. I stay. I stay because I too had that terribly human longing to hit some of the heady heights of immortal divinity, shock and awe my enemies and usher in an enlightened world peace. Besides, supposing all this stuff was true, then it would be worth the sacrifices involved to become a saint, I mean, self realised. We had already experienced phenomena the normal, straight world would not believe, why not this stuff? Anyway, by this time I had seriously lost the plot, despite its thickening on several fronts.

A few of the sisters had never managed to keep a man and were envious of those who could, such as Aneeta and me – though I admit, I wasn't doing too well in this particular scenario. With Aneeta gone, two of them organised a campaign for a distinctly sisterly revenge. Perhaps relevant, Martin is focusing a lot of his Tantric teachings on one of them and I noticed that she began to place a rather proprietorial hand on Martin after some of the meditations. Bitter? Moi! They both now avoided me. Can't say I blame them, I was eaten up with a fury that spat at them. One afternoon, she discovered a scorpion in her bed; I wondered if my witch's evil eye might have put it there.

The core team of this project to raise the vibrational level of the planet, met twice daily, to tell the truth, though 'this is a lie' would have been more truthful than what we did say. We were also responsible for decisions about finance, administration, the future of the project etc. To help along the process of dissolving our boundaries, our decision-making was consensual. (In a fractal echo of the neo-Reichian alternative, socialist commune in Leeds, there was also an orgone pyramid in the grounds.) We twelve were each paid a monthly salary. These two sisters had the bright idea my salary should be cut by half – I am not losing my humanity quickly enough. Plus I had flown back to spend Christmas with Tim, further proof of my lack of commitment.

Freud said the secret that binds the men of all communities together is the shared guilt at their wish to murder the father. But what about the hidden secret of women, as much as they give birth and nurture life, their bitter envy destroys it? At least the men feel guilty, such women as these think they are right. But I guess if you cannot keep a man through your own charms, you must annihilate any woman that threatens you. And there were more men here who loved me than loved either of them. I was keeping it real, not pimping my ride, and perhaps being no angel meant with me, the men were free to be fallen angels too.

I stare around the room at this dream team.

'Don't you realise, I am going through all this so you don't have to!' I tell them. 'Without my suffering the need, anger and chaos that is our human lot, none of you would be going anywhere. Don't you get it? I am intrinsic to this whole project. I should, if anything, be paid more because my job here is the toughest!'

They have no idea what I am talking about. None of them. I am gobsmacked. From thinking I was the dunce here, I suddenly realised they haven't a clue. I haven't much of one either, I admit, but at least I understand that for a tribe or family to survive, when the going gets tough, the tough stuff is projected onto the toughest and they get going dealing with it, while the rest can get on with their lives. The scapegoat, the black sheep, the sacrificial lamb, whatever you call him or her, is normally honoured for their love-sacrifice; there is no such integrity in this tribe. They are splitting me off. They do not know what they are doing. We had made a joint commitment to find our transcendental interconnectedness, yet here I am being isolated and rejected, by the arrogance of their ignorance. Like I said, this is no ordinary envy.

Several argue that they do not like this idea. The others can't really see the point either but these two are determined. Even in my devastation I must have remained a force to be reckoned with, because they are not going to give up.

In democracy the richest and most persuasive wins, in consensual politics, as I had learned in our Leeds commune, the most vindictive and vehement wins – because the others want their dinner and we'll be here all night if we keep arguing.

Eventually all but me agree, my cut should be cut. They look at me. I look at them. If I am to continue this journey with them, I will not agree. If I give it up, I will agree, and we can go for dinner.

They say the first cut is the deepest, but here, as in Hollywood, it is the last that cuts the deepest.

I sit on the sofa in silence and look around at these people, some of whom have been my 'family' for over ten years. I suddenly see that during this six months project, whatever was our mission statement to go beyond our separateness, we have each been working on our separate agendas the whole time. And in my project to love the world into loving me, I had lost myself. Now there is no one to save me.

I briefly wonder if I have failed so completely, I really am such a worthless creature and they are right to ex-communicate me, cast me into outer darkness. For a timeless moment the Last Judgment sounds, and I fall into the darkest hell of them all, where Satan himself smiles in greeting. The evening sky slowly darkens. The last of the blackbirds ceases its song.

I agree.

We are released.

My enemies think they have won.

A war, however, is never really over until everyone is dead – even then there are ghosts. And I play a very long game.

There is a Chinese saying not written in Sun Tzu's *Art of War*. 'If you sit by the river and wait, you will see the bodies of all your enemies float by.' Is it the river, the waiting, or that they are your enemies which orders this re-meeting? Or is it the same mysterious ocean currents that one day move even the darkest water to the surface?

Chapter 20
Revelations of A Serpent

I did not look back when I left the Villa to catch the plane from Milan. I was less successful in London. I tried, but selling the house involved dismantling the dreams woven into this home for me, Martin and Tim. Everywhere were reminders of the life that had gone. Even sorting through the crockery, what to keep, what to throw away, I had frequently to sit down as a stabbing pain shot through me. I saw us relaxing before dinner, curled up on the sofa gossiping, lazy breakfasts on Sundays, drinking wine with friends, and it made me gasp when I was shocked all over again by my loss. Memories were distributed all over. Everywhere hurt.

I found the presents we had given each other over the years. On the mantelpiece was the statue of Kali I had given him when sorry for smashing his family's china. On the bed was a blanket I had knitted for us both. In the back of a drawer lay the silver belt he had brought back from Pune for me so long ago.

At least he was not here in person smiling at another and not me. Martin and I planned to split the proceeds and go our separate ways; he onto the team's next project to cruise further into outer space, me to go to ground. I was so hurt and angry, only the earth could absorb me.

Occasionally someone from the Villa called, how was I, they were 'worried' about me. I was cold and distant. How the hell did they imagine I was? But when Martin called there would be a forest fire and I would scream across Europe how I hated him. One of my comrades from our old Oak Village gang of four, called with a message from Paul. She delivered the message coldly, as if on orders from the boss to fire one of the typists. She told me, although part of this team, I was not welcome back at the Villa until I had got beyond my anger. Did they imagine I wanted to return?

It was all over. They were still living in the myth. There were not even the tattered remnants of friendship left. My last attachments are gone.

Not quite.

I went away for a weekend to drown my sorrows in the English countryside. Late on Sunday night, a friend who had been staying with me called. He had returned that evening to find the house had been broken into and everything stolen. Including the food in the fridge. Including the fridge.

I rushed back. The house was empty of beds, furniture, jewellery, clothes, bags, computers, cameras, kettle, and bed linen. Even curtains and lampshades were gone. Neighbours had seen the van arrive and take everything away, but had presumed we were simply moving out earlier than planned.

I wandered through bleak and violated rooms that reflected my own desolation and emptiness. I had nothing at all now, other than the clothes I wore, the contents of my bag and the odd tea towel and broken pencil left on the floor. I walked through to the back of the house into the kitchen and saw the table had been left. On it, lying on its side was a brass Buddha.

We are supposed to fall to the feet of the Buddha, not the Buddha fall over for us, and I placed him upright. As I did so, I suddenly realised what Martin and the others were doing was their affair, not mine. This was my life, I must chew on what had happened, swallow it, digest it and discover its meaning. The Buddha had spoken.

I did not want this. I wanted someone or something to blame, and then someone of something to save me. But it was too late; I had heard the Buddha and knew it was true.

I borrowed some foam and a sleeping bag and for the next six weeks, until the house sale was complete, lay in what had been my bedroom and gazed at empty walls in my own private Zazen. Stripped of all that had defined me and given me an identity, even the objects I had owned, I got ready to meet myself, without even a midsummer night's gossamer dream left between me and life as it is lived on this planet rather than those starry heavens. Though there were many dreams each night.

I dreamed Paul and I did psychic battle. Night after night, we sat opposite each other across a low chessboard, though with no pieces, just our naked psyches meeting in immortal combat. Each time we met, the game grew more menacing. Finally, in our usual places, the low table between us, Paul called Martin over. Paul stared at me with compelling mesmeric eyes.

'Anne, you are insane, but because you are mad you do not know this. I will prove it. Martin also knows you are insane, and he truly knows you. We are here to help you. We want to rescue you from your madness, to help you realise, all you think and believe about yourself is self-delusion.' He called Martin over. They look at me with what, if I didn't know better, I might imagine was compassion.

I saw laid out in front of me all the love I had longed for from Martin, reconciliation with the papal spiritual patriarch and forgiveness from God for all my sins. All this would be mine; the wounds in my soul healed, and a deep peace descend on me, if I would only surrender myself to them. My self-doubt has pulled the carpet from under my feet so often, 'I fall therefore I am' could be my motto, yet, for the first time in my life, I felt not a flicker of uncertainty. I stood, stared down at them both with contempt, and walked away. I knew I would never return to sit at that table again.

In another dream I am a billion year old astral travelling shark, swimming back and forth across light years. I am the most perfect killing machine biology can create, I always catch my prey. I prowl the universe looking for Martin. I will find him, however long it takes, and destroy him. Martin has let loose this monstrous creature, that now tracks him across time and space – it is his fate to meet me and be destroyed by me.

Another night I am a witch with long red fingernails whose green eyes flash with delight when I catch sight of Martin on the far reaches of the universe. I fly through space at the speed of light, screeching my revenge, and gouge out his third eye. He has forfeited all rights to any psychic knowledge. This is my domain. In my generosity I had allowed him the freedom to roam; I now take back everything I gave him that he has falsely thought was his. I curse him. His life force will shrivel, worms will eat at his intestines, his heart will be smashed into tiny pieces, just like mine, and he will burn in a hell of remorse and regret forever.

I think that covers it.

He writes to me, he has worms. Ha! The curse is taking root!

Yet every letter and call from him inflames me further, the wound is jolted and the pain runs through me all over again. I do not want this. I tell him I want no more contact with him but he does not understand and continues to write and call. I throw all his letters, unread, into the bin and when he calls I tell him, 'Never contact me again' and put the phone down. Martin has committed the immortal sin against me, has stolen the fruit of the tree of my knowledge. I exile him from myself. He is banished from my Eden. An angel with the flaming sword now stands between us.

When you have been betrayed, hatred is a deeper healing than tears and there are now flames within me and around me. I build another bonfire to burn our past. Onto it go photos of Martin and everything I can find connected with our past together. I systematically annihilate all trace of him from my life.

Waves of rage alternate with tides of grief. I lie in the makeshift bed and weep for all I had loved and lost. My efforts to create a better world have led only to failure, my longing for family, to loneliness, my creation of a home, to a piece of foam and a borrowed sleeping bag. Even my money was gone; our house has been sold during the price slump. That year an Iranian airline was shot down by USS Vincennes, a Pan Am Boeing Jumbo jet was blown up and crashed in pieces all over Lockerbie, Nelson Mandela was still in prison despite the Wembley Concert. Tragedy was everywhere. It appeared to me we are born in pain, die in pain and, in between, live in pain.

Once I went to the market to buy some vegetables and saw carrots with fresh leaves. I heard their screams at having been wrenched from the ground and rushed home in tears. Buddha was wrong, it is not only sentient beings that suffer, the vegetation does too.

There was no respite. I could not watch TV because I would cry out in pain at not only the suffering of others but at their joy too. If I saw a family sitting together, or a man and a woman holding hands, a child laughing, friends meeting with a hug, the tears would fall. Because when your love has been your escape from yourself, you have to be completely alone to find yourself. Even Tim no longer lived with me but with John and his girlfriend, a mile away.

Every Tuesday, Thursday and Saturday I'd go round to see him. We wandered over Hampstead Heath, where he showed me his latest bike manoeuvres, and we gossiped of skateboarding, could he have a kitten and did I know if you leave goldfish too long in the dark, they turn white? No, I didn't, but I did know when we humans stay too long in the light, we don't turn golden, we become dark. But he didn't hear. He had whizzed off on another foray into the bushes.

Later we'd sit in his bedroom munching take-away Kung Po Chicken from Fong's Kitchen round the corner, gossip, struggle over homework, or Tim played games on his computer while I lounged on his bed and flicked through the latest self-help manual. I no longer expected to find the answer, but you never know, an insight or two might leap off the page, making everything suddenly clear. Though I don't think the book has been written that would have helped me – 'Women who throw themselves to the wolves and love wrong things too much, on roads no one in their right mind would travel.'

I tried not to cry with Tim, not to burden him with my tears, but occasionally the tears would fall. Tim would put his arms around me.

'You'll be alright soon mum, I know you will.'

He had no doubt. I wished I'd had his confidence.

My last night in this house arrives, a house I had tried to make into a home with so many dreams. Tomorrow I will be walking away from that life, though with no idea where I will be sleeping. After Martin and I have paid our debts, I will have £500, my Levis, a couple of T-shirts and a jacket. I have no profession, no home, no partner and no possessions. I have friends, but none as intimate as the others had been. But thank goodness for these friends anyway. One calls and offers to rent me a room in her house in Knightsbridge. Another, a homeopath sees my tormented fever of devastation, rage and loss, and gives me a remedy – Lachesis, the most potent snake venom on Earth. I am to take three powders at 6am, mid-day and 6pm.

I am in bed, writhing in my familiar fever of helpless agony when I take the third. Within two minutes the howling winds of the betrayals of Martin and my friends, that have devastated and wrecked my life, cease. The storm passes. From one moment to the next, the fever has broken; I am out of the torture and left with simply the loss. Without those relentless, persecuting winds wailing around me I can hear a new silence as I come to rest in my sweaty tangled sheets. I am grateful for the stillness, even though it is the silence of a death. A love that has driven me my whole life has died.

When something dies, however something else is born.

A serpent, with wisdom older than the Bible, older than humanity, uncurled from where it had lain dormant at the base of my spine. Kissed awake by the venom of its homoeopathic sister, it began its Kundalini journey to my consciousness. My inner worthless worm had at last turned full circle and revealed itself to have been a snake all along. As it slowly moved up my spine, it spoke to me and I saw visions and dreamed different dreams.

The first knowledge the Serpent revealed was of the good in evil and the evil in good, and who better to speak of this than one with a forked tongue.

The second was of the good in myself, and its evil.

IN THE DARK AND STILL MOVING

The third was of the evil in myself, and its good.

The fourth was the true nature and beauty of the Beast, though that is a book in itself.

The fifth was of itself.

This serpent has two heads, one at each end. These heads have many names: Gog and Magog, Lucifer and Satan, alpha and omega, Male and Female, You and Me, but their real name is no name, because this reptilian Serpent is older than the mammalian Word, even the one that was with God. The mouths can swallow each other; or the mouths can open. If one swallows the other, all form contracts into a single point of intense potential that will explode into another universe, with a Big Bang loud enough to become the first Word of another story. If the mouths open, out roll tongues as long as time. On each is written the history of the human race and its destiny, one in black, the other in red. No one knows whether these stories are the same or different, because if you read them you die.

The cunning of the serpent joined the innocence of the babe. I systematically sorted through all my beliefs and ideologies, discarding every second hand spiritual, psychotherapeutic, political, religious, New Age idea that I had wrapped around myself to protect me from the harsh winds of reality. I threw out all false prophets from the temple, and kept only what I had learned through my own experience.

There is no greater authority than that of your own experience, not even God, and after having stripped all this away, I stood before Him, with not even fig leaf to hide my nakedness. If He didn't like what He saw, tough, I'd stick my finger in His third eye and blind Him. Because God had to submit to my gaze too. And I found She and He and their love, were not what I had been told.

This was the sixth lesson – the Creator is created by the Creatures created by the Creator created by the Creatures... And the love they make between them is what gives birth to the universe.

And the seventh lesson – after a good day's work plumbing the esoteric mysteries of the universe, put your feet up with a glass of Chablis and relax.

And that is how I learned homoeopathy holds a powerful healing, though not one that scientists can measure.

In all universes enfolded in the dimension of time, however, Monday always comes round and I had to spiral back into another round of work. This time to learn the lessons of my own history and re-build my shattered life here on Earth, not just in the archetypal and transcendental realms, in the mundane and personal.

I remembered Ram Dass had told me as we walked through the beautiful gardens of the Tibetan Monastery in Tuscany, we have two hearts. One heart is the human heart of feeling, compassion, active service to help ease the suffering of the world; the other heart is the divine heart that knows everything is an unfolding of a deeper mystery in which there is nothing we need to do. And both hearts must open.

If only the human heart opens, we rush around exhausting ourselves in an endless whirl of activity trying to help everyone and end up burned out. If only the divine heart opens we sit on top of a mountain detached and unengaged, a cold unfeeling observer of life. He had told me I had lived in the humanity of my heart and now needed to discover its divinity.

My attempts to open my divine heart in the villa had failed spectacularly. Yet ancient permafrost does not just melt in the sun and though the heat of my anger, the bonfire of my vanities and the flames of angels' swords might help, I wondered if both my hearts had been so frozen by the fears of generations, they had had to be broken open. I certainly needed a new understanding of love; my old one had got me nowhere.

I began to dismantle my assumptions about love and enquire afresh, what is this thing called love. I had lived in relationship because I had hoped through loving others to avoid the heartbreak that lay in me, yet those relationships had broken my heart anyway. I had hoped to draw back together the fractured fragments of my family through embracing each element in my love, yet my own family was in pieces instead. I had loved others because I could not love myself, and my love had to go somewhere; but they did not love me in the same way, naturally, they loved themselves more.

I sat raking through the ashes of my old life to discover, I was the one who had betrayed me, not the guru, false prophets, my old comrades or even Martin. Me. I had dreamed impossible dreams, broken my own heart and had fallen into an abyss of my own creation.

Dark clouds threatened rain. There was a cold wind blowing. One afternoon in early May, I sat on the edge of my bed. The dreadful knowledge of my own complicity in what had devastated me had been creeping towards me for weeks. I felt it coming, like a tsunami that travels so fast there is no point in trying to run run from it. Then it crashed full force into me.

Love had not betrayed me; I had betrayed love. The most mortal of all mortal sins.

I sat unmoving and bowed over, utterly smashed by my own design, and fell into this awful truth, the seventh circle of hell. This is the end. I will never rise again.

The sun came out from behind the clouds. As it shone in through the window, I was touched lightly on the shoulder by a great and awesome Presence and lifted up from where I had fallen. I sat back on my heels. A tremendous peace and light filled the room and I felt touched by the hem of a garment belonging to a different God from the one of my childhood. Love itself had come to me. Personal and intimate, yet transcendental and vast, this awesome being, so far beyond my understanding, knew all about me yet loved me still. The circle was complete. I had come truly home at last and now belonged to this mystery. Life had been what I had been seeking all along but had not known it. I remembered the final Buddhist vow, to fall the feet of Life itself, *Dhammam Sharanam Gaachami*. Life itself had become my Beloved.

I dissolved into the love beneath all grief. My love had never left me, it had been in me all along. But not a sentimental one, a love so nakedly powerful it kills what is false and break our hearts if it has to. Yet love's most dangerous secret is, this killing is better than any living. Because in the way we love, is the way God will be with us.

In a strange synchronicity, maybe I sat on the remote, the sound system clicked on and Mark Knopfler's 'The Long Road' filled the room. I stood up and began to dance. An ordinary ecstasy in just being alive ran through me. I laughed and whirled around the living room. It had, for sure, been a long road to here. Perhaps all roads lead to this, even if they are the road to nowhere. And I'd certainly walked that one.

Chogyam Trungpa described enlightenment as like a cow pat falling, splat, on your head. Now I understood. The life lived by this ordinary person called me, was as utterly amazing and divine, as it was devastatingly heartbreaking and mundane. I had not known such love and joy could be found in life, not in my life anyway. I had thought my beloved had been many things – freedom, truth, Martin, my family, Bhagwan, yet all along, Life itself was what I had been seeking.

The one who went to do some celebratory shopping was not the one who had fallen. Or rather it was she and 'not-she', which is why I needed new clothes. As good an excuse as any to pop round to our local corner shop, Harrods. After all, one cannot go scruffily into a dark night of the soul.

Everything had changed and nothing had changed.

The weather forecast shifted from violent storms to outbreaks of rain with occasional sunny spells. No longer so continually either enraged and sobbing in grief, I could walk through Hyde Park without rushing back in tears when I saw a couple walk hand in hand, or a group of people laugh in a bar. I began to forget for moments my devastation and once or twice may have even made a joke. In my new Nicole Farhi cardigan and Max Mara dress, I was equipped to dive down and plumb the depths again.

I decided to check out old haunts in case I found new truths there as well. I even went to see a Franciscan monk, the parish priest of my sister. He was, she told me, a wise man, not at all of the 'old style'. We met. He was intelligent and kind, but not wise, and there was something about him I did not trust. My lack of faith he called it. His repressed energy I called it. But what did I expect from a celibate priest, after all, to damn your sexuality completely is the ultimate perversion, the deepest turning away from what has made the love that has made us.

Back into another lion's den, I went to see Barry Long, an Australian journalist turned spiritual teacher. Several hundred of us, stacked in rows in an auditorium at Regent's College, listened to his words of wisdom. I liked him immediately in his Marks and Spencer's sweaters and corduroy trousers, not a jewel or Rolls Royce in sight. I liked too what he said – we must experience the hell of the world in us, before we can encounter the truth of Earth. Though he had a puritanical streak. He announced there was no need for twenty varieties of cheese, one would do, as so much choice distracted us. I suggested so many cheeses reflected the creativity of the human spirit, let's enjoy them, and the eating of them would be the teaching. As a Tantrika, of course I would say that. But he said the path was hard enough without making it any harder.

I didn't tell him shopping for cheese might help us through the hard times, because, dressed as he was, it was clear he was not into retail therapy. But though he may not have shopped in Bond Street, he was certainly one of the wisest people I have met.

I wrote to him saying he had helped me make sense of my experience, thanks mate. Just before the tea break he asked if there was an Anne Geraghty in the house. I panicked. I was living rather close to both worldly and Earthly realities at the time and thought my cheque for the weekend may have bounced. But he was just inviting me to have tea with him.

'I recognise you' he told me.

'I don't think so I replied, 'we've never met before, you must be thinking of someone else.'

''No' he said, 'I recognise what has happened to you. You have fallen off the karmic table and are now free.'

'Ah that' I replied. 'I know what you mean, though I'm rather bruised from the fall at the moment!' Over the chocolate digestives we gossiped about friends we had in common, who was doing what and to whom, though not about shopping or cheeses.

I also visited Mrs Tweedie, a woman about eighty years old, who had written of her journey with her guru, before the movement east of a generation. Even with her pre-feminist assumptions of what is a woman, I enjoyed her story, and when I met her felt she was genuine and had soul. It was dawning on me such creatures are fewer and further between than I had once imagined. I liked the silence and sweetness of her presence, but after sex, drugs and r&r, and a Tantric guru, it was not really my cup of tea.

Meanwhile, my new life took shape. John and his girl friend moved out to Reading where John now worked, and I took over the lease on their flat. I put up new curtains, bought pots and pans for the kitchen and planted some herbs. Tim and I got a kitten from the local pet shop.

This two bed-roomed ground floor flat in Savernake Road, near South End Green, became our home.

Hampstead Heath lay beyond the railway line that ran along the bottom of our garden. During the day I would walk over the Heath, even in the rain, finding ways through wild thickets of nettles and brambles as well as along the more populated paths to Kenwood. When Tim came with me on his bike, I tried to point out the beauties of nature but he was more interested in practicing skids around tree roots.

In summer, I would make my way to the women's pond and swim in the dark water with baby moorhens scuttling out of my way. Occasionally a heron flew over in wide sky-circles. Each night, after years of communal living, communal showers, communal kitchens, and dormitories, it was wonderful to lie in bed and know, at least in one direction, there was no one out there in the darkness. No one at all. Just birds, foxes, mice and the Heath.

Despite its scruffiness and pokiness, its threadbare carpets and cheap standard rented property furniture, I loved our little flat. It was where I came back to Earth and found out I liked it here after all. It was where I discovered how much I enjoyed to cook, sit and read, wonder what to do next, chat on the phone, invite friends to dinner, watch TV, listen to the radio, buy cushions to brighten up the faded furniture, iron clothes, go back to bed in the morning with a pot of tea. Tim too loved having a home with a kitten that played with him endlessly when he dangled bits of string, going to sleep every night in the same bed with his tiger blanket on it. And a mother who was there when he woke up each morning.

I began to teach Maths in a centre for children having difficulties in ordinary school. My old ability to connect with the fragmented and broken came into play, and 'un-teachable' children began to learn Maths. Once again, when asked what were my teaching methods that produced such striking results, I could not explain, because I did not know. Psychologists observed me and discovered it was very simple.

At the beginning of the lesson we took time to gossip of more important things than long division and quadratic equations, such as football and computer games. Then I would wander around and sit next to the children, so we looked at the Maths together, united against a common enemy. When their answer was wrong or they had not understood, I would say 'sorry, I haven't explained that very well' and explain again in smaller bits of information. I knew, if a child can understand $1+1=2$ then they can understand maths. It's a matter of the child's confidence and the teacher breaking down the units of explanation small enough so they can be digested by the child. Oh and the last point, which they didn't think was important, but I reckon they were wrong, I knew the names of their hamsters, rats, guinea pigs, cats and dogs.

There were still times when I wept over my losses, but as often I found myself full of a new happiness. I was no longer seeking myself, I was finding myself. I even found myself in a sweet love affair. My shattered life was reforming very nicely thank you.

One morning my bike had a puncture. Not having the time to mend it, I leaped onto the number 24 bus to Camden Town. Coming home I saw a man about to get off the bus who looked remarkably like Martin. I was checking whether this reminder left me coolly untouched or there was an unwelcome flutter, when I saw this guy's shoes. I knew those shoes. I'd helped buy them. It was Martin.

I lurched towards him. 'Hello, Martin.'

He staggered in shock. He was in London for the afternoon to see his dentist while in England to visit his parents. We walked over the Heath to Kenwood House where we had a surprisingly easy gossip over tea and cakes, both avoiding certain subjects – enlightenment, old 'friends' and love affairs among them. Though I did mention I no longer saw a good reason to leave a planet which produced such chocolate cake, however amazing the stardom. I was out for dinner that evening and as we said goodbye, Martin began to cry.

'I am so sorry, Anne, I didn't know what I was doing. I am so, so sorry.'

I can think of nothing to say. We sit in the car in silence. There is an old intimacy in this being together, which is no longer right. I turn to him.

'We cannot just be friends; the meeting between us has been too deep to return to that. Either we get back together or we say good-bye and never meet again.'

Martin turned to me. 'I cannot go back. I cannot do the same as my father did with my mother, and my grandfather did with my grandmother. I cannot leave, be with another woman, and then return. I cannot be the same as them. Not after all the work I have done to try and be different.'

I looked at him and smiled. 'Then we should thank each other for all the love there has been, wish each other well and say good-bye.' To my surprise I meant it. And that is what we did.

I weep into my pillow that night, but just a little, for old times sake. The next day I pack Tim's lunch, send him off to school and am back teaching geometry to children who would prefer to be kicking a football. I walk in the door just as the phone rings. It's Martin.

'I've been calling you all day. I love you. I want to be with you. Please can we meet to talk about this. I'll drive over tonight.'

He drove up from his parents' home in Hampshire. It was late when he arrived and Tim was asleep in bed. We sat in the living room and talked. He told me he had driven back to his parent's and arrived to find his mother in the middle of afternoon tea with her friends. He had rushed in wailing 'I am in love with Anne. I want to be with her. What am I going to do? I have made a dreadful mistake!' Then he'd sat on the sofa and wept. The silver teapots, china cups, sandwiches and cakes were quietly and politely put aside as the worthy women of the village discreetly took their leave.

I had a clear picture of the kind of man I wanted; this man was not Martin. Martin made hardly a single tick on my checklist of what I wanted – stable, reliable, successful, rich... Yet there was something here I could not explain. The talking finished. There was a long pause during which it gradually dawned on us there was only one way to find out whether we should get back together or not. On the Tantric path you follow your energy, not your checklists. And, as the guru had warned us long before, once you have stepped onto the Tantric path, that's it, there's no other road for you ever again.

We moved into the bedroom, took off our clothes, climbed into bed and made love.

It is two years since we have been intimate like this. Even as I look into the eyes of this devil-man, who makes me smile as much as he has made me cry, a part of me is pissed off. The devil you know is not necessarily better than the devil you don't. Maybe another would not be a devil. Yet if I am a failed and fallen angel, what other than a demon lover could be my partner? And a love that has resisted all attempts to kill it, does not argue. It simply is. So we let it be.

Ancient Buddhist teaching tells us, 'Entering Tantra is hellish. It will either destroy or enlighten you'. I have discovered, it does both.

Chapter 21
Familiar Strangers

Martin and I moved gradually closer. Sometimes I made quantum leaps of trust, other times I punished him. He had to pay for what he'd done and I extracted that payment. One revenge would have seen my wielding the stick of moral superiority for the rest of our lives. I could have gone with that, but he would have gone, and I didn't want that. Yet if you want to sleep with the enemy, first you must wound him, and there are many ways to cut a man who loves you. I'm just being practical – a saint, I ain't.

Four months after we had re-met, Martin returned to London, and moved in with me and Tim. The three of us were a family again. Martin and I set up a therapy centre where we offered individual sessions and ran groups and training courses in counselling, relationships, psychodrama and group dynamics. In the security and routine of home, regular school and family, Tim felt safe, and when you feel safe, parts of you that had run away, feel safe too. Like refugees who flee to the hills when their homes become battlegrounds, return once the war is over, lost parts of Tim emerged from their hiding and returned home too.

It was our first Christmas back together. The cold damp and frequent, even colder freezing rain, meant the pile of wet coats hanging in our narrow hallway never got dry. But I didn't mind. I didn't mind either there were no clear frosty nights, bright mornings with snow, crackling logs on an open fire – just grey clouds, an old gas fire, and a fake plastic tree from Pound-Stretcher in Kentish Town.

Our flat looked festive, welcoming and cosy. We put decorations around the doorways, hung the tree with golden apples, chocolates, flashing lights, and on the top, an angel. Tim helped me lay out bowls of dried fruits and nuts, and we loaded the fridge with food. I wrapped presents in brightly coloured paper with stars, snowflakes and reindeers, and laid them in their intriguing shapes around the tree. Even Nelson, our cat, had a stocking made up with catnip mice, feathery toys and cat treats, which he was not allowed to sniff until Christmas day. But a storm was brewing.

The closer Christmas came, the more Tim seemed to pull away from us and into his own world, as if this Christmas reminded him of how few such times we'd had together. I hoped when we gave out the presents, he would be happy again, knowing that this was how it would be every Christmas from now on.

On Christmas morning I lay in bed and could hear Tim playing with the toys Martin and I had put into his stocking. I snuggled into the duvet and looked forward to our day together.

After breakfast we went into the living room to give out the presents. I noticed two parcels had appeared under the tree screwed up in newspaper, on one was scribbled 'Mum', and on the other was 'Martin'. Something was up.

Mine was a pack of cards and a jar of bath oil. Martin's was a ball bearing.

'What's this?' Martin asked perplexed, perhaps it was part of an elaborate game that Tim had yet to explain.

'It's out of a jumping bean. The jumping bean broke but I gave you that anyway.'

Martin and I looked at each other. This was not a joke.

'What's this about?' Martin asked, shaking his head as he looked at his ball bearing.

'I don't know.'

Martin is hurt and angry and goes into the kitchen to avoid a fight.

'What's up Tim?' I ask.

'Nothing.'

'Is there something wrong? If so let's talk about it. Maybe we can help.'

Tim does not reply but gets up, goes into his bedroom and slams the door.

Martin and I decide that we will not push it at this point, we'll play some games together and when Tim is more relaxed, we'll talk with him.

I knock on his room.

'Can I come in?'

No answer. I open the door and stand in the doorway.

'How about a game of Cluedo?' I know this is his favourite.

'No. It's boring.'

'Well, would you like to play a game of cards with my new deck? I can teach you Poker.'

'No.'

'How about Monopoly then?'

'No. It's silly.'

'Scrabble?'

He looks at me with hooded eyes that cannot begin to tell me how stupid I am to think he would want to play Scrabble.

I felt lost. Every idea I put forward was rejected as boring, silly, and pointless. I suggested he was feeling angry and hurt about past Christmases and it would be good to talk about it so we could unravel what he needed. I said I understood; I often felt sad too for what we'd missed. If he would come and talk with us, I knew we would sort it out and get through it.

Tim stood up and stared down at me.

'You should have thought of this years ago. When I wanted to play games with you, you weren't there. It's too late now'. And he walked out.

I sat on the edge of his bed, not knowing what to do. This was all my fault. I had made a mess of one of the most important things in life, creating a family and raising a child. I had completely failed as a mother. What could be worse?

It grew dark. I sat alone, without lights, no Christmas joy, just a broken family, a broken relationship with my child and a broken heart, none of which would be mended, however hard I tried. Tim wandered the streets. Martin felt helpless in another room. I sat in darkness, bowed over in despair. For a long time.

Suddenly a fierce determination arose in me. I was going to repair our family, whatever it took. I stood up, wiped my eyes and went down the corridor into the living room. I told Martin I was determined to sort this out, whatever that might involve, and he immediately understood.

When Tim returned I let him know that next Thursday, and every following Thursday, we would meet together as a family, to explore everything that had happened.

'We will meet in the living room at 7.30pm and stay until each one of us agrees we can finish. And whatever it takes, we'll keep going until we get to the bottom of this. If one of us wants to rearrange this meeting, the other two have to agree because nothing is more important than mending our family.'

My determination was clear, Tim did not argue.

Tim had been born into a nomadic unsettled existence with an insecure mother on a pilgrimage to find herself. My hope was we could go on another journey, together this time. I hoped to show Tim the very search that had taken me away from him, had given me myself and now I could be with him in the way he needed. The same understandings that had cost our relationship so dear, could be the means through which we rediscovered each other. Maybe just as every dream has in it the seeds of its own failure, so every failure has in it the seeds of it own redemption. Perhaps we would value our relationship all the more for having so nearly lost it.

My fear was that it was to late, we had drifted too far apart, and too much harm had been done. But what would it profit me to have found myself if I then suffered the loss of my son? Yet which might we prefer? To have a mother who loves us and values freedom, both hers and ours, but who has not been there for us enough? Or a mother who has always been there, loves us but not our freedom, because she has not known it for herself?

Tim and I were about to find out.

Even before the meetings began there was a subtle change in the atmosphere at home. Tim seemed to feel our commitment and determination, his baseball cap moved up so we could see more of his face, even if what was revealed was angry and resentful.

Thursday evening arrived and at 7.30 we assembled into the living room. Our first family meeting did not go well.

Rather than sit side by side on the sofa presenting what might look like a united front 'against' Tim, I sat on the sofa, Martin on a chair. I had hoped Tim would sit next to me, but he took another chair and sat in the corner. Arms folded, his baseball cap pulled over his face, he looked at us with hooded eyes and sneered when either Martin or I spoke.

I began. 'I want to deal with everything that has happened between us because I want to make our family work and I am absolutely committed to this. I know I have made mistakes, and I regret some of what I have done, but I am determined to redeem it all as best as I can. I want us to be a loving family again and I'm ready to do whatever is needed for this.'

Tim shifts in his chair but his expression and posture remain the same – hostile, unforgiving, resentful and withdrawn. I continue.

'I want us to be honest and share what we think and feel. And I am willing to look into everything I have done that hurt you Tim, I am not just going to sit here and expect you to do it all.'

271

Martin leaned forward, placed his elbows on his knees, his chin in his hands.

'I am absolutely here too, and like your Mum, I am willing to go with the process of these meetings wherever it takes us.'

He looks directly at Tim who does not look at him. 'I have not taken care of you Tim, as I now know I should have done. And I am very sorry about that and I want to put it right'

We wait for a response from Tim. There is silence. He continues to sit in the corner throwing disdainful sneers in our direction. I had hoped our willingness to have these meetings would show Tim how much we cared and if we talked openly, then Tim would do the same. No. Tim's scornful looks merely took on another level of contempt.

I tried every way I could think of to persuade, motivate, cajole, influence, tempt, and convince Tim to talk to us. Nothing worked, and the baseball cap sneered at all my efforts.

I bent over, my head in my hands. There seemed no way through this. All I could see was I had failed as a mother and my son was lost to me. However much I loved and cared for him, my mistakes had been too great, too many and this was too late.

Suddenly I heard myself cry out – 'I wish I'd had a mother like me!' I don't know where that had come from, but it opened up a well of tears and I sobbed.

Tim moved from the corner to give me a tissue from the box I had earlier made sure was in the room. I had thought they were for him and had never imagined I would use them first. He put his hand on my shoulder as I wept.

When Tim handed me the tissues and put his hand on my shoulder, we had begun the journey, just not as I had imagined. I had hoped Martin's and my warmth and sincerity would be enough to encourage Tim to talk, slowly the ice would thaw and we would naturally come back together again as a family. It was clear after this first meeting, however, all of us were on the line. Of course. For these meetings to work I had to be myself, not me the 'good' mother, facilitating therapist, wise source of love and understanding or whatever other role I may assign myself. My long journey to escape the pain that lay in my family, had taken me right back into the heart of that same pain within my own. There is a terrible vulnerability in being a parent. You suffer both your own pain and your children's.

I left Tim to be cared for in a community where I thought he would have all the freedom and variety of experience I was so earnestly seeking for myself. He felt lonely and insignificant. I felt he had had a rich and exciting childhood. He felt unsettled and insecure. I thought he would be grateful for so much travel, so many people to relate with. He felt over-whelmed, lost and missed being close to the person he wanted most.

I recalled a story of Buddha. When he got up from under the Bodhi Tree and returned home from seven years seeking enlightenment he too found his family hurt and angry he should have left them for so long. His wife challenged him,

'If what you have found is the ultimate truth, then surely it is every-where and you could have found it here with me.'

'Yes' he replied, 'but I had to leave in order to discover that I need not have left.'

At this, his wife had become one of his disciples.

Such enlightened wisdom may have worked for the Buddha but such talk would not work with Tim. He needed real engagement not just more deep and meaningful words. Besides he and Majid would stick fingers in their mouths and pretend to puke if they heard anyone spouting such words as 'enlightenment', 'surrender', and 'consciousness'. Buddha had it easy.

Another Thursday evening arrives. I tidy away the books and newspapers, re-arrange the cushions and sit in the armchair to wait for the others. Nelson is asleep in front of the hissing gas fire. I have cut some of the Forsythia that grow outside our front window and brought it into the warmth. The buds are beginning to open with their yellow promise of spring. I feel low and dispirited. It has been a particularly difficult week. Tim has been even less communicative than ever.

Martin and Tim arrive together. We sit in silence. Finally Martin speaks.

'I am fed up with what's happening, Tim.'

Tim flicks his eyes towards Martin before looking back down to the floor.

'You do not get up in the mornings. Every day we have to drag you out of bed and you are late to school. You refuse to do any housework unless we stand over you. Your room is a complete tip, the floor is littered with dirty clothes. It's like a rubbish dump with waste paper and overflowing ashtrays all over the place. We talk to you and you walk away. You are rude and selfish and I do not like it.'

Tim's eyes flash with rage, then he sneers and turns away. He looks as if he doesn't care what we say and wishes he were far away.

'Well fuck you too' says Martin. He stands up. 'I am sick of this. Sick of you treating us like shit. I'm not going to put up with it anymore. You are going to have to deal with this whether you like it or not.' He is shouting now.

Tim stands and heads for the door. He is so angry he only knows how to leave. Martin leaps to the door and stands in front of it.

'You are not leaving!' he shouts. 'You'll have to get past me and you won't manage. I'm stronger than you.'

They bristle with anger and stare at each other. A potential for violence hangs threateningly between them.

A tight-lipped Tim tells Martin 'Get out of my way.'

'Sit down. I'm not going anywhere and neither are you Tim.'

'You can't make me.'

'Yes I can if it comes to that. I hope it doesn't but if you want a fight, you can have one.'

They glare at one another.

I am afraid. Both of them loom large in a small space, male beasts, unpredictable, irrational, capable of hurting each other and between them wrecking our living room. They jostle each other. Tim tries to get past Martin and open the door to leave. Martin grabs his arms and won't let go. The fight that I have dreaded looks like it's about to erupt into violence.

Nelson wakes up and runs under the table. He is afraid too.

'Be careful of Nelson!' I cry, though really I am calling out to them to be careful of each other. I know neither will back down. I don't know what to do and anyway sense this is for the two of them to sort out.

'Let's see if we can deal with this another way' offers Martin. Though he has let go Tim's arms, he remains in front of the door.

Tim sits down. Martin sits next to him.

'Thank you for sitting down Tim. I really want to work this out, that's why I'm so fierce. I care about you don't you see?'

'No I don't' says Tim. 'It doesn't feel like you care about me at all. Neither of you.' He glares at me this time.

It seems a deep tension between him and Martin has gone. An instinctual meeting has happened and like two male stags after locking antlers, they are more relaxed with each other.

I stroke Nelson who has taken refuge on my lap.

'I think you are more angry with me than Martin.'

'What do you mean?'

I put the cat down whom, sensing danger is over, at least in one form, sits in front of the fire and washes himself.

It seems important for Tim to express his anger to me directly yet I sense he is afraid the force of it will drive me away. Yet his behaviour is expressing it anyway, through his untidiness, his sullen reluctance to help around the house, his refusal to communicate.

'I have an idea. We can act out situations where you were unhappy and play them out again here. Like when you wanted to see me and I was in a session and didn't answer your knock. Or when I went away to run a group and you were left behind. That way we can find out what was really going on.'

Tim gives a non-committal shrug. I take that as a yes.

I sit on the floor in front of a cushion and pretend it is a client. I listen intently to their troubles with a total attention that blocks out Tim. Tim crouches down near me and knocks on an imaginary door.

'Mum. Can I come in? I want to show you something.'

'Not now I'm busy. Later. Let's meet later.'

'No, not later. Now. I want you now.'

'Tim, I'm working. We'll meet later, for two minutes before dinner.'

'No! I want you now. Stop talking to that stupid client. Pay me attention. I need you more than they do.'

'But Tim you must understand. I have to do this. I'll come and see you later in the Kids' House. But not now. I'm too busy.'

Tim kicks the cushion. He is surprised at suddenly how angry he feels.

'I hate you and your stupid therapy and your stupid clients and your stupid work! I hate it. I hate all of it. And I hate you.'

'Now Tim, that's enough. You know I have to work. Go and play with your friends and I will find you before you go to bed. I will read you a book before my meeting. For a few seconds.'

That's done it. He's furious now.

'You never gave me any time! You always put everyone else first. You never stayed with me long enough. You were always too busy for me. You were a terrible mother. I hate you for what you did to me. I hate you for leaving me so much. When I wanted you, you were never there. Now you want me I am going to get my own back. You can do all you want playing these stupid games with stupid cushions, but I am never going to care about you again. And I'll never forgive you. Never!'

I sit there and look at my son while he spits his hatred at me.

'And you needn't look at me like that. You're just doing this so that you can ease your guilt. Well I'm not going to give you that satisfaction.'

He sits back on the sofa, a tense ball of anger, arms crossed, tight lips, refusing to look at me.

'It looks like you hate me yet you need me. That's a hard place to be.'

'Shut up your stupid therapy talk! I am never going to speak to you ever again. Leave me alone!'

'That, Tim, is the last thing I am going to do. Push me away. Go on. Try and get rid of me.'

He comes over to me and shoves me. I fall back and pop up. He pushes me down again. I pop up. He pushes me down; I fall and then pop back up again. And again. And again. Neither of us can stop even though after a while we are laughing so hysterically we can hardly breathe. Tim and I are playing. Laughing. Shoving. Shouting. Saying things. Crying. Arguing. And playing. Real playing.

I remember Winnicott said, when a child is free to play, they work out everything they need to through their play, and no other therapy is needed.

One Thursday meeting, Tim picks at bits of thread on the arm of the chair.

'Why have you not stayed in one place and done one job so we would have money and a home with old toys and things that have been lying around for years. Why have we kept moving and moving?'

Tim's English homework a short while previously had been to write about the different homes he had lived in. The other kids had two, maybe three or even four to describe. We had sat down at the table and counted up, including our time in a Victorian semi, a Marxist-Feminist commune, a manor house in Suffolk, a hut in India, an apartment block in Köln, a ranch house in California, a back-to-back in Leeds, a terrace in Islington and a flat in Hampstead, he had lived in seventeen different homes in twelve years. Homes. Not just places we travelled through, where we rested for a while with our real home somewhere behind us, supporting us. These were complete landings with all our possessions.

I can feel the anger and hurt in his questions. Should I address that directly or approach him more cautiously, through his questions? I sense I need to move into his deeper feelings gradually, like moving towards a wild animal, slowly, no sudden movements, no direct challenge.

'The truth is Tim, I don't really know. There are so many levels to it all. The best I can do is tell you as much as I can.'

But how to explain I had taken on the fragmentation of my family and tried to heal it within myself? How, shattered in pieces, I had wandered the Earth seeking to make myself whole. How this broken-ness sent me spiralling repeatedly into further heartbreak. How to also explain a broken heart is an open one, and in its ruins many more creatures can find a home than can when it is a walled city, fortified, unbroken, with its defences intact? And how do you tell a fourteen-year-old boy struggling to mend his own broken heart, to heal his own ruined city, his own well of sadness and loss, that perhaps it has always been this way? I try to tell him anyway.

'I am so sorry you had to suffer with me, Tim. I am so sorry.' I wept. Tim came over to me on the sofa and passed me a tissue. He kept one for himself.

'Thanks Tim.' I reach out and hold his hand. 'We've both been hurt. I wish with all my heart it could all have been different. But it wasn't.'

Tim is crying now. I hold his hand. My touch and Martin's silent presence across the room hold him in a way he has longed for. The ice around his heart begins to melt and flows down his cheeks as tears. He squeezes my hand unable to speak. There is nothing to say anyway. In that moment there is no blame, no guilt, no resentment, just the profound is-ness of a universal pain, that teaches us one of the great mysteries of the human heart – that its capacity for love and its capacity for suffering are the same.

The cat scratches at the door. Martin opens it and Nelson walks in. He sits in the middle of us, looks around, yawns and begins to wash himself. We all laugh. No broken heart there!

Martin makes us hot chocolate. We sit squashed together on the sofa being silly, laughing. I hope we have many more such times together ahead of us. As many as we have missed and then some more.

Despite our broken hearts.

Perhaps because of our broken hearts.

Our Thursday evenings fell into a routine. We had dinner together, though did not talk about 'things' over the meal, we saved that for the meeting. We would clear up the dishes and take our drinks into the living room. This particular evening Tim and I are on the sofa, Martin in the armchair.

I begin. 'I've been thinking about all the times we have said good-bye to each other. And I feel sad about how often we waved goodbye, sometimes not knowing when we would meet again.'

'What's the point in going over what we already know' says Tim. It's a statement, not a question but Martin answers him.

'I think you and your Mum have both been hurt by your separations. And for both of you that needs to come out.'

'I don't see why she's been hurt, she was the one that left. It was her choice. It wasn't mine. I was just something she could sweep aside in her search for the perfect life.'

I want to protest.

'I was not just searching for the perfect life in some self-centred narcissistic obsession! It was for you too! It was for so many things!'

But I restrain myself. Now is not the time to defend what I've done, or even explain it. Instead I listen to him, hear his sense of helplessness.

'If we go over our separations, it will give us the chance to deal with them differently. Instead of running blindly into what I thought I had to do, I can stop and feel what I am leaving behind – most importantly, you. And you can tell me how you felt. You can argue with me, get angry, tell me whatever you want to, instead of just having to put up with it.'

I want Tim to argue and fight with me about the times I have left him. I hope it will help him feel less helpless if he can make me stop and listen to him this time. But this evening would not go the way I expected.

'OK' he reluctantly agrees. 'But you know more than me because I can't remember what happened when I was very small.'

'Wait a minute' says Martin, 'I am going to write it down so we have a record.'

He returns with pen and paper. 'Move over you two. I'll sit on the sofa too then we can all see.'

We sit squeezed together on the sofa, Tim and I either side of Martin.

'Well, I'll start with the first time I left you Tim. It was to go for a conference in Scotland on 'The Politics of Experience and Alternative Socialism'. You were a year old and stayed at home with John. I was going on a quest to sort myself out, to find a better way to live. I had tried to find help but nothing seemed to work so I had to go looking. I cried in the car as I drove away seeing you waving, quite happily it seemed to me, in John's arms on the doorstep. I didn't want to upset you so hid my tears.'

Tim is fiddling with his watch, but he's listening.

'Then, after John and I had separated, there were many times when I waved you goodbye as you left to stay with John for a few days. I can still see you walking down our garden path with your furry monkey in one hand and the other in John's, with a little bag packed with your favourite toys. I would cry every time after you had gone. I felt a terrible guilt that John and I had failed to create the perfect family for you, that you were split between two homes. I felt I had failed you and I could imagine nothing worse.'

'Well I didn't know that' said Tim, surprised.

'Then came the first big separation, when I went to the ashram in India for six months. I knew you were safe with John but it was too long to be away from you really. You had only just had your fourth birthday. But I had to go. I was driven by inner forces, you could call them demons, you could call them selfish, you could call them longings of the human spirit, but whatever you call them, I followed them to find a better life for us than the one I knew.'

Tim and Martin exchange looks. They know my tendency to go on rather esoterically about such things.

'We can listen to tape number 42 on longings of the spirit later' says Martin. 'Let's get back to the good-byes.'

'What about the time you went to London, to Oak Village? You left me with Martin and John' Tim offers. He's getting into it now. 'Then all those times you left me at Medina and went around the world running groups.' There's no stopping him now. 'And when I left Germany to go to Rajneesh School I didn't know when I was ever going to see you again! Then when you went to the Villa for six months. On the day you left, Ratty, my mouse died. That was a terrible day!'

Martin holds out the list. I look at it feeling tears well up, yet just as when I said the goodbyes, I hide my sadness from Tim and Martin. I do not want them to know how sad I am. I am afraid once I start to cry I will not be able to stop; I will dissolve into a sea of tears and drown. Anyway, I feel responsible. I had initiated most of these separations; surely it would be self indulgent to cry about what has been my own creation? An echo from my childhood reaches down through the years – 'There's no point crying over spilt milk, you've made your bed, you've got to lie in it!' I blink back the tears and swallow hard.

We stare at the paper. It is written like a shopping list, a schedule of places and dates that could be of holidays, not the chronicle of separations and loss it really is. There is nothing to say. I can hardly read it anyway; the writing is blurred through the tears I am blinking back.

Eventually Martin speaks. 'You are sitting here, the two of you, hardly breathing. I think you should act out some of these separations to find out what was really going on.'

I stand in front of Tim and say goodbye as we play out the separations one by painful one.

By the time we reach my leaving to join the commune in Oak Village, Martin has joined in, and I say goodbye to him too. John is represented by a cushion as I say goodbye to them all. Again and again. My tears are falling as I keep on saying good-bye to the people I love most. 'Goodbye' I weep. 'See you soon. Take care of yourselves. I'll write. I'll call. I love you. Good bye.' Each time I leave the room sobbing and come back in for another goodbye still in tears from the one before.

Something strange happens.

I am feeling a well of sadness and loss, Martin also has tears in his eyes, yet the more I struggle to speak my goodbyes through my tears, the more Tim sits up, bright eyed. The more I feel my sadness, the lighter he feels.

'I don't understand it' he says. 'I feel happy. Why am I not feeling sad like you two? Mum, you never told me how sad you were. You were always so together, I thought you didn't care that much. I'm glad you were sad, it makes me feel you loved me even though you kept leaving.' He is struck by a new possibility.

'That's what I've wanted – to know you loved me!'

I suddenly feel lighter too. Tim needed to know how painful our partings were for me, but I had protected him, and deprived him of that knowledge. He has known that something cold lay buried in his heart and had thought it was my absence, now he realises it was a fear that he had not been loved.

'Mum. Martin. Come here!' He sits in the middle of the sofa, smiling, and his arms out to hold us, in a reversal of our more usual reaching out to him.

We sit either side of him and he hugs us to him.

Martin and I look at each other in a wordless exchange that acknowledges what we are doing here may save Tim from having to do the painful searching we have had to. As our tears release us, they release Tim. The creaky vessel that is our family, that contains and carries us through the deep waters in which we keep finding ourselves, seems to shift and find a new balance.

A Zen story comes to my mind. A seeker goes to a wise monk and asks for the secret of a happy life. The monk tells her 'First the grandmother dies, then the mother dies and then the daughter dies.' The seeker is outraged. 'What are you talking about? That is not happiness, that's unhappiness!' 'Ah, you are wrong. Unhappiness is, first the daughter dies, then the mother dies then the grandmother dies.'

Our family is learning the right of order of suffering.

Tim, Martin and I met most Thursdays for the next two years. We went back into our memories and feelings; we enacted old dramas and replayed them in new ways. We struggled, shouted, wept and laughed. We explained, listened, spoke what we did not know could be spoken. We shared dreams, fears and longings. We brought to light what had been lost within and between us, however painful, and found each other all over again.

Each meeting ended with one or other of us weeping in the middle of the other two, or with us falling about laughing. Mostly it was first the tears, then the laughter. We not only re-discovered each other, we found, family love has the power to heal many other wounds within and between us, ancestral pain from generations of struggle as well. It also gave us a raft to help keep us afloat through the inevitable on-going turbulence of north London life.

Haverstock Comprehensive School had far heavier people, and much harder, than Tim had ever met in the commune. Many of Tim's struggles were every bit as much about what he encountered there as they were from his life as a sanyassin, though that is not what most people want to hear. They want to hear about how dreadful the commune was. Certainly, because of difficulties in the commune, many people reading Tim's book judged me as an awful mother. Reviews of it described me as 'a ghastly mother', 'one of the most selfish mothers you could imagine', 'one of the world's worst mothers'. But I knew the truth. I had met Tim's gaze, even when he resented me. I was a good enough mother to understand he had to feel his anger to find his freedom. I loved Tim enough to let him hate me with the same fury that had released me – our first guru is, after all, our mother. I let him do his worst to me and still loved him – that's how good enough a mother I was.

Over the two years these family meetings worked their magic. Tim became more communicative and was doing well in school. He roamed London with his gang of friends in a shuffling phalanx of baseball caps and skateboards. I heard only a fraction of their adventures I'm sure, and like most parents there were times I worried. But whatever happened, we now had a forum we each trusted could deal with whatever happened. Eventually we had a meeting only when one of us called for one.

The final family meeting I remember ended with me in the middle. I had wept in the first, and now I was weeping in the last. A group of sannyasins had been spreading vicious lies about me, trying to do me and my work harm. I couldn't understand why it was happening. Maybe so much unquestioning devotion to the guru inevitably involves a hate-figure somewhere else to balance things, maybe I had once again bonded in with what hated me in a futile effort to make it love me, I didn't know.

'Why do so many of them judge and attack me without knowing me!' Martin and Tim listen but don't know what to say. Then Tim speaks.

'You know, mum, It's very difficult to see you because you twirl round spinning worlds for people which they think are real. And they never see you because you are spinning in the middle of it all so fast, you have become invisible.'

'That is true' adds Martin. 'They think they see you but they don't. They see their projections, not you. It took me years to realise I had to be very still and wait, like for a wild creature, then you could come to me. Just as you. And that's who I love. You.'

'Me too, mum.'

They sit either side of me and hold my hand. The two people who mean the most to me have seen me, want to see me, and having seen me, still love me.

Their love reaches into corners of my psyche lying frozen and unloved. Like the snow that lies in hollows on hills, long after the sun has warmed the slopes, eventually melts in the full heat of summer, I come home, at last, into the warmth of my family. I look at Martin and Tim and smile. They smile back at me. Fragments of an Eagle's song come into my mind – 'One thing's for sure, we'll never be here again, so you'd better let somebody love you, before it's too late.'

Chapter 22
A Tantric Marriage

A group of people set off up a mountain and they climbed until they reached the peak. The view was so magnificent they lost all sense of time. Darkness fell and they realised no one had brought a torch. There was no moon and the night was pitch black. The temperature dropped. Wolves began to howl. What could they to do? One of them said 'Let's hold hands in a line and walk down in single file'. In this way they edged slowly down the mountain and eventually reached the bottom. They threw themselves to the feet of the one who had led them down. 'Our guru!' they cried. 'But I had no idea where we were headed anymore than you did,' he said, 'it was just that someone had to do it.'

We teach what we most need to learn and I had ample opportunity on the courses I ran, in counselling skills, psychodrama and group dynamics, to explain the brighter the light, the darker are the shadows it casts. Somewhere between Freud's Oedipal Complex and Jung's Collective Unconscious, I could expound my theory the humanity of the parent/leader/ guru does not demean them, on the contrary, it makes them more courageous and their mistakes more forgivable.

Still blinded by the light, most sanyassins did not like my saying Osho, though a remarkable channel of energy, was also a man, with all the flaws and frailties that entailed. Or that our commune was no different from the society we had been so keen on bettering in its inevitable abuse of power. They had not gone through the rage that kills the guru within you, freeing you to re-meet him as a fellow flawed human being. But if your devotion goes past its sell by date and you don't kill the Buddha when you should, I guess you will kill someone or something else instead.

A group of sannyasins held meetings to plan a campaign to destroy my work. Our centre was broken into, our mailing list stolen and everyone sent a letter describing me as abusive, power crazy and 'just like Sheela', though most on our mailing list hadn't a clue who Sheela was. I was threatened with court cases and falsely accused of a range of sins – embezzlement, racism, corruption, tax avoidance, wrongful dismissal, lies and all sorts. None of which came to anything because there was no substance to any of it. Such things take their toll, however, and even my friends began to doubt me.

Yet our enemies teach us what we don't want to learn, else we would not need them; our friends would have taught us more gently long before. My enemies finally taught me to let go of what had driven me my whole life and I abandoned my project, begun as a child, to become a saint/goddess/enlightened healer/angel who could provide the love missing in the world around me. Which anyway had always ended in my becoming a fallen angel who'd failed. But though I'm no angel that does not mean I cannot fly.

One morning, I was at home alone, when a friend called me. Osho had died in the night. I sat down winded, hit in the solar plexus. I could hardly breathe. Cars swished softly by in the road, the wisteria brushed against the window, the house creaked in the wind. In between the sounds lay a silence like an abyss.

I moved to the back of the flat, into the conservatory, and looked through to the trees on the Heath. I sat on a pile of cushions among the leaves and tendrils of plants. A curled, dry leaf fell to the floor. A small brown moth crawled up the window. A spider span its way between stems. From far away the phone kept ringing. For over an hour I sat unmoving. Empty. Beyond myself.

Suddenly I was astonished. Osho was in front of me.

'You have learned what I wanted you to', he told me, and smiled.

We sat in a companionable silence. The wind blew through the trees. Then he went. He disappeared into the movements of insects, the flights of birds and the way of white clouds. Into the songs of the wind, the flow of tides and the slow meanders of rivers towards seas. He dissolved into life. And was gone.

Later I wished we'd had a deep and meaningful dialogue that I could repeat to impress others, but the real meeting had been in the silence. We had said all there was to say in a language beyond words. Besides he had a lot of people to visit on the long farewell of his final surrender into the Dharma.

Who killed this Buddha?

Had the loneliness of a guru so far adrift from his natural Sangha been so great he had pined away, like a deep-sea fish in a fresh water lake?

When Vivek, his partner, committed suicide, when his favourite disciples turned against him, when the commune had shattered into pieces, was Osho's heart also broken in pieces? So completely he died of heartbreak?

If, as the ashram claimed, the poison he'd been given in the Maryland prison, killed him, why was there no autopsy to prove it?

Or had Osho asked one of his close disciples to kill him, according to some old pact made long before? If so, was this because of his despair at the failure of his vision or because his work was complete? Or are they the same? The Dalai Llama has reportedly said, Osho was the re-incarnation of a Tantric guru who many centuries earlier, in his previous life, had ordered his disciples to kill him the day before he was due to die, so that rather than step off the karmic wheel into the eternal bliss of nirvana, he could return one more lifetime to finally complete his work.

Maybe it was simply time for him to rest in peace as those disciples who were to 'get it' had got it, and those who were going to kill him, already had? According to Chogyam Trungpa, the Tantric guru is always 'in league with death' anyway. So perhaps we all killed this Buddha and the Buddha killed himself.

For many years after his death I dreamed of Osho. We would drink tea and discuss things with the relaxed freedom of two people who have done their worst to each other. In the very last of the series I asked him why had he not run off with Vivek into the hills, to live in a simple happiness to a ripe old age. Surely he deserved that if nothing else.

He smiled. 'Life has no meaning without death. I died as I had lived, my way, with no regrets. Such a death is not what it seems.'

Such a multi-dimensional fable, with as many depths and intrigues as a four dimensional Machiavellian labyrinth, can never be completely told. The best we can hope for are periodic flashes of light that reveal glimpses of a myth with meaning for us all. There is always a mystery. We can never know it all.

In another mystery, I had moved through the intimacy of love into the freedom of aloneness, while Martin had moved through the freedom of aloneness into the intimacy of love. He told me he had been afraid of the commitment to love all his life, but was now ready for it and asked me to marry him. I agreed. The power of our love had proved greater than our separateness, and we had both surrendered to that love; not to each other

– God forbid! – but to the mysterious workings of love in our relationship. This love was now our most intimate teacher, healer and guide, it made sense to honour this, yet ... parts of me were deeply ambivalent.

Several weeks before the wedding everything about Martin irritated me, how he sat, the clothes he wore, the way he breathed. Then one evening I left our therapy centre to return home. I went down the stairs, out to where my bike was waiting, and found Martin had locked his bike to mine and gone off with the key. I stormed back into the centre in a fury. A friend heard me raging.

'Anne, surely all this anger cannot be simply because Martin chained your bikes together and took the key. There must be more to it.'

I stop in my tracks. Suddenly I realise I am terrified of the commitment of marriage. I feel I will be trapped, unable to run free. Caught in a room with no exit. Stifled, smothered, imprisoned. I am as afraid of the vulnerability of intimacy as Martin had been. As soon as I realise this, I am no longer irritated by Martin. He had anyway, he told me, only chained his bike to mine because he had noticed I had forgotten to lock it. It was just parked there; any stranger passing by could have walked off with it.

We created our own marriage ceremony full of vows to support, nourish and love each other forever. Friends read poetry and sang. My sisters showered us with rose petals. We drank champagne and danced. In the evening, Martin and I were at last alone. We had commitments at the centre and so were not going away on a honeymoon yet, but Martin had booked a hotel in Kensington for the night. We drove into central London and parked.

Martin cannot remember the name of the hotel, but never mind, the night is young, we can wander around, and he will soon remember it. We stroll arm in arm in the warm evening air, gossiping, smiling, happy to be together. After a while I become restless. The night seems to be cooling and I want to lie with my love, in bed with champagne and candles not stroll the streets of London. We walk around more quickly now. Martin tries but fails to remember the hotel. I am annoyed. This is typical; he has messed up our special night. I remember other occasions when he has messed up.

I remind him of them.

Martin is silent, though I can feel the tension in his arm. More walking around, more looking, more trying to remember the hotel's name. But, no hotel. No longer arm in arm, we walk briskly. I point out to him other things I remember he has done wrong. He begins to mutter under his breath but I do not listen. I am too busy explaining to him everything he does fails simply because he *is* a failure.

We arrive back at the car and climb in.

'I am so angry' I spit at him, 'I will never forgive you!' I sit next to him, a righteous unmoving statue of hostility.

Martin turns to me and finally speaks, pronouncing every word with precision.

'I hate you with every fibre of my being.'

There is silence.

I try to repress it but cannot. I begin to laugh. Martin joins in. We cannot stop. Soon we are in hysterics. All those sincere vows to cherish one another, to always listen and love each other forever – and here we are hating each other absolutely! It is so funny we choke on our laughter, tears run down our cheeks. Finally we manage to calm down.

'Now we are truly married' I say.

'Yes,' he agrees. 'We are.'

Martin wound down the car window to let in some fresh air and caught sight of the name of the hotel next to us. He recognised it. We had been parked outside our hotel the whole time.

How else are two Tantrikas to be together except in a Tantric Marriage, which contains, as well as boundless love and freedom, deep rage and hatred? And when you have done your worst to each other, and still there is love, your marriage, like the vajra hell, is indestructible. Love and hate, two more names written on the heads of the Serpent with no name.

Chapter 23
I Promised Me a Rose Garden

After Osho died, a management team of twenty-one loyal disciples took over the running of the ashram in Pune. Perhaps they imagined they could do it better. For a while I thought so too, that I had learned the lessons of our communal failure and would not, therefore, make the same mistakes. Nine years running our centre taught me I could do it differently, but no better. Though my reign as guru-ess was in a therapy centre in Tufnell Park, north London, not the exotic landscape of Koregaon Park, Maharastra, India. Except the landscape of the human heart remains much the same in all weathers, in all terrain.

Not long ago, I met one of the current '21' at a dinner party, a woman who had been a friend in the commune. We had broken the rules, sneaked off and smoked fags in the toilet, gossiped about our love lives when we should have been silently pondering the mysteries of the universe. We had risen through the ranks in parallel, and had occasionally run courses together. And like sisters, we'd had our fights as well. We had not met for nearly twenty years. She looked much the same with her dark hair and Jewish American flashing eyes. She told me I did too, but I think she was being polite because later she told me I should dye my hair back to its original flaming red.

She described how she flew around the world running courses, a respected elder of the tribe, supported and held by the community. I, on the other hand, lived at that time in an isolated farmhouse in the mountains of north Spain with no phone line, no English-speaking people nearby, and no radio or TV. Wolves regularly came down into the forest where we lived and the month before had killed a horse just 50 meters from our house, a few weeks previously, twenty-three goats. While she described the hundreds who came to her courses, I described the hundred scattered bones of dead animals. She patted my arm in sympathy for my tough and isolated existence. Perhaps I would like to visit Pune, she suggested, where the sun shone on peaceful green gardens and a splendid silence lay in the marble meditation room that was Osho's tomb.

I was rather envious of the ease and security of her life and her serene confidence that what she was doing was so right and good. The price of freedom is far greater than eternal vigilance; a lioness in a zoo is sleek and well fed, is applauded for jumping through hoops, while a wild lioness has scars, old battle wounds, memories of starvation and fights. Yet I would not have swapped places with her for the world. Though I didn't tell her this; she would not have understood.

We talked about the book my son, Tim, had written about his childhood in the commune – 'My Life in Orange'. She asked if he had written it himself or had someone else and used his name. I was surprised and assured her that it was his own work. I also told her he was thinking of coming to Pune to revisit scenes from his childhood and experience, as an adult, the meditations and groups. She told me to give him her email address and she would show him around when he arrived, a child of the Sangha being welcomed back home.

When Tim emailed her he got a curt reply telling him the management team had decided he was not welcome, his book was 'not doing Osho's work.' He went anyway. He sat in the reception while a keen young sannyasin told him there appeared to be something wrong with the computer as when she typed in his name a warning flashed up. They laughed and joked while waiting for the security to arrive to sort this out. He told her he had grown up a sannyasin, one of the original children of the Sangha. She was impressed and moved closer. 'It won't take long' she said smiling, flirting as sannyasins do so easily.

Like travellers all over the world who, at Passport Control, are told 'Please step this way, something's come up on the computer', Tim was thinking, 'There is nothing wrong with the computer. I am an undesirable alien.'

Security arrived and it was explained to Tim he was not welcome.

The young woman put her hands up in horror and shrank away from this dangerous man she had only minutes previously been deceived into thinking was attractive, funny, intelligent. Tim was escorted from the property and told never to return.

'Us' and 'them' and no dialogue. God is on our side, not yours. Another religion is born. But if we become what we hate, and I hate those who become what I hate, does that make me the same as them? Or are our differences the stuff of love, then war, and then love again?

Without the bio-diversity of difference there would be no culture or language to ponder such things anyway, yet in all tribes the diversity that gives a community meaning is also what threatens to divide it. In our neo-sannyas commune there had been many potential fault lines of difference running through it. The necessities of the material and the demands of the spiritual. The different cultures of East and West. The struggles and surrenders between love and power, the individual and the collective. The different vulnerabilities of women and men, and too their samenesses. The opposing polarities of all societies which spin a culture into being – order and anarchy, commitment and spontaneity, responsibility and freedom; all of which demand not merely conformity to the law, but personal integrity and creativity.

Every one of the different groupings within the commune, which constellated around these dynamics, and there were many, used their power with love, and every one abused it with greed. And in between each and every one of these differences we made love, then war, until a different love arrived. For those who made it that is.

Yet every love leads to some kind of war, just as every war leads to some kind of love. War, because the otherness of the difference that feeds us, also threatens us. Love, because through our differences we make the love that makes all the difference. And there is no other love; the rest is narcissism.

Love of what is different extends beyond ourselves. This love lets the other be itself, unique, different, a mystery, and able, therefore, to love us in return. It is the only love that can save us from ourselves. But I came to the redemption of this love only after I had suffered several wars.

Whatever had been our original dream of making love not war, in every commune, collective, community I have known, we made love, then war, until some of us discovered a different love – a love that doesn't need to make everything 'better' but can let it all be. Yet unreconstructed love, with no fallings out into conflict or war, is one of the sweetest dreams of all; even if every dream not rooted in reality turns eventually into a nightmare. Though some dream to remember, some dream to forget; perhaps what matters is who is dreaming the dream. As a Bushman from the Kalahari told Laurens van de Post, 'It's difficult to explain things because there is a dream dreaming us.'

A child grew up in a concentration camp. He survived by hiding during the day and coming out at night to scavenge for food alongside rats. He ate like a rat, hid like a rat and thought he was a rat. Yet he dreamed he was a child.

A boy lived for years among a pack of wild dogs in Moscow. He forgot he was human. He bared his teeth, growled and bit the men who trapped and 'rescued' him. And that only after several failures as the dogs fought to protect him as one of their own. He later said he was cleaner with his new human family, and less hungry, but he had felt more loved when he lived with the dogs. And more dogs visited him in his dreams than humans.

Whatever may be our waking fantasies, our dreams reveal our reality.

The loves and wars of a whole tribe, the birth and death of a religion, the collective enlightenment and endarkenment of a generation, such a story, though written on the tongues of the Serpent with no name, is never completely told. Perhaps what matters is each individual that lived it. Sheela said recently that the whole adventure had been Osho's work to bring her to her enlightenment. When he insisted on another Rolls Royce and the commune desperately needed a combine harvester, when he told her to tell outrageous anti-Jewish jokes on American TV, when he threatened to have a devotee kill him if he did not get what he wanted, these were Tantric koans of impossibility. Just for her. Why not?

In our omni-centric universe, where every point is at the centre of a vast expanding universe, each of us is the story. Each of us creates the meaning. Each of us embodies the myth. Like the love of our parents that made us and what lies on the other side of death, none of us can understand the whole story, because we are part of it. We both create and are created by this vast geo-Mystery.

Yet in our mysterious bio-diverse universe, with its evolution of difference and uniqueness, gods too are bound by the laws of their own creation. Even Zeus cannot interfere with Fate, the law, the Dharma, the Tao. Neither can Buddha, Shiva, Allah or Yahweh. But though Gods may know this, we, thank goodness, do not. And each generation will try again to live the dream, save the planet, ease the suffering, and bring love and peace to the world. Until they discover what is happening *is* the dream.

But it's the dreaming that keeps the human spirit alive.

In the courses I run now, I no longer know what should happen. (Not that I ever did, I just thought I did.) A group of us gather together to explore what is dreaming through us, what is being dreamed up by us all. We listen to the greater geo-Mystery, and as it reveals itself to us, things happen. Consciousness, good and evil, all three burst into existence simultaneously, and are connected in mysterious and enigmatic ways. Perhaps what is being dreamed up is their re-union. There is an ancient Greek saying – 'Called or not, God will be there.' I now know Satan will be there too. To deepen the Mystery.

For a long time I did not want this. I locked away my demons. When they broke loose, I ran from them. When I could run no further I tried to exorcise them with therapy and meditation. I travelled the world seeking ways to rid myself of my despair, my anguish, my pain, to send my demons far away, to live somewhere else, somewhere I would never visit. I dived into shamanic rituals and esoteric mysteries, hoping to become the serene person I so much wished to be, rather than this one who suffered so excruciatingly at times. I tried to heal my 'broken' heart, not knowing there is no other kind of heart and an unbroken heart is merely a stone in which nothing can live for long. I did not realise, if I do not live with my darkness, someone else will have to suffer it for me.

The pain and anguish in our own hearts has to live somewhere, and if not in us, in an innocent other – a child, a lover, a friend, a stranger, our bodies, animals, this beautiful Earth. I tried everything I could to exile my darkness from myself until I discovered the awful truth – if I do not allow my demons to live in me, I project them out onto others. Banished from their true home, they wander existence with nothing to contain them. Free to do their worst, they cause untold harm.

For most of us, our individual happiness has become the most sacred thing in the universe and in our determination to be happy we send our misery overseas. Like damaged ships with dangerous cargo are sent to poorer countries that can be bribed to take them, we banish our unhappiness to where those with less power are forced to deal with it for us. We are each entangled with each other in a vast dynamic homeostasis and responsible for it all. Palestine and Israel struggle in a conflict with meaning for every one of us. Innocent animals everywhere suffer the consequence of our human material greed. If I smile in the mirror and make affirmations proclaiming how powerful I am, someone who perhaps cannot afford a mirror is likely to smile a little less and feel a little more powerless. Happiness may offer a veneer of comfort, but it is not wisdom. Neither is it love, freedom, truth or beauty.

Not long ago I went to a weekend seminar run by a very experienced workshop leader who works with the deep psychology of conflict. I have a lot of respect for this man and have read many of his books. He stood in front of us and told us every morning he leaps out of bed delighted to be alive, full of excitement at the coming day and how wonderful life is. Great stuff. Inspirational. Except I felt a strange inarticulate pain. Perhaps because this was a gathering of people from all over the world, Africa, Australia, Europe, Russia, the Middle and Far East, yet the only American present was the one telling us how fulfilled he was. And a week previously the Bush administration had extended their war into Iraq. Besides, on the mornings I lie in bed in anguish, I don't want to know others are leaping about with none of the insecurities I know so well. Anyway, why is leaping out of bed better than lying in it? Most of my deepest insights have occurred when I'm wrecked and on the floor, not when I'm flying high.

It seems the American way, where the rights of the individual are paramount and more significant than the responsibilities of community, has been adopted by us all now, in the psycho-spiritual realms too. Yet our inter-connectedness and entanglements with each other are as absolute as is our singular aloneness. One of the psychic roots of the conflict between fundamentalist Islam and fundamentalist Judeo-Christianity is this polarity – between a God that is a 'We' and a God that is an 'I'. Yet whatever the god, each has his or her array of demons dancing behind them.

Our collective experiment in the Rajneesh communes to find out what happened when we freed the array of demons incarcerated in the deepest dungeons of them all, the hell humanity collectively runs from, the dark instinctual battles in the underbellies of all societies, turned out to bring us face to face with our own. These, the most intimate demons of all, then showed us that this darkness is an old friend.

I did not want my demons and fought hard against them. As a consequence I have had to spiral back into these dark truths again and again, my lessons hitting me harder each time, until I finally learned – darkness is intrinsic to our dualistic existence where life is divided into 'good' and 'evil' and 'you' are not 'me', 'we' are not 'them'. I learned by falling, repeatedly, into my own darkness. When yet another city I had built on the sand of myself was destroyed and I fell through the cracks of my psyche into the ruins. When I sat in the rubble and met again the fears, dreads, shame, guilt, confusions and hurts that lay under my attempts to bring peace, love and freedom to the world. When I realised my commitment to the light had taken over my life and annihilated me as completely as had any darkness. When I found my compassion, my healing, my passion for freedom had become the same demonic bullies I had run from. When I realised the inescapable human predicament that confronts us all – to be and not to be are equally unbearable.

It was then I learned our human darkness, in all its anguish and despair, is the inextricable soul mate of the love, freedom, truth, friendship and beauty I have also found.

I can now answer my old question, whether good can vanquish evil, or are they forever intertwined.

I can also answer questions I had not known I was asking. Especially when I discovered an even deeper truth. Our demons are our love, in a strange disguise.

The systems I had been born into had not loved my parents and had beaten the love out of me, but it hadn't destroyed my love. With no home in me, my love too had wandered the planet seeking fulfilment, trying to find expression, looking for creatures to love. And my love had broken my heart to find the way to get back home too, back into me.

The real knowledge of good and evil is that in good there is also evil, and in evil, good. But it doesn't say that in the Bible, only in our own hearts. But perhaps this wisdom comes to us when we eat not only the apple, but chew and digest every bit of that Serpent – including both heads and those forked tongues as long as human longing.

Only to find, it is the Serpent that has eaten us.

Chapter 24

Redemption Songs

Several years ago, there was a competition on BBC Radio 4 to find the new deadly sins. Pride, gluttony, avarice, wrath, sloth, lust and envy, apparently don't cover the full spectrum of our modern age with its expanded freedoms and possibilities to sin. I thought of animal experiments, corporate lawyering, e-mail spamming, destroying rain forests, organised religion, wearing fur and listening to manufactured pop cover versions of the greats. Then Philip, my opera singer friend, now far from blind, came up with 'unconsciousness'.

Strictly speaking, if I remember my Catechism, though ignorance is no defence in law, when we do not know what we are doing we can be forgiven, whereas the deadly sins take us straight to hell. Yet surely unconsciousness is the root of evil, the deeper grammar that generates all sin, and not what I like to blame, corporate greed, and organised religion or crap pop music. After all, what is unconscious serves our unconscious desires, not the sensitive and loving kindness we might fondly imagine motivates us. And our unconscious is always with us. Wherever we go.

Martin and I live now at the end of a quiet road on a stunning tidal estuary. Each evening at dusk, flocks of birds fly into the bird reserve in the dunes. The beaches are magnificent and empty. Inland are lakes and mountains. We are surrounded by a wild beauty that has been left gloriously unspoilt ... because to the north, lies one of the UK's most famous nuclear power plants.

Despite the periodic radiation checks on the beach when we moved in, the village seemed peaceful enough – until the battle lines that criss-cross all communities gradually revealed themselves. Boundary disputes, territorial fights, acts of sabotage and escalating revenge – all we are missing, to complete our microcosm of the macrocosm, is a religious war. I could manage that, no problem; but I must have learned something on my travels because when I hear the stories, I listen, nod, take no side and say I am happy to lead a boring life. Then I go for a walk with the dog into wilderness. But even there, there are echoes, for our dog is from the RSPCA and you can see in his eyes that he too has his stories of dark losses and abuse of power.

I have found the same dark and painful stories in every patriarchy, matriarchy, sisterhood, neighbourhood, consensual, collective, co-operative, commune, I have come across, whatever their mission statement about love and peace. I have found them in every person I have ever met. Furthermore, most intimately of all, I found them within myself; my own dark losses, made even darker, because I have been so blinded by my own light.

However, while I may have cast myself centrally in a starring role, as a source of a love and light, the darkness I needed to complete myself, kept finding me all the same. Because my darkness, too, wanted to come home. Besides, without the deadly sins there would be no need for virtue. Though I did not want to know this for a long time.

I had seen how the hidden dynamics of society hurt the vulnerable, the poor, children, the mentally ill, my parents, me, so I tried to save everyone. I tried to make my parents happy by being good and peeling potatoes. I tried to save the souls in purgatory, the working class, the starving in Africa, Vietnamese peasants, the hurt children of Harrogate, the depressed women of Bradford. I tried to free demons. I tried to save the whole world, including – while I was at it – a few other dimensions of reality as well. However, my repeated failures turned out to be my salvation, because – eventually – I turned around and began to save myself at last.

Thus, all that effort had not been wasted after all. My struggles and failures, through a range of messianic projects, had cooked up the very person I needed to save me from myself. I have become the 'wise woman' whom I had looked for all my life but had not found – because she did not yet exist. Now, I have fulfilled my promise to the young woman who had stared into the sacred mirror in Nottingham so long before. I have become the one who can save me from myself.

I have repeatedly wandered off the path and into wilderness and often, therefore, travelled alone, as do we all in sections of our journey. Part of my solitude had been that no one in my family understood me. My ancestors had lived in a poverty that either killed them, or made them hard. In contrast, I was given opportunities they could not begin to imagine. Few working class men and women of their era ever went to university; but in my generation, we went in droves. I was one of the first generation of women to have sexual freedom without the worry of endless pregnancies. My ancestors jigged to the penny whistle and the Irish pipes, while I danced to an electric acid feedback wall of rock, reggae, disco, punk and re-mixed dance tunes with a heavy bass beat. Housing was cheap; and with commercial air flights I could travel anywhere in the world – and through inner worlds too. Like thousands of others, I did not let a chance like this go by.

We took it and ran into worlds and adventures, many more than I can describe here, taking our struggle to create a better world into new realms. And when you are a pioneer carving out the path through brambles that later becomes a motorway, you have no one to show you the way. You *are* the way. Thorns scratched me and my mother was right, I looked like I had been dragged through a hedge backwards. Yet, I have created a woman, despite the hair, who did not exist before. And I am no longer driven to change the world, transform it, heal it, make it over, and improve it. I might try of course, because it's natural to want a 'better' world. But then again, I might not. I might just let it be. After all it's a kind of subtle violence to life to relentlessly 'improve' things – including oneself.

I have not become the serene and self-contained beauty with silky wafting hair that I had so much wished to be. Neither am I the totally together person who always knows what to do and how to do it. Yet, I wouldn't have objected to becoming her either, with or without the hair. Though I have become more, just more of myself. Yet there is something else. A 'not-me' has arrived, a presence rather than a person.

Gurdjieff used to say, we are not born with a soul, we have to work for it – the grit of our suffering is what makes the pearl of great price. I have somehow managed to grow my soul.

Collectively too, we can grow the Soul of humanity, we can become what will save us from ourselves. After all, what good is it if only the 'good' are saved? Especially if being good is nothing to do with it and being real is. We cannot escape our individual or collective darkness anymore anyway; the accumulated darkness of our whole civilisation is confronting us across the globe. We can no longer just turn away; we must deal with it or die.

Our collective darkness is full of abuse of power, innocent suffering, gratuitous cruelty and despair. This is hell. There is no other. Just as our laughter, creativity, music, humour and friendship create the only heaven. Most religions do not want to know this and teach it is possible to escape the hell that we create for each other if we sign up and follow the path mapped out by them. Yet, there are dangers which lie that way. Obedience can become more important than personal integrity, the creative spirit of humanity stifled by religious dogma and the next life more important than this one. Yet, there is another way.

Tantra is the only spiritual teaching I know that makes us responsible for it all and does not dangle a heavenly carrot or shift the ultimate responsibility onto gods and demons, except that they are us. However, Tantra is a spiritual force and not a religion. There are no priests, no rules, no rituals, unless you choose to invent them. You are the ultimate authority, your own energy the god. You do not witness or transcend your desires; you follow them – to the sweet and bitter end. Yet are we not all pretty much doing that now anyway, whatever churches, synagogues, mosques, shopping malls or Reality TV shows we worship at?

The sinister or left-handed Tantric way of which Osho was a Master – where you live out your dreams, follow your impulses, listen to the siren song of your own energy – is not a road less travelled. In fact, it is not a road or a path at all. It is not even really a way. It is a becoming. You enter the heart of darkness, not to vanquish it, but to experience it. And Tantra's secret teaching, that we need now more than ever, is that deep in our animal bodies, hidden in the vast darkness of the Earth before the word was spoken, before we split the glorious life of the body into good and evil, and divided life in order to rule over it, there lies a great truth. There is only one body, the body of us all. 'All this is my Body. All this is my Blood.' In the holy communion of life, we are one Body, members of each other – one Body, one Love. We are the mysteries of the universe and the mysteries of the universe are us. The last knowledge lies in the first – before the Word. As ancient Tantric sutras proclaim: 'This very body the Buddha, this very Earth the lotus paradise.' Incarnation not transcendence is what it is all about.

In this body, on this Earth, the darkness of the collective unconscious may be the source of evil; it is also the source of good. Yet, if we are to continue living on this beautiful Earth, it is not enough any longer for only Tantric mystics and shamans to know this. All of us need to understand such things. Perhaps those with the colossal power of global technologies most of all. Because if we do not, we will find out the hardest way of all and when it is too late.

During our years, stumbling with wolves in a Galician wilderness, Martin and I discovered new ways of working with what we have learned, part of which involves a group that meets regularly for planetary homoeopathy. Through energy configurations, psychodrama, music and dance, we explore the complex interconnections and interdependencies of global issues. The list seems endless: what is happening in the oceans, to the rain forests, to the water, the rise of religious fundamentalism, global warming, endless conflict in the Middle East, famine and poverty, dwindling fish stocks, the last polar bears, AIDS in Africa, etc. Many make their contribution through the physical world, they take medicines to disaster areas, dig wells for clean water, campaign to save the environment, teach people to conserve energy. Our work is in the inner realms, with the dream that dreams us rather than its manifestation in form.

Barely one molecule of the original substance is left in a homoeopathic remedy yet this can trigger a healing in the whole body; maybe in a world confronted by forces beyond the powers of our individualistic culture to deal with them, our efforts may be as good an offering as any. What happens when we are together, and the energies unfold, is mysteriously sacred and sometimes shocking. However, the point is not to change things into how we think they should be; it is to become more conscious of how things are. Everything has a meaning, a purpose, and a part to play, however strange, threatening and unfathomable. And this living awareness is our contribution, our art, and our guerrilla consciousness.

We record these events and plan one day to broadcast them, perhaps also to invite others to witness the geo-mysteries as they unfold, in the raw. After periods of chaos and struggle, a new order of consciousness has always emerged – so far. Though we never know in advance if it will; and all involve surrender to what is greater than us. This is not something that our western materialism, with its magnificent science and technologies, is particularly keen on.

Many personal development processes too assume we can achieve anything if we just do it, remain positive, define our goals, walk on fire, eat raw food, re-configure our beliefs, and do yoga, whatever. But this is clearly not true. Once a liberation of the human individual spirit, such individualistic therapies will not help us in relation to what we have created as a collective, and what is, therefore, greater than any one of us and beyond our individual control. Our planetary homeopathy is one such way. Yet, in order to discover it, I had to turn everything that I thought I knew upon its head. Or perhaps it was just me who turned upside-down.

Many describe the journey towards wisdom as like climbing a mountain. You struggle through many difficulties, you reach the summit from which you can survey the whole world and the view from this peak of enlightenment is so breathtakingly beautiful, it is worth every effort of the climb to reach the top. But in my experience, a deeper wisdom arrives through falling. Falling in love. Falling out of love. Falling to the floor in despair. Falling out of dreams and illusions. Falling in love again. Falling and giving up all thought of getting up again. Falling off the top of that mountain so far into darkness that, like the creatures who live on the ocean floor where no light reaches, you have to create your own light. And when you can fall no further, you become a source of light yourself.

That is when I discovered the hidden knowledge of inner temples, covert sects, and esoteric mystery schools in cultures all over the world. A secret so dangerous that you would once have been killed for revealing it: that light is the source of darkness, and darkness, the source of light – and one can never vanquish the other.

The struggle between good and evil is the dialectic of our human existence, the Gaia of this planet. We, with all our 'unnatural' alienations from nature, are nature too. It all is. We are the part of Gaia that fell away from Her in order to become aware of Her; the part that left Earth and looked back so Gaia could see Herself. We are Her consciousness of good and evil. Further, because we know death, we are Her knowledge it is good to be alive.

However, this knowledge will soon be apparent to everyone, come what may. We all sense the great death coming over the horizon, whether we let ourselves know it or not. We can now foresee the end of our civilisation, with its white heat and black blood; with its magnificent cities, its gleaming spires, gothic follies and skyscrapers, its art, exquisite gardens and music, its markets, souks, department stores and shopping malls that sell billions of things we don't need until we see them; with its 'trains and boats and planes', and nuclear submarines, its brutal political regimes, arms manufacture and nasty cruelty to children behind closed doors. With its attempts to escape the gravitational pull of Earth, to land on the Moon, to reach the stars, to meet gods – and then to kill them in order to take their place.

Yet, as all mountain climbers are well aware, however high you climb, you have to go back down, back into the valley you came from, back home. Where you meet sisters, strangers and old comrades, people you know and people you don't know, but you know them just the same. People who have climbed and come down other mountains, with different war wounds, different tales to tell of what a long strange trip it's been.

And you can see in their eyes that they have seen what you have seen – that up there, beyond the snowline, there is no path and no guide. You climb alone, sometimes snow-blind, sometimes with magnificent views; but the panorama from the summit is so glorious that you fall down once more as its loveliness breaks your heart all over again. However, by this time, your heart has been broken so many times on the journey to get there; you know it is simply the pain of opening to yet more love. A love that, even as you fall, invites the darkness too into the ruins of your heart. And out of these ruins comes the song.

Can you hear it? In the cries of geese as they fly south for winter; in the whispering of the wind through pines; in distant thunder and the humming of insects; in the dawn chorus and conversations of whales? It is in the shock of bomb blasts, in the screams of war and the howls of the dispossessed, in the whispers of lullabies, the sighs of lovemaking, the rustle of tiny creatures through leaves. It is in my song, in your song and in ours. Because, whether we climb mountains, fall to the ocean floor or stick to gardening in our own back yard, all roads – however long and winding – lead to here. Where we find loss, fury and death just as much as life, love and laughter.

But, then, if we were never lonely, we would not reach out in friendship. Without our being stricken by inexplicable needs and fears of wounding loss, love would be no more than a pleasant way to spend an afternoon. Were it not for the dreams of the drunk and insane, there'd be no new wisdom under any sun. Without the blues, there's no song; and without the song, there's no soul – because it is the song that makes us sing.

Once upon a time, a generation dared to dream a great dream. Enough were dreaming this dream to give birth to it in forms all over the planet. Yet, though all form changes, the dream was real. And the dream lives on.

To those who see visions, dream their dreams and then dare to live them, comes an innocence and experience that those who live more sensibly cannot know. Such sensible people might criticise what they do not understand. They judge us, condemn us and think they know what it's all about. But we who were there, we are the ones who know. In communes, magic buses, eco-feminist collectives, radical politics, experimental theatre, self-sufficient farms, falling to the feet of gurus in ashrams, dancing in streets all over the world, it happened. Life is not now the same as a result of what we did back then, of what we dreamed and what we lived.

So dream on sisters, strangers, comrades, friends and enemies; dream on. Let us dream a dreaming that enfolds us in its heart – all of us and everything. A dream that embraces even our wounding use of power and darkest losses. I say this because I have seen what happens when we try to exclude them.

Are there enough of us to make this dreaming real? Because, if we do not, there is no one else who will dream up the Soul of the Earth – and we need that Soul now, as never before.

Bibliography and Further Reading

Some of these books are classics and have been re-printed many times. I have, therefore, given either the dates of their original publication or of a later edition. I have also tried to group the books into some form of relevant category, albeit personal.

THE COUNTER CULTURE OF THE 1960S AND 1970S
On the Road Jack Kerouac, Signet (1957)
Howl Allen Ginsberg, City (1967)
Turn On, Tune In, Drop Out Timothy Leary, Ronin (1999)
The Greening of America Charles Reich, Crown/Allen Lane (1971)
The Whole Earth Catalogue twice-yearly (1968-1972)

POLITICS & FEMINISM
The Dialectics of Liberation Conference ed. David Cooper, Penguin (1968)
The Second Sex Simone de Beauvoir, Jonathan Cape (1953)
The Tyranny of Structurelessness Jo Freeman, Berkley Journal essay (1971)
The Women's Rights Movement in the U.S.: A New View Shulamith Firestone,
    New York Radical Women essay (1968)
Toward a Radical Movement Heather Booth, Evie Goldfield & Sue Munaker,
    Lililth Gallery essay (1968)
The Female Eunuch Germaine Greer, Abacus (1972)
Wedlocked Women Lee Comer, Feminist Books (1974)
Our Bodies, Ourselves The Boston Women's Health Collective (1973)
The New Our Bodies, Ourselves The Boston Women's Health Collective,
    eds Angela Phillips & Jill Rakusen, Penguin (1978)

PSYCHO-POLITICS
The Function of the Orgasm Wilhelm Reich, Farrar, Strauss & Giroux (1927)
The Hidden Persuaders Vance Packard, Penguin (1957)
The Barefoot Psychoanalyst John Southgate and Rosemary Randell, Gale Centre
    (1975)
The Divided Self R. D. Laing (1961); reprinted Penguin (1965)
Playing and Reality D. W. Winnicott, reprinted Routledge (1982)
The Myth of Mental Illness Thomas Szasz, Harper & Row (1963)

SPIRITUALITY
My Way: The Way of the White Clouds Osho, Element (1995)
The Great Challenge Osho, reprinted Rebel (1993)
Be Here Now Ram Dass, The Lama Foundation (1971)
The Lion's Roar Chogyam Trungpa Rinpoche, Shambala Mew (2001)
Only Fear Dies: A Book of Liberation Barry Long, Barry Long Books (1986)

OTHER READING
My Life in Orange Tim Guest, Granta (2004)

Acknowledgements

I want to thank all my friends for the comradeship, the walks, the parties and the shoulders I've cried on through the years. Without you I don't know where I'd be. In relation to this book I want to thank especially Lyn Webster-Wilde, Aleine Ridge, Sandra Hailes, Prem Savita, Barbara Karagosian and Barbara Gladstone, for all their encouragement and helpful feedback, and most of all, Stuart Booth who has been a brilliant editor and mid-wife.

I also want to thank Osho Rajneesh and each of my teachers along the way, for their generosity and courage in daring to say things not said before. And thanks too to the musicians of the world who made the music that made us dance.

Plus, I want to thank my family – my parents because without them none of this would have been possible, my sisters and brother for being my oldest allies, and my son, Tim Guest for his inspired creative writing tips, and the champagne and meals in fancy restaurants which inspired me in a different way. And most of all, thank you Martin, without whom … it doesn't bear thinking about!

A.G.
www.annegeraghty.org